D0318792

The Arms Trial

The Arms Trial

Justin O'Brien

Gill & Macmillan

Gill & Macmillan Ltd
Hume Avenue, Park West, Dublin 12
with associated companies throughout the world
www.gillmacmillan.ie

© Justin O'Brien 2000

0 7171 3062 2

Design by Identikit Design Consultants, Dublin
Print origination by Carole Lynch
Printed by ColourBooks Ltd, Dublin

This book is typeset in MBembo 10.5pt on 13pt

All rights reserved. No part of this publication may be copied,
reproduced or transmitted in any form or by any means
without permission of the publishers.

A CIP record for this book is available
from the British Library.

1 3 5 4 2

To Darina and Élise

Contents

Preface

ON Friday 23 October 1970 a jubilant Charles Haughey addressed the crowd gathered in the central lobby of the Four Courts in Dublin. He thanked them for their support, and then began a short-lived push for political power based on his position as a vindicated patriot. For the former Minister for Finance, dismissed in ignominy from the Fianna Fáil Government six months earlier, it was a moment of triumph. Haughey had just been acquitted along with a leading Belfast republican, a military intelligence officer and a Belgian-born businessman of attempting to illegally import weapons for Northern nationalists.

Throughout the trial, Haughey, one of the most influential figures in Fianna Fáil, had maintained a physical and psychological distance from his co-defendants. He claimed that while he had used his position to gain customs clearance for a consignment, he was unaware of its contents. The three others had not attempted to hide their culpability. Their defence was disarmingly frank: the entire operation had been sanctioned at the highest levels of the Government.

The jury concluded that the divergent defence strategies amounted to an immaterial legal technicality. All four were deemed to have operated under properly delegated authority. The charges could not be sustained.

The decision to dismiss the charges marked the dénouement of a dramatic and destabilising controversy whose implications still resonate today. It was a controversy that undermined political consensus in the

Republic while playing midwife to the Provisional IRA. It was also a controversy that raised fundamental questions about the ideological limits of Irish nationalism. The green card of nationalism was played, and its currency as the central legitimising mechanism of the state devalued. Ultimately, however, the arms trial itself centred not on the legitimacy or otherwise of arming Northern nationalists but rather on a power play for the soul of Fianna Fáil.

In the highly charged atmosphere on the Dublin quays that October afternoon, as Haughey demanded the resignation of the Taoiseach and as the others claimed they had been victims of a political show trial, the crucial distinction in the defence strategies was momentarily forgiven. However, for those determined to use force to secure the republican aim of Irish unity it was not forgotten. It would be another eighteen years before the republican movement was again prepared to reach out to the political establishment; a further six before the IRA cease-fire of 1994 laid the foundation for a potential settlement.[1]

It is difficult to exaggerate the impact the Northern Ireland civil rights movement had on the politics of the entire country. By August 1969 the situation had become uncontrollable. The sectarian forces lurking just below the surface erupted in a rage of fury as the Stormont government buckled under the weight of its own contradictions. The conditions had been created for an Irish Government to have a profound influence on a territory whose very existence was an affront to the ideological underpinnings of the state. In short, the cataclysmic events in Northern Ireland provided an opportunity to complete the unfinished business of the Irish revolution.

The catalyst for the crisis was the interaction of a political vacuum in the North with the machinations of an internally divided Dublin Government, paranoid about the threat a coalescence of the radical left with the IRA and the wider republican movement posed to its conception of the nation. A genuine fear of a pogrom prompted many—including those who were later to make their careers by denouncing republican violence—to demand military support from the Republic. That support was forthcoming, though not necessarily because of an attempt to complete unfinished business.

In the immediate aftermath of serious sectarian violence in Derry in August 1969 the Taoiseach, Jack Lynch, made a television speech in which he made it clear that he felt the security situation in the North was spiralling out of control. He maintained that the Government 'could no longer stand by and see people injured or perhaps worse.' As the violence spread to Belfast, he turned Northern policy over to his most influential rivals in Fianna Fáil. A Government sub-committee was established under the direct control of Neil Blaney and Charles Haughey to co-ordinate intelligence and to map out policy. In a separate decision, the Government gave Haughey sole discretion in how to dispense Government aid to the Northern minority. By the time of the sackings, £100,000—a considerable sum in 1970—was spent, much of it in attempts to supply arms.

The way in which Dublin responded to the crisis provides a compelling insight into the working of nationalist politics during times of upheaval. The actions taken by a deeply divided administration in the pivotal years 1969–70, operating to a myriad of competing agendas, hastened the split in the militant republican movement and set the scene for the emergence and eventual dominance of the Provisional IRA.

This book, based on new research, is the story of how initial acceptance of calls for weapons turned into a conspiracy with grave implications for democratic Irish government. The intrigue surrounding the involvement of Military Intelligence in fomenting a split in the republican movement, acting under orders from Government ministers openly hostile to their party leader, reveals clearly the relationship between high politics and events on the streets. From the first burnings in Belfast, the priority in Dublin was ensuring that if confrontation with the RUC and British army were inevitable, then the Government would have to have some control over the situation, at all costs preventing the contagion from spreading south. If that meant supplying arms and expertise, then Military Intelligence was quite prepared to do it.

In many ways the success of this strategy was evident from as early as January 1970, with the formal split in the republican movement. On a more fundamental level, however, the schism had repercussions far beyond the confines of extreme nationalism. It transformed the balance of forces within the Government and gave Lynch much more room to manoeuvre. If the IRA was split, and split openly, then the danger of the threat of anarchy so graphically depicted by Military Intelligence was neutralised.[2] The fact that the conclusion of this power struggle took place in the aftermath of the Ballymurphy riots in Belfast in April 1970 is a crucial fact often overlooked. The riots marked the first overt confrontation between the Provisional IRA and the security forces. Dublin was in effect making it clear that it was one thing to be the moral guardians of the nation's ideology, quite another to take on the British army. The republican card was now operating at a discount, and the ministers most publicly associated with a hawkish line were fundamentally exposed.

It is by tracing how that balance of power shifted that one can reveal the real reasons behind the decision to prosecute Haughey and his co-defendants. This also reveals why the prosecution ultimately failed. From eye-witness accounts, interviews and recently released Government papers and intelligence reports, a disturbing picture emerges that forces a reassessment of contemporary Irish history and politics. By tracing concrete links between Fianna Fáil, Military Intelligence and members of the IRA it is possible to demonstrate not only the ambivalence towards political violence inherent in nationalist ideology and all too present in the heady days of 1969–70 but also a direct correlation between elite politics and paramilitary activity. This in turn suggests that intransigence had a specific function, that chaos was, to some, a valuable political commodity. As the *Irish Times* editorial acidly pointed out the day after the acquittal,

> overall, the casualness was startling, casualness about large sums of public money and ultimately casualness about human life. It was Harry Truman who first publicised the dictum—'This is where the buck stops': he meant on his desk. Very few people in Government circles seemed to be clear about where the buck stopped in Dublin.

The Arms Crisis represented the greatest threat to the stability of the state in a generation and arguably since its formation. It emerged with a terse statement by the Government Information Bureau in the early hours of 6 May 1970 announcing the forced resignation of Charles Haughey and Neil Blaney. Kevin Boland, Minister for Local Government, resigned in sympathy, along with Paudge Brennan, a parliamentary secretary. It quickly transpired that the resignation a day earlier of the Minister for Justice, Mícheál Ó Móráin, was also inextricably linked to the self-destruction of the first Fianna Fáil Government of the post-revolutionary generation.

The unprecedented three-day debate that followed remains arguably the most riveting piece of political theatre ever witnessed in Dáil Éireann. If the initial debate unmasked the dangers inherent in appeals to nationalist ideology, the subsequent arrests and prosecution neatly encapsulated not only the viciousness of internal Fianna Fáil politics but the magnitude of a crisis that was ultimately to necessitate a fundamental shift in the country's ideological underpinnings.

Yet for such a pivotal event, remarkably little has been written on the Arms Crisis and the questions it raises about the nature of politics in the Republic.[3] In large part this can be traced to the refusal of both Charles Haughey and Jack Lynch to answer any questions about their role in the affair. It also reflects what Professor W. J. McCormack has described as a propensity in Ireland to reflect on the past only 'if it is possible to blame an agency sufficiently remote in time, or space, or conception.'[4] That appears to be changing following the comprehensive vilification of Charles Haughey in the aftermath of the tribunals of inquiry into his tenure as Taoiseach—though in the rush to pass sentence certain fundamental truths have been glossed over.

The issue has also received cursory attention in specific histories of the IRA. A standard history of the Provisional IRA by Bishop and Mallie rejects as 'characteristically fanciful and vain' any suggestion of a Government-inspired conspiracy 'to replace dangerous leftists [such as Cathal Goulding] with the manageable stooges of the old tradition.'[5] That account takes into consideration neither the significant gains made in the Dublin trade union movement and media circles nor the perception in Fianna Fáil of the threat this posed to the stability of the Southern state. There are similar failings in Tim Pat Coogan's writings on the Arms Crisis. He views attempts to link Fianna Fáil—or even a section within it—to the formation of the Provisional IRA as an attempt by the Goulding faction to 'maximise its own pre-1969 importance.'[6] Coogan also uses his résumé to criticise the 'skin-deep knowledge of Dublin's drawing room left,' while somewhat contradictorily accepting that the consequence for Fianna Fáil was that it 'underwent the greatest upheaval in its history.'[7]

The inconsistencies in the public record about the factors that led to the emergence of the Provisional IRA reveal a profound gap in our understanding of the most ruthlessly efficient paramilitary organisation seen in western Europe. It is beyond question that the Provisional IRA was a product of the sectarian conflict that erupted in the aftermath of August 1969. Even if Dublin had adopted a more uncompromising and unified stance, the Provisionals would have emerged—but not necessarily in December 1969, and not necessarily with such reserves in ideological cohesion or financial clout.

The truth of what really happened during the Arms Crisis is not to be found in the official archives alone, a fact well articulated by Maurice Hayes.

[The files] miss out on much of the real muscle of decision taking, the private unrecorded conversations, the chance meetings, the nods and winks, the pressures of the political process, the ebb and flow of emotion, the arcane processes by which individuals and groups think their way out of one crisis, and into another. Officials do not commit to file the struggles that politicians make to keep parties from splitting apart, or to induce splits in others, or the interplay of ambition and envy, and the efforts individuals make either to make a name for themselves or to find a way to recreate careers which previous miscalculations have endangered.[8]

The files have been compared with contemporaneous newspaper and periodical reporting, political memoirs and interviews with central political and paramilitary figures to sift out bias and deconstruct competing agendas. Much new evidence has been collected that sheds significant light on the genesis of the most protracted period of civil strife in western Europe since the Second World War. Extensive interviews with senior members of the IRA who took opposing sides in the split provide crucial new insights into both its timing and its implications. In particular the testimony of the first chief of staff of the Provisional IRA, Seán Mac Stiofáin, makes it clear that the Citizens' Defence Committees, ostensibly formed in the immediate aftermath of August 1969, had a longer pedigree and a deeper purpose than was heretofore understood. John Kelly was on a mission to buy weaponry for the Provisional IRA from the very beginning, his search made much easier by the financial support offered by sections of the Dublin establishment. His visit to the United States in November 1969—paid for by Mr Blaney out of the Government grant in aid—reopened contacts with Irish America. Interviews with George Harrison in New York and other senior Republican figures whose identities cannot be revealed at this time again provide compelling evidence of the importance of the American connection to the Provisionals from the beginning.

Significant evidence has been uncovered to question Lynch's protestations that he knew nothing about the plots of his ministers. Against a backdrop of a quickly deteriorating situation in the North, Lynch was to prove that he too was not averse to using highly suspect measures to preserve his position. If this meant tampering with a criminal investigation, then he was quite prepared to do it. The implications of the arms trial really became apparent only after the failure to convict. Lynch determined immediately to institute a hearing by the Committee of Public Accounts into the dispersal of the Government grant in aid.

Testimony from Garret FitzGerald makes it clear, for the first time, that the committee's hearings were designed specifically by Government and opposition alike not to ascertain the truth but 'to buttress the state against the greatest threat to its security since partition.'[9]

Chapter 1 of this book outlines the ideological positions that animated political life in Ireland from partition until the formation of the civil rights movement. It connects the rise of the civil rights movement with attempts by the republican movement to embark on its most ambitious shift in policy since the initial split with de Valera led to the formation of Fianna Fáil. It reveals how this realignment threatened not only Stormont but also the ideological underpinnings of the Republic and of Fianna Fáil in particular.

This provides the context for the initial Government response to the outbreak of violence in Derry, examined in chapter 2. This demonstrates just how seriously the Government took the threat posed by the civil rights movement of infecting the Southern state. The rationale behind contrasting positions taken by senior figures in Fianna Fáil is teased out and placed in the context of an intense power struggle within the party. The chapter demonstrates how the transfer of power to the post-revolutionary leadership of Jack Lynch seriously eroded the cohesion of the party's base; it outlines the reasons for the continuing fragility of Lynch's leadership and reveals the full extent of the secret power struggles taking place in the party.

Chapter 3 reveals for the first time the scale of the involvement of Military Intelligence in fomenting the split in the republican movement and the rationale behind it. It examines the role played by Captain James Kelly in infiltrating the IRA and the manner in which the established IRA leadership in Dublin was sidelined and eventually cast aside. Particular emphasis is placed on the American connection, given its subsequent role in the nineteen-seventies as a vital source for Provisional IRA weapons and financial support, a theme developed in chapter 4. In revealing the various attempts to import weapons, this chapter unravels the web of intrigue and brings to light the murky world of paramilitary organisation and intelligence operatives. It examines the breakdown of trust within the Government and reveals just how far the various factions in Fianna Fáil were prepared to go to further their political ambitions.

Chapter 5 reconstructs the pivotal Dáil debates following Lynch's decision to sack the ministers. The extent to which there was a direct correlation between events on the ground and the high politics in

Dublin is reflected in chapter 6, which provides important new evidence about how a new political compact was established that would change fundamentally the trajectory of Northern politics.

Chapter 7 investigates the reasons behind the decision to prosecute. It critically examines Lynch's stated position that he knew nothing of the plans to import weapons and finds the explanation wanting on a number of counts.

The final chapter examines the impact of the arms trial on the politics of republicanism and combines this with an analysis of how the workings of the Committee of Public Accounts saw the birth of a new conception of the nation, in which irredentist nationalist rhetoric could no longer be used as the primary legitimising ideology of the Southern state.

The Arms Crisis did not result merely from the logical working out of nationalist rhetoric but was predicated on a bitter power struggle *within* Fianna Fáil. The failure so far to take into account the machinations of a Fianna Fáil power struggle in the formation of the Provisional IRA seriously impoverishes our understanding not only of both organisations but also of the trajectory of nationalist and republican politics. This book is an attempt to redress that imbalance. A complete exposition of such a pivotal event is not only essential from a historical point of view: it is also crucial for the development of research into such varied areas of interest to political scientists as elite politics, nationalism, escalation imperatives, conflict regulation, and political succession. As a new generation of political leaders grapples with the enduring political power of militant republicanism, we do well to understand the past. It is only through the acceptance of sometimes brutal truths that the body politic can hope to reach out, to break the impasse that has led to the destabilisation of the whole country. It is in this spirit that this book is written; it is in this spirit that its central argument should be understood.

Acknowledgments

THIS book owes its genesis to a BBC documentary I produced on the arms trial, broadcast on 10 March 1998. The skill of the reporter, Shane Harrison, in helping to conceptualise the final format of the programme is gratefully acknowledged. The new evidence brought to light by the programme prompted a recognition that our knowledge of the beginnings of the Troubles was deeply suspect. In this core belief I am indebted to Professor Richard English, who encouraged me to investigate the topic further for an MA in Irish politics at Queen's University, Belfast, and who now acts as joint doctorate supervisor, along with Professor Paul Bew.

Professor Bob Eccleshall, Head of Politics at Queen's, provided financial backing for research in the United States; Professor Henry Patterson and Dr Patrick Maume provided much stimulating debate about the nature of republican politics and its interaction with Fianna Fáil. I am grateful to Dr Jim Grant for sharing many insightful comments about the reality of living in Belfast during the white heat of the August 1969 disturbances. He cast a critical eye over an earlier draft, and his suggestions improved the text considerably.

My former colleagues at the BBC, in particular Chris Moore, Shane Harrison, and Kevin Magee, gamely interpreted their reporting brief as covering current affairs from a thirty-year distance, allowing me the latitude to delve into the past.

Fergal Tobin at Gill & Macmillan was supportive of the project from the beginning. Peter and Mary Blake provided hours of conversation and sustenance, while Darina and Élise simply put up with endless hours and days of my non-appearance.

I would particularly like to thank all those who agreed to be interviewed, including those who wish to remain anonymous. The book could not have been written without their co-operation. Any errors of fact or judgment remain my responsibility.

CHAPTER ONE

The Retreat from Certainty

Civil Rights and Revolutionary Thinking

O N 26 February 1962 the IRA called on its members to dump arms. A campaign designed to break the Northern state seemed only to reveal the durability of partition, exposing just how hopelessly out of step with contemporary realities the republican movement had become.

A statement had long been expected; when it eventually came it was distinguished by its defensive tone. It castigated the nationalist establishment for paying mere lip service to the goal of unity, and proclaimed that 'foremost among the factors motivating this course of action has been the attitude of the general public whose minds have been deliberately distracted from the supreme issue facing the Irish people—the unity and freedom of Ireland.'[1]

The movement's transformation from leading player to walk-on part appeared complete. An audience whose tastes had changed, and changed dramatically, no longer required its service. Public support for what the IRA termed the 'primacy of armed struggle' had waned even in the republican heartland. It was an embarrassment to the Republic and nothing more than an irritant to the Northern Ireland administration. Indeed the stage appeared set for its final exit from Irish politics; yet a mere seven years later both states were convulsed by violent disorder of such magnitude that the IRA emerged from the shadows to begin reasserting a position in Irish society it had not held since the Civil War.

The reason lies primarily with the progressive unravelling throughout the nineteen-sixties of the contradictions buried deep within the fabric of Northern Ireland. These chronic imperfections had been masked by the central role the national question had played as a legitimising mechanism for the status quo in both jurisdictions. The decision by the Northern Ireland civil rights movement to agitate for change *within* the constitutional status quo provided a crucial new dynamic. It transformed the course of Irish history, reopening in the process the constitutional question that had bedevilled Anglo-Irish relations for much of the late nineteenth and early twentieth centuries.

The demand for home rule had been successfully rebuffed in 1886 and again in 1893, but by the turn of the century the writing was on the wall. The extension of the suffrage and the vagaries of British electoral politics meant that the Irish Party became an influential broker in the British Parliament. Some form of home rule for Ireland was now an unstoppable political reality; the question was to what extent and over what geographical area. The campaign was in large part an outpouring of resentment at the perception of native impoverishment by a rapacious empire. In the north-east, successive population influxes, particularly from Scotland, and rapid industrialisation created a very different reality.[2] Belfast had become a powerhouse; it dominated the trade in linen, and its shipyards were among the most productive in the world. Ulster, and in particular Belfast and its hinterland, had benefited greatly from association with the Union. Its leaders were determined that market access would not be threatened by economic or social rupture. As a result the rationale for maintaining the Union against the wishes of the majority of the Irish population retreated to the heartland of Ulster and specifically to the defence of Protestant self-interest. That interest was increasingly expressed through mass mobilisation and the threat of violence.

The process of retrenchment accelerated significantly with the establishment of the Ulster Unionist Council in 1905, formal recognition that Ulster's concerns were fundamentally at variance with the rest of Ireland. Its formation coincided with a shift in leadership and emphasis away from the landed gentry and towards the business and merchant class of Belfast. This realignment had other benefits for the mercantile leaders of Ulster unionism: it obviated any cross-cutting allegiances such as class, particularly in the rapidly industrialising hinterland of Belfast, where job opportunities were already heavily weighted in favour of Protestant applicants.[3] To cement over the vertical and horizontal fault-line of Ulster, the new establishment had rehabilitated the Orange Order as early as 1886, bearing witness to the overt sectarian dimension of political life as well as giving tangible expression to wider questions of belonging and identity. The ideological component of the re-articulation of the provincial case against home rule was to become an important weapon in the unionist argument as the battleground shifted away from the exclusive domain of the Palace of Westminster.[4]

The general election of 1910 forced the leader of the Liberal Party, Herbert Asquith, to rely on the Irish Party to secure his government; the price was to be a third Home Rule Bill. The passing of the Parliament Act the following year, blocking the power of the House of Lords to thwart the will of the House of Commons, gave notice that Ireland would have its own self-government.

When the Liberal government published its long-awaited bill in April 1912 the consequences were immense. For nationalists the modest measures did not go far enough; for Ulster unionists it represented nothing less than the threatened destruction of their way of life. Gun-running expeditions were organised, and the Ulster Volunteer Force was formed, a paramilitary organisation designed to augment, or if necessary supersede, its political argument. The message to London was clear: Ulster was prepared to take up arms against the very empire it pledged allegiance to. The conflict had mutated from constitutional wrangling to one over the preservation of identity.

Throughout the immediate crisis of 1912–14 and beyond, as unionism became synonymous with the position in society of the planted stock in Ulster, a sense of bitterness prevailed that was to infect the nature of the eventual dispensation. The *Portadown News* commented in May 1912:

> Should the British Crown place in jeopardy the property and the lives of the loyal subjects of the North of Ireland, history could record no baser betrayal. From time to time within the last 300 years, our forefathers came to this country on the invitation and under the guaranteed protection of the British Government … The lapse of time has brought no fusion of races in Ireland. Between Saxon and Celt there is at best only an approach to friendship. The minority still requires protection, the only change in the situation being that if outside protection is withdrawn, they can and will protect themselves.[5]

This threat was formalised by the swearing of a 'Solemn League and Covenant'; and the mass demonstrations that accompanied the signing of the Covenant on 28 September 1912 were symptomatic of both the retrenchment to Ulster and the conception of loyalty to that Ulster as an exclusively Protestant enterprise. More than 200,000 thronged the streets of Belfast alone in a display of defiance. The Covenant proclaimed that home rule would be 'disastrous to the material well-being of Ulster as well as the whole of Ireland, subversive of our civil and religious freedom, destructive of our citizenship and perilous to the unity of the Empire.' A banner allegedly carried before William of Orange at the Battle of the Boyne was unfurled by the unionist leader Edward Carson, who declared: 'May this flag ever float over a people that can boast of civil and religious liberty.'[6]

The phrasing of the Covenant is instructive and makes it abundantly clear that home rule would be damaging for Ulster and its way of life first and foremost. The linking of autonomy to the future of the empire was instrumental in gaining Conservative support.[7] However, at its core is a belief that the Union should be defended to protect a Protestant way of life;[8] the Covenant represented, therefore, a formalisation of the contractual limits to Ulster's loyalty to Britain. As the *Northern Whig* commented, 'men do not deliver themselves to perpetual shame by signing a public vow of courage and sacrifice which they do not intend to keep.'[9]

In a comprehensive reassessment of the home rule debates, Paul Bew suggests there was 'no shortage of writers who were prepared to denounce the bigotry of the Ulster party, but this is not quite the same thing as a refutation of the opposition's principal thesis.'[10] Bew is undoubtedly correct in arguing that it is a severe distortion to depict Ulster unionism as a monolithic force hell-bent on imposing its domination on a servile Catholic population: his central project is to tease out the economic and social case against home rule, in the process revealing the disquiet within sections of Presbyterianism, in particular, about the naked sectarianism associated with Ulster politics. Nevertheless it is also a fact that as the unionist cause retreated to the heartland of Ulster in the face of a resurgent nationalist and Catholic Irish identity, the subtleties of this position were obliterated, a point Bew himself concedes.[11]

The distancing of the North from the rest of Ireland and the shift towards an Ulster identity required the invention of Protestant—as opposed to British—rights to Ulster. As one researcher acidly points out, 'this entailed the usurpation of Ulster both from Ireland and from Ulster Catholics, a process which continues today.'[12] This was particularly so because of the tacit contract unionism had made with Protestant workers during the industrialisation of Belfast, a deal made explicit with the formation of the Ulster Volunteer Force. A similar emphasis was placed on culture and the development of racial theories to buttress ideological points. Throughout the crisis and later on in the creation of a separate Northern state, attempts were made to use sociology and science to demonstrate the special characteristics of 'Ulster man'.[13]

There is a further illustration of this exclusion in the mythology over the Battle of the Somme. The Ulster Volunteer Force enlisted *en masse* in the British army and was metamorphosed into the 36th (Ulster) Division. On 1 July 1916 this division suffered unimaginable losses in a senseless battle, a slaughter that emphasised for the union-ists their commitment to preserving the link—a down payment in the blood of Ulstermen. What is conveniently forgotten is that serious losses were also inflicted that day on the 16th Division, a unit made up primarily of members of the Irish Volunteers. Mostly supporters of John Redmond, they were serving in large part to demonstrate constitutional nationalism's commitment to what it perceived to be the central goal of the First World War: the right of small nations to self-determination.

The failure at Versailles to include Ireland in that project, coupled with widespread revulsion at the execution of the leaders of the Easter Rising, spelt an end to the constitutional accommodation offered by Redmond. In the general election of December 1918 Sinn Féin swept the board, gaining seventy-three seats to the Irish Party's seven. Sinn Féin refused to take its seats in the British Parliament and established a separate parliament in Dublin, which issued a Declaration of Independence. The decision not only brought nationalism into direct conflict with the British empire but also ensured that unionism would be able to dictate the terms of the Government of Ireland Act, then passing through Parliament. For Joseph Devlin, the former barman who succeeded Redmond as leader of the Irish Party, it amounted to a strategic mistake of momentous proportions. He declared: 'Once they [the unionists] have their own parliament with all the machinery of government and administration, I am afraid that anything like sub-sequent union [with the rest of Ireland] will be impossible.'[14] It was a remarkably prescient statement.

During the parliamentary debates the unionists reduced their demand for a separate dispensation for the nine counties of the province of Ulster to six of them. Their calculations were made on the grounds that this would ensure control while maintaining a viable territorial entity—though even this reduced area contained a Protestant majority in only the four north-eastern counties. The debates were accompanied by severe disturbances throughout Ireland. As the War of Independence raged in the south, Ulster drew up a mental drawbridge to any accommodation with Sinn Féin or indeed with its own Catholic minority. The overt sectarian campaign waged by the IRA in the south-west, which in effect depopulated Protestant communities, added to the sense of foreboding.[15]

But if the IRA campaign in west Cork displayed vicious undertones, it was more than matched by loyalist atrocities in mid-Ulster and in Belfast in particular. Between July 1920 and July 1922 more than 550 people were killed as pogroms raged in the principal towns. The veteran journalist James Kelly recalled that even going to the shops on the tram from the Falls Road to the city centre in the summer of 1920 involved a journey of hazardous dimensions.

> There were certain danger points when it crossed Cupar Street, Conway Street, Northumberland Street and Dover Street, long streets leading from the Falls to the Shankill. Across these streets, at moments of tension, the report of rifle fire rang out as snipers on both sides opened up. The tram speeded and clanked past these streets as the driver crouched down on the deck behind the controls. The passengers took their cue and huddled down on the floor, which the Tramways Department thoughtfully provided with a carpet of straw. There was always audible sighs of relief when the neutral Castle Junction hove in sight.[16]

Ostensibly the cause of the violence was the assassination of an Ulster-born policeman in west Cork on 18 July 1920 and the difficulties encountered in getting his remains back to Ulster.[17] In reality, however, an ugly mood was already brewing in Belfast, inflamed by Twelfth of July demonstrations at which Orange leaders adopted an increasingly hard-line position. Carson, for example, told the main demonstration in Belfast that he was sick of words without action to protect Ulster from the Sinn Féin threat.[18] A letter published in the *News Letter* days before the start of the pogroms makes clear the wider sense of fear and defiance that Carson's speech touched on:

> Look at Londonderry city. The increase of population there has been so considerable as to give them the government of the ancient city and the fortress of Protestantism. One should look facts in the face. The Roman Catholics are pouring into Ulster and increasing rapidly in this province where Protestants are emigrating and disappearing.[19]

On 21 July, following a mass meeting called by the Protestant Labour Association, Catholic workers at Belfast's second shipyard were forcibly expelled. That night the Falls Road district in west Belfast came under attack, and three people were killed. The widespread looting and intimidation of Catholic residents of Ballymacarret in the south-east of the city also typified the sense of isolation felt by Catholic residents.

> The air was thick with burnings all day long and throughout the night. The various sections of a very efficient fire brigade were sorely over-worked and much handicapped by the frequent cutting of the hosepipes by the frenzied Protestant mobs, who in their strength defied a weak and indulgent police.[20]

St Matthew's Church in Bryson Street, off the Newtownards Road and in the shadow of the shipyard, came under sustained siege, forcing the military to open fire. Clonard Monastery in west Belfast also came under attack. Mass expulsions from the linen mills and factories followed, and thousands were forced from their homes as the fighting continued sporadically into August.

A curfew announced on 30 August curtailed further serious dis-order; but so grave had the situation become that the government authorised the formation of an Ulster Special Constabulary to main-tain order. This was made up almost exclusively of members of the Ulster Volunteer Force. A contemporary account maintains that the violence was deliberately manipulated to arm the Protestants and as a plot to destabilise the province.[21] It is more likely that it was designed, at least in part, to underline the depth of feeling in Ulster about the truce negotiations in London, making it clear that Ulster was determined to retain its distance.[22]

The formation of the Special Constabulary did little to quell further outbreaks of violence, and the flames were fanned by an increasingly effective Southern boycott of goods from the North. As Michael Laffan points out, 'the boycott reinforced psychological par-tition and the erection of an economic frontier encouraged both sides to see Ireland in terms of two mutually hostile peoples and states.'[23] Partition was effectually formalised with the opening of a parliament in Belfast on 22 June 1921; but the creation of a parliament did little to reassure unionists increasingly fearful of British intentions and increasingly hostile to Sinn Féin. Violence and the threat of wider instability were the *leitmotiv* of organised unionism. That this was so is amplified by the timing of incidents.[24]

The pogroms returned to Belfast the following July and coincided with a truce between British forces and the IRA. The night before the truce was due to come into operation at least 123 Catholic houses were burnt to the ground and fifteen people were killed on what became known as Bloody Sunday. Mobs went on the rampage, and the curfew announced the previous August was openly defied as Ballymacarret again came under fierce attack. The leader of an American White Cross delegation expressed shock at both the level of intimidation and the conditions that those living in temporary halls and hostels were subjected to.

> As an American citizen, I cannot comprehend how such a thing could occur in a law-abiding community. It is a very terrible thing to contemplate that people should be burnt out of their homes and left without anything but the clothes on their backs.[25]

As the negotiations in London proceeded, the sectarian conflict in Belfast had a very clear purpose: Ulster had to maintain its separate identity. Nationalists viewed the violence as an expression of hostility to Catholicism; unionists, on the other hand, maintained that it was directed at Sinn Féin's project, not at Catholicism *per se*. Nevertheless the pogroms were to colour each side's perception of the other for generations. When Northern Ireland disintegrated in 1969–70, the sectarian demography of Belfast ensured that many of the areas attacked in 1920–22 were again vulnerable. Northern Ireland was truly a prisoner of its past.

It is clear that from the beginnings of the state the first Prime Minister, James Craig, sought to make every election a plebiscite on the maintenance of the Union. Failure to do so would, the Unionists claimed, mean the submergence of the fledgling state in hostile waters controlled by a legitimised IRA. The Northern Ireland electorate, according to the unionist view, could not have the luxury of developing class-based politics. Accordingly, privileges were defended not because they were privileges but because the defence of every privilege was locked into the defence of everything.[26] The people had a fight on their hands to defend their identity; this meant in effect an attempt to create a state in which the quest for internal Protestant unity precluded any attempt to reach out to a disillusioned and resentful minority.[27] The Catholic community simply did not count as far as policy was concerned. The decision by Fianna Fáil to forsake its revolutionary ideals by entering Dáil Éireann in 1927 served only to strengthen the resolve of the Ulster unionists to protect their state as de Valera sought to create a new language of politics.

Fianna Fáil was formed out of a realisation that republican moralism of itself was not a panacea for Ireland's problems. The defeat of the republican side after the Civil War left it with a stark choice: adapt the fundamentalist precepts of the revolution or retreat into obscurity. Long-term strategic thinking created a new template that successfully disarmed any attempts by the opposition or interest groups to assert their own agenda. In effect Fianna Fáil inculcated the belief that it alone represented the true national interest, as opposed to the selfish sectional interests of those who would betray the goal of the revolution. That goal centred not on partition but on sovereignty, the creation of an independent state. This strategy fundamentally transformed the politics of the Free State and created a framework that still informs political realities in both jurisdictions. It had little to do with the national question *per se* and everything to do with the skilful manipulation of interest groups whose needs were clothed in the respectability of being championed by a national movement rather than a mere political party.

De Valera recognised that once the political state had been established, and its legitimacy solidified by successive elections, the appeal to republican certainty became ever more irrelevant. By 1926 he realised that unless republicans embraced the parliamentary system a new political order would be firmly established that had the potential to permanently exclude them. His chief lieutenant, Seán Lemass, a founder-member of Fianna Fáil, put the position succinctly in a series of articles for *An Phoblacht* in 1926. 'We must forget all the petty conceits and formulae which bedevil us, like rouge on the face of a corpse and face the facts, the hard facts, which we must overcome.'[28] Here was an acceptance that an appeal to mythical republicanism alone had rendered Sinn Féin obsolete. The strategists realised that it was necessary to create a political machine that could exploit the very obvious weaknesses presented by Cumann na nGaedheal's structural base. The dichotomy between republican moralism and nationalist pragmatism is therefore a less than perfect framework for assessing the nature of Fianna Fáil politics.[29] A more likely explanation is that Cumann na nGaedheal's failure to act rationally in the deteriorating circumstances of the nineteen-twenties opened the way for Fianna Fáil to steal the very ground so carefully established in the early years of the state.

The founding fathers of Fianna Fáil were helped considerably in this project by the progressive undermining of the government's reformist credentials. Large voting blocs such as the small farmers and the urban working class were alienated by alliances that solidified the vested interests of large-scale farmers, known as the rancher class, and the chambers of commerce. A government that prided itself on its pragmatism appeared callous to many; it also made the government a hostage to fortune when a viable alternative emerged. De Valera was determined that it would be Fianna Fáil that would take advantage of the opportunity.[30]

Outrage alone, however, was not going to deliver the kind of change envisaged by de Valera and the wider Fianna Fáil leadership. They wanted to create a new focus for the state that would ensure the reproduction of its own centrality. The use of old IRA commanders helped to improve the social cachet of the new party; former rebels such as Ernie O'Malley helped propagate the message abroad.[31] There were, however, carefully defined limits to Fianna Fáil's radicalism, both on the national question and, more importantly, on social and economic policies.

The republican left was neutered by the appropriation of the campaign against the payment of land annuities to the British state in lieu of rent to landlords. Similarly, care was taken not to transform anti-rancher sentiment into 'operational reality',[32] and in its dealings with the urban working class Fianna Fáil was careful not to allow the development of class-based politics. A combination of enhanced housing programmes and increases in social welfare provided important electoral cushions for the party as it sought to develop a new national bourgeoisie, which allowed it to appeal simultaneously to both business and the trade unions. This was to be achieved by a reliance on protected industry producing for a home market, which proved incapable of stopping the downward pressure on wages. Neither for the first time nor for the last, Fianna Fáil astutely propagated the view that the shortages caused by the Economic War with Britain were part of the necessary pain of securing national freedom.

The threat from the right was equally neutralised. Academic opinion is divided over the threat posed to democracy by the emergence of the Blueshirt movement;[33] it is beyond dispute, however, that the violence associated with it provided de Valera and Fianna Fáil with a strong law-and-order mandate. The result was the marginalisation of right-wing politics. A realignment that saw the creation of Fine Gael did little to stem this. The politics of Fine Gael seemed increasingly irrelevant, indeed carping, particularly over the 1937 Constitution.

Fianna Fáil was again able to don the national cloak by accusing the right of conspiring to restart the civil war.

In many ways the Constitution marks a defining moment in Fianna Fáil's successful attempt to cement its centrality in Irish politics. As Richard Dunphy demonstrates in his deconstruction of the document, it represented an astute cocktail of Catholic thinking and paternalism; it successfully managed to keep the dream of unfinished business alive while ensuring that nothing was done about it. For de Valera—as for most of Ireland—there was now no justification whatever for IRA violence. A new 26-county state had been delivered into the hands of a national bourgeoisie that owed its very existence to Fianna Fáil and its continued perseverance with protectionism.[34]

In short, no alternative vision was able to compete. The republican movement found itself out of kilter with de Valera's vision of an Ireland of frugal comfort at peace with itself. Fianna Fáil's careful wielding of state power while paying lip service to the republican ideal placed the republican left at a severe disadvantage. The labour movement was equally marginalised, unable to capitalise on the inherent weakness of Fianna Fáil's socio-economic policies because of the latter's astute handling of urban constituencies, particularly in Dublin.[35]

In essence, the threat to Fianna Fáil came from within. Intellectual and strategic torpor caught unawares an organisation that prided itself on its organisational abilities. The emergence of Clann na Talmhan in 1938, galvanising the rural vote, and Clann na Poblachta in 1946, targeting the working class and disgruntled white-collar workers, particularly teachers, fits into this analysis. The dissatisfaction within the rural and urban sectors demonstrated that a valid alternate to Fianna Fáil could be fashioned. The shaping of a unified constituency, which Fianna Fáil had so carefully built up, was wilting before its eyes, and the party had no answers. Appeals to stability, to ideology, to ending partition, though central to Fianna Fáil's conception of itself as the guardian of the nation, were not sufficient to keep its cross-class appeal and contributed significantly to electoral defeat.[36]

It was this lapse of purpose more than any other reason that created the conditions for Fianna Fáil's loss of power in the 1948 election. It was the shock of this collapse that refocused the minds of the party strategists in refashioning the powerhouse. Policy revolved around re-creating the dichotomy between Fianna Fáil as guardian of the national interest, operating beyond the petty conceits of class politics, and coalition politics aimed at breaking that model. Following the declaration of the Republic, the first salvo in the battle to re-invigorate Fianna Fáil was detectable in the manoeuvring surrounding the Anti-Partition Campaign. Henry Patterson is undoubtedly correct in describing both episodes as evidence of little more than a 'self-interested scramble' to determine nationalist credentials.[37] Despite the obvious weaknesses as a mobilising strategy, it did prove remarkably successful in bringing a new generation of politicians into Fianna Fáil. These included Charles Haughey and Jack Lynch, men who were to take opposing sides when the conflagration in Northern Ireland in August 1969 once again brought the issue of 'unfinished business' to the top of the agenda, exposing the ideological deceit at the heart of Fianna Fáil's policy pretensions.

For its part, the remnants of the republican movement mis-interpreted the Anti-Partition Campaign, in particular, as a signal that the political establishment in Dublin was prepared to step beyond rhetoric. The IRA began a process of steadily building up its arms net-work. Raids were confined to Northern Ireland and Britain; among those involved were Cathal Goulding and Seán Mac Stiofáin, later to become the most influential figures in republicanism for fifty years. Goulding was sent over from Dublin to help Mac Stiofáin raid the armoury at a public school in Essex. It was, according to Mac Stiofáin's own account, a fiasco, and the pair, along with a third accomplice, were imprisoned for eight years.[38]

The dismal and predictable failure of the Anti-Partition Campaign increased alienation in Northern Ireland, however, and offered poten-tially more fertile ground for a republican movement increasingly out-manoeuvred in the new Republic. Yet even here the ultimate decision to move towards a military campaign was predicated not on arguments over viability but on the premise that unless military action was taken the movement would split again. The most significant expression of this negative potential surrounded the election of Liam Kelly as MP for Mid-Ulster in 1952. Kelly argued passionately:

> I do not believe in constitutional methods. I believe in the use of force; the more the better, the sooner the better. That may be treason or sedition: call it whatever you like.[39]

Behind this bellicose statement lay the sub-text that Kelly was prepared to countenance recognition of the Republic as declared by Seán MacBride, a step that would involve ending the purist policy of abstention. To prevent a drift towards split, the movement began to drift towards war.

The perception of underlying popular support for armed struggle was heightened by Sinn Féin's unexpectedly good performance in the 1955 Westminster elections, which provided victories in Mid-Ulster and Fermanagh-South Tyrone and secured the highest nationalist vote since partition. Sinn Féin coupled this increased militancy with an analysis that ascribed the deteriorating economic conditions of the nineteen-fifties to continued British occupation of the six counties, rather than the systemic failure of the autarchic economics of protectionism. The 'one more push' school of thought flourished. Republican strategists argued that the use of violence would force the national question to the top of the agenda, the Nationalist Party could be swept aside, and the paradigm underpinning the 1922 settlement would be irrevocably altered.

It was buoyed up in this strategy by a policy of inaction in the Republic. The IRA was in effect operating with impunity, in large part because of the influence of MacBride. A statue commemorating the IRA leader Seán Russell, who died while on a mission to arrange weapons from Nazi Germany, was allowed to be erected in Dublin; IRA internees were released; and the bodies of those executed by de Valera's government were returned to their families. When Fianna Fáil returned to power from 1951 to 1954 and again during the new coalition Government of 1954–7, the IRA was careful not to provide an excuse for repression and made a policy decision not to engage in confrontation with forces south of the border. In turn the IRA was viewed as representing little or no threat to public order and went unmolested, much to the anger of Britain.[40] Emboldened, it launched Operation Harvest in 1956, carefully sticking to this policy so as not to alienate public opinion in the Republic. The South was used merely as a base from which to launch campaigns against economic and commercial targets on the northern side of the border.

The strategists in the Army Council argued that limiting its sphere of operations to areas in which the Catholic community was in a majority would minimise the danger of a loyalist backlash and therefore of sectarian conflagration. Early propaganda victories, such as the death of Seán South in Brookeborough in December 1956 following a botched raid on an RUC station, brought thousands of people onto the streets in a show of sympathy. Little thought was given to the impact attacks on Northern Ireland would have on the position of Catholics in the entire province, or indeed to how such attacks would feed and subsequently buttress the siege impulses of Ulster unionism.[41] The gains were, however, to be short-lived. The 1957 general election in the Republic may have brought about a significant increase in Sinn Féin's representation, which abstentionism rendered ineffective anyway, but it also returned to power a much more formidable enemy, Fianna Fáil. De Valera quickly reintroduced internment, and the campaign disintegrated.

By 1957, at the end of de Valera's career, the person who had steered his party to dominance told his supporters that force could not be justified and that the best way to achieve unity was to break down the high levels of distrust. When Seán Lemass took over as Taoiseach this thinking was formally introduced as policy, representing, according to Martin Mansergh, 'far more continuity than is generally acknowledged.'[42] Mansergh argues that an address by Seán Lemass to the Oxford Union in which he proposed that Britain should act as a persuader for Irish unity represented a logical conclusion of Fianna Fáil policy enunciated by the party from its inception. This was a brand of republicanism 'formally based on a majoritarian ethos with regards to the constitutional position, while prepared to allow maximum latitude on other issues.'[43] The new policy involved a major change in emphasis: the replacement of antagonism with rapprochement. Events within Fianna Fáil and within the wider republican movement, however, were to destabilise the grand project of redefining the nature of patriotism.[44]

Within Fianna Fáil itself Lemass found himself riding the tiger of opposition to the scale of Government cut-backs throughout the early sixties. His grip on the party was weakening with the economy. As Todd Andrews acidly pointed out, 'it would be impossible to organise cabals in the cabinet or the party [in de Valera's time] but they were certainly organised in Seán Lemass's time.'[45] The Government and the party were becoming increasingly nervous about the lack of direction in policy or, more accurately, a belief that the technocratic approach had more in common with the Cumann na nGaedheal government of the twenties than the humane social republicanism bestowed by de Valera. Calling for closer links with Northern Ireland had taken away an important ideological crutch, with little benefit.

When Lemass finally decided to go, he left behind a party riven by factionalism. Speaking notes from his old adversary, Seán MacEntee, unearthed by John Horgan, for a party meeting at which the Taoiseach announced his intention to retire reveal a remarkable prescience.

MacEntee accused the party leader of squandering de Valera's inheritance, leaving behind an organisation 'at its lowest ebb,' which

> in the minds of the general public appears to be riven apart. The devious
> course which he has pursued not only in relation to his leadership and on
> the succession but on other issues as well, have confounded the members
> of our organisation so that none of them know where we stand on any
> issue.[46]

Far from organising a smooth succession, Lemass's prevarication allowed the protagonists to sharpen their knives, with dangerous consequences. Lemass had unsuccessfully attempted to persuade Patrick Hillery and Jack Lynch to take over the leadership. Fianna Fáil was becoming unmanageable; both individuals had witnessed a weakening of the iron control; neither wanted to carry the can of ignominious defeat. The rising stars of the party, George Colley and Charles Haughey, had no such compunction: both had the capacity to tear the fragile fabric of Fianna Fáil asunder.

As the feuding intensified, farmers demonstrated on the streets outside Haughey's Department of Agriculture. Neil Blaney, the ultimate party machine man, conferred with Kevin Boland, who perceived himself to be the political soul of Fianna Fáil and put his name forward, creating a three-way race. Lemass sought to placate the rival factions by eventually securing the nomination of Lynch; Blaney and Haughey immediately retired from the race, neither prepared to openly flout the decree of the ageing Lemass. Colley refused to back down and was humiliated in the ensuing battle. Haughey and Blaney sensed that Lynch's hold on power was fragile and plotted his downfall.

The leader of Fine Gael, James Dillon, watched the developments with wry amusement. During a debate in Dáil Éireann on 11 November he predicted with remarkable precision the power struggle in Fianna Fáil. 'There is not an hour, or a day, or a week until they break his [Lynch's] heart, that the clash of knives will not be heard in the corridors of Fianna Fáil.' He proclaimed Lynch as a man of integrity but viewed him as expendable to those who 'are now sharpening their knives and whirling their tomahawks, not only for their enemies but for one another.'[47]

A similar rupture at the highest echelons of the IRA mirrored this power struggle within Fianna Fáil. For the republican movement the disastrous 1956–62 campaign, with its retreat to the primacy of armed struggle and ideological purity, had again stymied the movement's

capacity to remain relevant. Lemass's warning in 1926 that the movement must forget the 'petty conceits that bedevil us' retained its
potency in assessing the reasons behind the failure of yet another resort
to fundamental precepts. There was a belated recognition that the
anti-partition campaign and interventions in Northern politics were
primarily aimed at Southern consumption rather than any real determination to radically alter the political landscape. The search was on
for an alternative that could compete with Fianna Fáil's conception of
the state. Its answer was found in the political path advocated by a
new IRA chief of staff, Cathal Goulding. It represented a return to the
politics of social republicanism.[48]

Goulding had emerged from prison in 1959 to witness the disintegration of yet another campaign of republican violence. His
former prison colleague Seán Mac Stiofáin attended a reception held
in his honour in Dublin. Mac Stiofáin, released earlier in the year, had
settled in Cork and had already begun working his way up the IRA
hierarchy. Despite the apparent futility of the IRA strategy, both men
remained committed to the cause and to the prosecution of the war.
Significantly, however, the two differed in their analysis of what the
future could bring. Goulding clearly believed that the lack of clear
political objectives had pushed the movement into a cul-de-sac. In an
interview in 1985 he declared:

> I and others felt that the movement as a whole had never given a thought
> to winning a war. They had only thought of starting one.[49]

His solution was radical: a revolution with the capacity to destroy
partition could be achieved only if the IRA was subsumed within it.
Mac Stiofáin agreed that social agitation had a crucial role to play; he
was simply not prepared, however, to sacrifice the IRA's capacity, or
right, to wage war. The movement was torn between awareness that
the use of force to achieve its core objective was no longer viable and
a recognition that the kind of change advocated by Goulding meant
jettisoning core beliefs. Throughout the sixties these conflicting visions
of the IRA's role in Irish society were played out to increasingly
polarised factions.

The IRA Goulding took control of in 1962 was a bitterly divided
and demoralised organisation. The armed struggle had again failed to
provide tangible benefits. As the prisons opened north and south, the
internees found themselves facing an indifferent world—indifferent to
their cause, indifferent to their sacrifice.[50] The first task facing the new
chief of staff was to find a way of reinvigorating the movement. The

strategy embarked on involved an attempt to awaken the nation from what was perceived to be the torpor of romantic nationalism alluded to in the statement calling off the border campaign.

The Sinn Féin head office in Gardiner Place in central Dublin became a base for those determined to create the conditions for a successful revolution. The great survivors of the republican left, Peadar O'Donnell and George Gilmore, found themselves back in favour and became part of the coterie surrounding the new chief of staff. Two academics, Dr Roy Johnston and Anthony Coughlan, active members of the Connolly Association in London who had recently returned to Dublin, gave the discussions a modern gloss, replete with the arcane language of Marxism-Leninism. This grouping produced a far-reaching diagnosis not only of the nature of the problem but also of future strategies to combat past failures. It concluded that previous attempts to use force had failed because the preconditions for successful revolution were not present. More importantly, it argued that these conditions could be manufactured only if the republican movement developed a wide range of social and economic programmes. The analysis was, of course, self-serving: by placing itself firmly on the far left of the political spectrum, a traditionally less than fertile position in Irish politics long since vacated by a conservative and timid labour movement, the republican movement could retain its vanguard position. There were, however, serious implications for the IRA.[51]

The Goulding strategy is succinctly explained in a document issued in January 1970 entitled 'The IRA in the 1970s'. The critique centres on the problems associated with the lack of an over-arching ideology and the absence of a solid political base. The realignment conducted by the IRA in the sixties centred on rectifying these 'major weaknesses'. A third ingredient of the revolutionary cocktail was the unsettling of Fianna Fáil and its conception of the nation. The document asserts that the IRA's previous emphasis on armed struggle in Northern Ireland was a strategic blunder: the southern state must be challenged.

> Free Statism had been left free of both military, political and social assaults and was merely attacked for its failure to take the six counties and for its coercion of Republicans. Free Statism is now a clearly defined pseudo-nationalist Catholic/Capitalist philosophy rooted in Griffith and de Valera and happy in its British designed geographical area.[52]

A policy of infiltration was used to develop links within the trade unions. This was coupled with an attempt to reveal what these proto-Marxists argued was the corrupt nature of the new breed of Fianna Fáil politicians emerging from the shadow of the revolutionary generation as power finally passed from Lemass to Lynch in 1966. The Land League campaign championed by O'Donnell in the nineteen-thirties and hijacked by de Valera was reintroduced in Mullingar as evidence of the duplicitous nature of Fianna Fáil and its failure to fulfil its radical promise. Attention in particular was focused on the activities of Taca, a fund-raising organisation that formally linked Fianna Fáil to the interests of the business class.[53] Perhaps ironically, the republican leadership joined in the campaign for the preservation of Georgian Dublin against the efforts to create a new indigenous vision of Ireland replete with concrete tower-blocks.

While the change in strategy was greeted with unease by some sections of the movement, the lack of an alternative stayed any immediate schism. Goulding himself had been interned as a youth during the Second World War in the Curragh military internment camp and had subsequently seen action with the abortive armoury raid in England in 1953. Seán Garland, his close associate in the IRA leadership, had played a major role in the Brookeborough raid that led to the death of Seán South in 1957. The unease turned to alarm, however, when Goulding proposed to an IRA convention in 1964 that the policy of abstention should be abandoned.

The policy of non-recognition of the London, Belfast and Dublin parliaments was an article of faith for the republican movement; ending it was not a step to be taken lightly. Indeed there were sound practical reasons for caution—not least the poor electoral performance of the left in Ireland. For Ruairí Ó Brádaigh, a schoolteacher from County Roscommon and chief of staff during the final phase of the border campaign, abstention gave the republican movement its moral status: it was not a mere tactic to be traded, however fortuitous the circumstances might appear in theory or in fact.[54]

He was to receive powerful backing. Seán Mac Stiofáin regarded the proposals as evidence of an 'unmistakable programme' and adopted an increasingly militaristic posture.[55] Reasoning that the changes represented the first step in the sidelining and eventual destruction of the IRA's capacity to wage war, he joined Ó Brádaigh in condemning the proposal. The two were to become important allies as the struggle for the soul of the movement intensified. Abstention was rejected, but, significantly, eight other policy departures were also debated that, if acted upon, could have profound implications. These maintained that economic and social agitation should be the primary goal of the republican movement. That goal, in turn, would be best achieved by greater co-operation with other radical groups: these included the Communist Party of Northern Ireland, the Irish Workers' Party and Connolly Youth Movement in the Republic, and the Connolly Association in England.[56]

Many regarded the new departure as at best a distraction and left the movement. One senior republican returned to Gardiner Place after a tour around Ireland and reported that there was no longer a republican movement.[57] For those who remained, however, the resentment smouldered on over what was perceived to be the undue influence that left-wing intellectuals—Johnston in particular—held over the chief of staff. Mac Stiofáin remembers being suspicious of Johnston from the beginning.

> We were in the cells after being sentenced [in 1953] and [Goulding] said to me this is wrong. We should make contact with Moscow. They have a policy to help people in revolutionary movements. When he was appointed chief of staff he went to London to the embassy of the Soviet Union and was told no, we do not help revolutionary movements, we help revolutionary governments. A couple of months afterwards Johnston and Coughlan returned to Ireland, and the connection was obvious.[58]

Coughlan remained outside the movement, contributing sharp criticisms of the failure of republicanism to offer any real theoretical justification for its position. Johnston was to become a pivotal figure as the IRA changed direction. To Mac Stiofáin, the influence of Johnston, with his doctorate of science and mastery of the nuances of Marxism-Leninism, was evidence of a fatal flaw in Goulding's character. 'He had a key weakness. He felt inferior to somebody with a better education.'[59] But the unease expressed by Mac Stiofáin was widely shared—a point conceded by the chief of staff himself.[60] Nevertheless, despite these misgivings, Goulding maintained that the theoretical input was vital: all that was necessary was the dissemination of the message to the volunteers.

Johnston was appointed to the Army Council with the title of director of education, despite not having taken even a basic training course, much to the consternation of at least two of his senior colleagues. One of his first tasks was to brief volunteers about the need for social agitation. To some it represented not only the stating of the obvious but also the first tangible evidence that the military capacity of the movement was being scaled down. The campaign to stop the sale of the entire County Cork town of Midleton to developers in 1965 was a case in point, an apposite example of the kind of social agitation the new policy ordained, in that it provided evidence of the continued influence of foreign landlords. Mac Stiofáin, as the senior IRA commander in County Cork, suggested that the IRA should go on the offensive by shooting the developer. Goulding, who instead ordered Johnston to give Mac Stiofáin and his men a pep talk, rejected it.[61]

> Johnston came to me in Cork to speak about political education and agitation. I said, 'Look, Roy, we know instinctively that we must do something about Midleton. We don't need you to tell us.'

It is clear that Mac Stiofáin found Johnston's critique irrelevant, self-evident, and irritating. That being said, it would be wrong to view the divisions brewing in the highest echelons of the republican movement as a re-run of the Civil War Sinn Féin split. This was not simply about pragmatism versus atavistic militarism.

> I supported the social and economic aspect, but I said, 'Look, you must have the army ready to act. In any agitation you come to a point when controlled force will help the campaign. You recruit, you train, you get new supplies of arms, new tactics, and wait for an opportunity.'[62]

For Ó Brádaigh and Mac Stiofáin what was at stake was the essence of the movement, the IRA. They agreed wholeheartedly in the analysis put forward that the republican movement had to have a coherent social and economic programme; where they differed was in the role the IRA would play in the new dispensation. There was a growing recognition from 1965 onwards that the logical conclusion of the radical new departure set self-imposed limits on the IRA's freedom of manoeuvre. A revolution might be required, but not yet.

> I went to [Goulding] and said, 'Look, Cathal, we were once friends. I want to sit down and speak to you about the movement. You want the movement to be radical. I agree, but what about the military policy?' He said, 'No, that's out for the time being.' The British army had a recruitment policy, and I wanted to blow up every recruiting office in the North—six of them. That would be good for us in Ireland and America. 'No.' So I encouraged economic resistance. When an English company closed a factory for shoes I sent one of my intelligence units to the main

factory in Nottingham and proposed to burn it. 'No.' So after that relations went down.[63]

Relations were further strained when Johnston condemned as a sectarian practice the tradition of reciting the Rosary at republican commemorations. When Mac Stiofáin objected he was suspended from the movement for two months. It was to be the combination of this attempt to reassure Ulster Protestants in particular about the intentions of the IRA and the wider and more fundamental debate about the army's role in contemporary society that would finally push the movement towards schism.

The northern units of the IRA had watched the manoeuvrings in Dublin with an increasing sense of exasperation. Many packed up their bags and turned their backs on a lifetime of involvement. Among them was Joe Cahill, a member of the IRA who was sentenced to death, later commuted to life imprisonment, for the killing of an RUC man in 1942. Cahill recently told an interviewer: 'We realised that if Goulding and this new leadership were allowed to carry on, republicanism would die a natural death.'[64] Others, not so opposed to the general direction, simply believed that the IRA had no longer anything to offer and returned to ordinary life. John Kelly, who was later to play a central role in the arms trial, explains:

> The leftward trend in the republican movement was fine in itself, but a lot of more traditional republicans would have seen it as getting away from the armed struggle, as getting away from the physical force element within the republican movement—too much concentration on politics and not enough on the physical force element; so there was that residual resentment within the republican movement that formed a catalyst in 1969 for a split that already existed in embryonic form.[65]

Kelly's recollection typifies a perception that has gained currency particularly since the Northern leadership of the Provisional IRA took control of the movement in 1986. This places Belfast at the centre of the movement and suggests that the split occurred primarily because of the failure by the Dublin leadership to retreat from the Marxist script when theory collided with fact on the streets of Northern Ireland. This was undoubtedly a serious factor in precipitating the split; but the roots went much deeper.[66] The reality was that Belfast was not only not powerful enough to change the direction of the movement but played only a minor role in either the development of republican strategy or the opposition to it throughout the sixties. The

Belfast component of the movement had suffered more atrophy than any other; for the commemorations of the fiftieth anniversary of the Easter Rising in 1966 the entire Belfast Brigade could not even fill a minibus to visit Dublin.[67]

The rising sense of resentment felt by the Catholic community in Northern Ireland in the changing social climate of the nineteen-sixties provided the IRA with its greatest opportunity since partition to maintain its relevance. The resentment, if harnessed, offered a synthesis for transforming the dialectic of the proto-Marxist analysis. The opportunity was to be provided by direct confrontation with the state through the Northern Ireland Civil Rights Association, which owed its creation—though not its drive—to Johnston. The civil rights movement was used to further the IRA's ends; but it was for a fundamentally different purpose than the histrionic interpretation put forward by loyalist opponents, and it was also done without the support of the Belfast old guard.

The genesis of the civil rights movement was a meeting of the Wolfe Tone Society established by Goulding as a way of broadening the policy contribution to the republican movement. Goulding and Johnston travelled to the home of a prominent Catholic lawyer, Kevin Agnew, in Maghera on 13 August 1966 to put forward a strategy for broadening the appeal of republican socialism. According to the analysis written by Johnston, delivered by the Cork writer Eoghan Harris and endorsed by Goulding, sectarianism and the resulting discrimination against Catholics in the Northern state were artificially fostered by the interests of British imperialism. If these base motives were exposed, the Protestant working class would realise that their true interests lay in unity. The southerners proposed adopting the policy of trade union infiltration to unify the working class. The meeting concluded that a civil rights campaign should instead be adopted. That campaign centred on the Northern Ireland Civil Rights Association, which held its first meeting the following February.

An influential history of the Provisional IRA suggests that the southerners found themselves gradually outnumbered by those of competing ideologies with more of a feel for Northern realities, a development 'which simultaneously irritated and gratified' the Dublin leadership.[68] This interpretation fails to take into consideration the thrust of Johnston's policy, which was to actively seek out alliances with the communists and trade union movement. It also fails to take into account the fact that a civil rights campaign centred in the North 'to shatter Ulster unionism' was mooted as early as 1955 by the Connolly Association in London, the organisation in which Johnston had made his name.[69]

The decision by the IRA to accept this analysis was the most important factor in hurling Northern Ireland headlong towards chaos. Stormont was for the first time forced to either live up to its democratic ideals or accept an uncomfortable reality that it was, at root, a state founded on base sectarian principles of domination.[70] The problem for the IRA was that it failed to think out the consequences of such a move. Those consequences quickly came to the surface as each civil rights demonstration attracted howls of conspiracy from evangelical firebrands like Ian Paisley. The rhetoric of Paisley and Ulster politicians about an IRA rearming and using the civil rights movement as a Trojan horse to begin another armed campaign missed the point: the emphasis for the Dublin-based leadership of the IRA was on demonstrating the inability of both states to deliver meaningful reforms to benefit the working class. By keeping the IRA under tight control and concentrating on a policy of reform, the republican movement hoped to reach out of the isolation and futility of yet another armed struggle.[71]

The problem for Goulding and Johnston was that in fanning the flames of resentment they were in danger of unleashing forces they would be powerless to control. One unintended consequence was a reawakening of the malign dialectic between militant nationalism and loyalist backlash that had traditionally informed political life in the north-east of Ireland.

Emboldened by an earlier protest in Dungannon, a decision was made to hold a march on 5 October 1968 in Derry, the citadel of Protestant culture and a glaring example of how gerrymandering and housing policy were used to artificially bolster Unionist electoral representation. While the march was organised under the auspices of NICRA, the driving force was Eamonn McCann and the Young Socialists. The route chosen was designed to maximise the chances of confrontation with the state.[72]

The Minister of Home Affairs, William Craig, banned the march on 3 October 1968. Despite the ban, the march went ahead, with senior politicians, including the Nationalist Party leader, Eddie McAteer, and the Republican Labour MP for West Belfast, Gerry Fitt, in attendance. When an RUC road block stopped the march from crossing the Craigavon Bridge into the city centre, trouble flared. Several people were injured, including Fitt. After a sit-down protest, during which there were calls for the marchers to disband, the Young Socialist component began throwing placards at the RUC, who responded with batons.

Serious rioting erupted in the Bogside housing estate in the west of the city as nationalist youths fought running battles with police equipped with riot gear and water cannon. Television pictures showing undoubted police brutality against the marchers were beamed around the world. The over-reaction of the RUC was of course exactly the result the Young Socialists had hoped for. As McCann himself points out,

> a howl of elemental rage was unleashed across Northern Ireland, and it was clear that things were never going to be the same again. We had, indeed set out to make the police over-react. But we hadn't expected the animal brutality of the RUC.[73]

Community relations plummeted. The Unionist administration commended the RUC for adopting restraint in the face of a communist conspiracy orchestrated by the IRA.[74] A fault line was created. As David Harkness points out, 'by condemning the civil rights movement as a republican plot the demonstrators were forced back towards the identification of ideology with religion, so apparently justifying their detractors.'[75] O'Neill's administration was in free fall from that moment onwards. McCann was correct: Northern Ireland would never be the same again.

The Nationalist Party leader, Eddie McAteer, announced that his party was formally relinquishing its position as official opposition at Stormont, a position it had taken only after pressure from Lemass after his meeting with O'Neill in 1965 had marked the beginning of a new rapprochement with Northern Ireland. McAteer journeyed south to see Lemass's successor as Taoiseach, Jack Lynch, who attempted to placate him with a statement that the root cause of the Derry disturbance was the evil of partition. This amounted to little more than a platitude, a retreat to the rhetoric of the past in the absence of any clear thinking about its potential destabilising impact.

It is easy to see why both governments reverted to type in the immediate aftermath of the Derry march. Lynch had more pressing matters to contend with, not least a debilitating power struggle that consistently undermined his position. He had retained the feuding ministers in his Government, but any hopes that the internecine bickering would end soon evaporated. Colley had publicly decried the danger of low standards in high places, a veiled criticism of the flamboyant Haughey, now holding the influential post of Minister for Finance. Blaney developed his position in the party through skilful by-election campaigns, most notably in South Kerry, and by the development of organised links between Fianna Fáil and big business.[76] All three were circling Lynch looking for signs of weakness.

Furthermore, partition had appeared to be copperfastened by successive governments in both jurisdictions, bellicose rhetoric notwithstanding. Fianna Fáil had established itself as the self-appointed guardian of the national interest; it continued to pledge that not only was the reunification of Ireland its central goal but that it alone had the moral authority to achieve it. The Derry violence occurred just as the party was attempting to push through a referendum to end proportional representation—the introduction of which in the North was a central demand of the civil rights movement. Blaney suggested that nationalists were mistaken in campaigning for civil rights: they should instead be concentrating on ending partition. The refusal of Northern nationalists to continue playing their appointed role as Fianna Fáil supplicants was a development that horrified him.[77]

The Ulster Unionist Party, on the other hand, actively fed off and indeed required an IRA threat to underwrite the security of the state. O'Neill's government, under pressure from London, announced a series of measures aimed at satisfying the basic civil rights agenda but in so doing only further infuriated his own community. What was becoming increasingly clear was that beneath the surface of an outwardly stable society, Northern Ireland was a fragile construct, a fact emphasised by an extraordinary television address by Terence O'Neill on 9 December 1968. He spelt out the choices in no uncertain terms. 'Ulster stands at the crossroads.' He appealed to nationalists to believe him when he promised change; to his unionist constituency he made it clear that there was no alternative.

> A Northern Ireland based upon the interests of any one section rather than upon the interests of all could have no long-term future ... Unionism armed with justice will be a stronger cause than unionism armed merely with strength.[78]

The speech was well received in moderate nationalist circles, and a decision was reached to call off all further demonstrations until January 1969, in order to give O'Neill's administration the opportunity to deliver. It was too late, however: the die was cast. The apparent

concessions—in fact the concession of equal rights to a minority community—upset the delicate balance. O'Neill's predecessor, Lord
Brookeborough, was characteristically blunt in a television interview.
'How can you give somebody who is your enemy a higher position
in order to allow him to come and destroy you?' The inability of the
Unionist establishment to deal with a coherent, articulate desire for
fundamental change in the province served only to bring back to life
the failings of partition, challenging the core assumptions of both
governments and of the IRA itself.

The IRA leadership gathered for a convention in early December
1968 against this backdrop of a rapidly disintegrating Northern
Ireland. Goulding, profoundly aware of the dangers of a sectarian
melee in Northern Ireland, was determined to act: he realised that the
execution of his plan to demilitarise and sideline the IRA in order to
further his wider revolution had to be pushed through at this moment
or not at all. The plans hatched at the 1965 convention had in effect
been shelved since then because of opposition in the Army Council
and the Executive.

Goulding proposed two motions to the convention. Firstly, he
wanted to abolish the Army Executive, a second tier that acted in
effect as a second chamber for the movement, and replace it with a
commission; this commission would be charged with gathering the
opinions of grass-roots republicans at open meetings to be held
throughout the country. Secondly, he suggested that the Army
Council be expanded, from seven to twenty members.

While it may appear somewhat esoteric to have been discussing
changes to the composition of the Army Council and the Executive
as Northern Ireland raced towards the precipice, these discussions
were crucial, and the eventual split in the movement can be directly
traced to this convention. According to Mac Stiofáin, 'the split was
inevitable from that moment onwards.'[79]

Traditionally, delegates to an IRA convention appointed a twelve-
member Executive; the Executive then appointed the seven-member
Army Council, which in turn elected the chief of staff. Though the
Executive acted mainly as an advisory body for the Army Council,
crucially it had the capacity to withhold support for the Army
Council. In extreme circumstances it had the right to sack the entire
Army Council and convene an extraordinary convention.[80] The root
desire of the Goulding move in the winter of 1968 was to ensure that
the Executive and the Army Council would do his bidding.

The convention refused to abolish the Executive, but it did accept Goulding's argument that an expanded Army Council could benefit from the insight of a wider social base. The proposal hinged on three interlocking objectives. Firstly, the traditional seven members who made up the Army Council were for the first time elected not by the Executive but directly from the floor of the convention; a further eight were to be elected at four provincial meetings of commanding officers or 'OCs' in those provinces. This was to be crucial. The OCs were appointed by the GHQ Staff, which was under the control of the chief of staff.

It was a shrewd example of Goulding's ability to force through changes, according to Ruairí Ó Brádaigh.

> What he was doing was going to people that he had himself appointed in the four provinces and having in each case people elected. And when the eight were elected they already outnumbered the seven from the floor of the convention.[81]

Throughout his tenure, Goulding had been sure of the active support of only two other members of the Army Council: Seán Garland and Séamus Costello. By expanding the size of the Army Council he shifted the balance of power dramatically. To stem any seepage and to consolidate his position, a further five were then to be co-opted. Those opposed to Goulding were thus rendered powerless. As Ó Brádaigh points out,

> clearly the original seven from the floor of the convention would be swamped by these two further additions of people; and it meant that not alone would Goulding have a majority but he would have an overwhelming majority.[82]

Goulding may have had control for the first time since 1962; but there was a fundamental miscalculation at the heart of his strategy: the reaction of loyalism to the civil rights campaign. Far from seeing the light, the loyalists saw only the dark hand of the IRA in fomenting trouble on the streets—their streets. The civil rights campaign was perceived as the planned destruction of the Northern state, not an honest attempt to end discrimination.[83] The consequences were to be immense, as Northern Ireland spiralled towards the kind of communal violence the IRA had pledged to avoid at all costs.[84] Mac Stiofáin proposed the immediate establishment of defence committees to protect nationalist areas from attack; but protecting Northern Catholics from a loyalist backlash ran counter to the entire strategy.

Even people from the North went to Goulding, from Newry, from Armagh—said they were very worried about the situation. 'We have no guns, any ammunition, and people are leaving the movement.' The response was that if the loyalists attacked the nationalist people then it is the job of the British army to defend them.[85]

By the end of 1968 the apocalyptic warnings from Mac Stiofáin and Northern delegates seemed to Goulding to be just that. Time and space had been bought by the decision of NICRA to suspend further marches. The crucial intervention of the People's Democracy in proceeding with a march from Belfast to Derry on New Year's Day was to destroy any hope of compromise; it was also to heighten the sense of unease within what was left of the republican movement in Northern Ireland. Within People's Democracy was a core of radicals, the Young Socialist Alliance, formed by Michael Farrell on his return from postgraduate study at the University of Strathclyde. He was determined that the impetus of the civil rights campaign should not be destroyed, and he engineered a coup to ensure that the march went ahead, despite widespread nationalist opposition.[86]

Farrell accepts that the march was planned to have profound implications:

> either the government would face up to the extreme right of its own Unionist party … Or it would be exposed as impotent in the face of sectarian thuggery, and Westminster would be forced to intervene, reopening the whole Irish question for the first time in 50 years.[87]

The RUC, despite the appearance of protection, made little effort to prevent attacks on the march, apart from advising its rerouting or cancellation. The marchers were attacked by jeering loyalist protesters on five separate occasions, the most serious on the approach to Derry itself. When the marchers were ambushed at Burntollet, a village outside the city, on 4 January 1969, Farrell's desire became a reality. The marchers were viciously attacked with stones and cudgels. When the parade eventually reached the safety of Guildhall Square, serious rioting with the RUC followed, which gave birth to 'Free Derry' as the RUC were kept out of the Bogside estate. The most complete history of People's Democracy sums up the significance of the march as follows:

> In short some PD members were now seeing their task as the destruction of the State, no matter what the consequences. The Long March began the long march from the policy of persuasion to that of polarisation.[88]

A march the following week in Newry descended into chaos as the RUC baton-charged the crowd. When Farrell suggested taking over Newry post office, the symbolism was apparent. The increased activism on the streets was accompanied by a general election, which led only to further polarisation. O'Neill was humiliated and the Nationalist Party swept aside as internal contests demonstrated the lack of middle ground in Northern Ireland politics. Throughout March and April street politics filled the vacuum at Stormont. Farrell was elected to the leadership of NICRA and immediately began planning a renewed campaign of street disturbances, which reached its height with six simultaneous protests against the Public Order Act on 22 March 1969.

The new left in People's Democracy were determined to use their influence to further the cause of revolution, and they organised a march to Dublin in April to raise the issue of civil rights there. It was a serious mistake and succeeded only in alienating left-wing opinion in the Republic. The following week the UVF blew up an electricity sub-station at Castlereagh to the east of Belfast in an attack blamed on the IRA. Right-wing unionists demanded the end of all concessions. Northern Ireland was fast becoming ungovernable; it became so when RUC men beat a Bogside resident, Sam Devenny, unconscious in front of his family following a riot in Derry city centre on 19 April. He died three months later.

Serious rioting took place after protests organised by NICRA in Belfast amid a series of bomb attacks against utility installations blamed on the IRA but carried out by the UVF to destabilise O'Neill. What was becoming clear was that the attacks were broadening and that the risk of civil war was a real one.

> My contacts in the North were saying there would be trouble here during the summer: get all the help you can. I went to Goulding. He said I don't think so. A meeting of the Army Executive proposed that arms would be collected from south and put in dumps in the north and issued to units in Belfast and elsewhere ready for trouble, but they didn't do it.[89]

Ireland was in turmoil as the Republic went to the polls in June 1969. The election focused almost entirely on Fianna Fáil's determination to destroy the credibility of any left-leaning policy alternative as being an attempt to impose 'Cuban socialism' in Ireland. Dossiers were collected on 'subversive' organisations to illustrate what the

Minister for Justice, Mícheál Ó Móráin, described as 'the new left-wing political queers who have taken over the Labour Party from the steps of Trinity College.'[90]

Fianna Fáil was returned to power with 46 per cent of the vote. While this represented a 2 per cent reduction, the failure of Fine Gael and the Labour Party to adopt a common electoral strategy regarding transfers gave Fianna Fáil seventy-five seats and an overall majority. The Labour Party, in particular, was handicapped by an injudicious use of socialist rhetoric, which allowed the Fianna Fáil strategists to skilfully use the red scare.[91] The result reflected the ability of Fianna Fáil to tap into the social conservatism of the electorate by concentrating on the collapse of old standards of morality in what had become a more liberal climate conducive to the rise of left-wing groups in the cities.

What should have been the crowning achievement of Lynch's career quickly soured. He collapsed at a function after smoking a different brand of tobacco offered to him by the Archbishop of Tuam. This exacerbated the perception in the party that Lynch was an interim figurehead whose leadership days were numbered. The failure of his attempt to demote Blaney after an election he believed he had won for the party signified not only his continued power within the parliamentary party but also the continuance of a high-level leadership campaign fought *in camera* within Fianna Fáil. Michael Mills, the veteran political correspondent of the *Irish Press,* gave this assessment of the pretenders' strengths:

> Blaney was a wonderful organiser. He was a very stubborn man but a massive man to have on hand for the organisation of elections. He played a major part in some of the best by-election victories that Fianna Fáil ever had. He was a very demanding leader of organisation. Similarly, Haughey as Minister for Finance had immense authority, and indeed many people in Fianna Fáil and in other areas regarded Haughey as practically running the country in this period, in as much as the decisions that really counted were taken by Haughey.[92]

The battleground for the control of Fianna Fáil was to be in the quickly deteriorating situation in the North, and the chief weapon the completion of the national revolution. Blaney saw in the coming conflagration an opportunity to reassert the party's control over the civil rights movement and over nationalist politics in general. Haughey was determined that Blaney would not outflank him.

Within the IRA, schism had already taken place, with the director of intelligence flouting Army Council regulations. From early May onwards Mac Stiofáin had been stockpiling weapons; in June he transferred the weapons to dumps no longer under the control of GHQ. The putsch had begun. Mac Stiofáin suggests that there was no alternative.

> I decided that my duty is to help the people in Belfast in particular, and any weapons I could get I said to friends, come and pick them up, and we raided two gun shops in the south. The Army Council didn't know.[93]

Within a month the first overt signs of schism appeared at a ceremony in Mullingar. The occasion was the re-interment of Peter Barnes and James McCormick, two IRA men hanged for bombing Coventry in 1940. Jimmy Steele, a leading Belfast republican and close associate of Mac Stiofáin, gave the oration. He criticised the emphasis on constitutional methods and suggested that armed force was the only method of securing the aim of a united Ireland. To loud applause, he proclaimed disdainfully that 'one is now expected to be more conversant with the teaching of Chairman Mao than our dead patriots.'[94]

Peter Taylor suggests that this provides evidence of 'the growing fracture within the IRA between Belfast and Dublin.'[95] While it is true that the Belfast IRA in particular was hostile to any form of socialism, Steele was articulating a wider sense of unease about where the IRA should stand in the new dispensation. Mac Stiofáin agreed with the sentiments but thought Steele was mistaken in going public, in particular because weapons had already begun to move into place in the North.[96]

The dissidents had no quarrel with the need to have a coherent social and economic programme. They saw, however, that an exclusive emphasis on parliamentary politics—particularly in the aftermath of a general election that comprehensively demonstrated the futility of adopting a position further to the left of the already discredited Labour Party—amounted to strategic suicide. As Mac Stiofáin made clear,

> it went without saying that agitation on social and economic issues was part of the struggle for justice. But I believed that we should not allow ourselves to get so committed to it that we would lose sight of the main objective: to free Ireland from British rule. Guerrillas who want to bring social and political change do not wait for conditions to become ripe for revolutionary action, because they could be waiting for ever.[97]

In reality Mac Stiofáin had to wait only a further two months. The uneasy construct was to be tested to its limit as the 1969 marching season reached its climax.

CHAPTER TWO

We Will Not Stand By

The Impact of August 1969

HE 'marching season' of July and August had long been a
source of confrontation in the north-eastern six counties of
Ireland. The practice intensified after partition.[1] Such a
palpable show of Protestant defiance within a Catholic
community determined on achieving what it perceived as equality
was a recipe for disaster.[2] As the civil rights campaign of the nineteen-
sixties developed, the confrontations with the RUC and the Special
Constabulary—ostensibly a police reserve but in reality a Protestant
armed militia—became commonplace.[3] Events on the ground created
new grievances and new grievances new demands, each in turn more
fundamental and thus more destabilising. The perception of threat
versus opportunity heightened demonstrably as the 1969 marching
season progressed.

There was an early warning of the trouble ahead on 2 August,
when the RUC came under attack from nationalists and unionists
alike over the policing of a Junior Orange Order parade through west
Belfast. The Catholic residents of the Unity Flats complex took
exception to the parade passing their area. Rather than rerouting or
banning the parade, the RUC response was to hem in the residents
and to force the young Orangemen through the estate. Skirmishes
between the police and rival demonstrators were contained, but by
the time the parade made its return journey, both sides were spoiling
for revenge. Rumours had swept the Shankill Road district that the
bandsmen were under threat, and large groups of loyalists gathered at
the edge of the complex. For several hours Unity Flats were under

siege. Every accessible window was broken in what the RUC later accepted was a frenzied attack. Residents claimed that the police allowed this to happen unhindered. The RUC countered:

> Citizens who are under attack cannot be expected to make proper allowance for the problems confronting the Authorities, or to recognise that it may be proper for the police to refrain from taking vigorous action in order to avoid a greater catastrophe.[4]

As frustration and anger came to the boil, the RUC was caught in the middle. Following the dispersal of the parade, the police turned on the loyalist demonstrators and forced them back into the Shankill Road area, prompting two days of severe rioting. Such was the level of animosity towards the RUC that the Ulster Special Constabulary was deployed in Protestant areas to assuage the loyalist population. The implication was clear: the Special Constabulary was loyal, untainted with the suspicion of sell-out to those who were determined to destroy Ulster, and therefore more acceptable to the Protestant community.

The RUC submission to the Scarman Tribunal is instructive. It argues that

> the extent and ferocity of the rioting in the Shankill Road area on the 2nd and 3rd of August and the forceful nature of the action taken by the police to deal with it have tended to be obscured. The police did not hesitate to use whatever force was required to put an end to it, many casualties were suffered and large numbers of arrests were made.[5]

What is also clear is that sectarian feeling in Belfast was running at such a dangerous level that the city was on the point of exploding. As Lord Scarman acknowledged in the final report on the causes of the violence, in such a volatile atmosphere it would take very little to spark a major disturbance.

> Their own interpretation of the events of 1968 and early 1969 had encouraged the belief among the minority that demonstrations did secure concessions and that the police were their enemy and the main obstacle to a continuing programme of demonstrations, while the same events had convinced a large number of Protestants that a determined attempt, already gaining a measure of success, was being made to undermine the constitutional position of Northern Ireland within the United Kingdom.[6]

On 12 August, Derry—a predominantly Catholic city controlled by the Protestant minority only through gross gerrymandering—acted merely as a detonator. The Apprentice Boys' parade marked the finale of the 1969 marching season, an event that nationalist Ireland viewed with increasing alarm. The Taoiseach, Jack Lynch, asserted that the Government had received intelligence that the parade would be held on a much greater scale than previously, in large part to demonstrate who controlled Northern Ireland. The Minister for External Affairs, Dr Patrick Hillery, asked London to ban the parade; the request was refused. According to Lynch,

> the holding of this parade at all could well have serious consequences but to enlarge participation in it threefold or fourfold, as we were reliably informed would be the case, we were convinced, would be highly provocative, to say the least.[7]

London, however, was not prepared to push Stormont any further, recognising that forcing its recalcitrant dominion brought with it risks of long-term involvement. At a meeting on 3 August the Stormont Cabinet decided on a number of security measures, including giving the Minister of Home Affairs more latitude in deciding when to use CS gas. The Cabinet also decided to contact the Home Office to alert it 'to the possibility that the assistance of the military might have to be invoked.' This request prompted an exchange of correspondence between the Cabinet Secretary, Sir Harold Black, and his counterpart in London, Sir Philip Allen, which demonstrates the distrust between the two administrations and the growing impatience of Westminster. The British Home Secretary, James Callaghan, said he believed that if the British sent soldiers onto the streets of Northern Ireland they might find themselves committed to taking over the government of the North. In his reply Black commented:

> The UK authorities should consider the situation that might arise if, in fact, they did decide to exercise direct rule from Westminster. There would first of all, be a frightening reaction from the Protestant community which could make anything that has happened up to now seem like child's play; a provisional government might be set up with extreme elements at its head and it was highly probable that wholesale sectarian strife would break out, not only in the streets but in the factories.[8]

According to Maurice Hayes, then a senior civil servant at Stormont,

> there is little doubt that his note had an effect, but it would not have been the only influence on the decision not to impose direct rule at that time. In the end, politicians have to face reality and the reality was of

really wild men riding around the place and the real danger of a protestant provisional government (based on the Portadown parliament and
dissident ministers) and a revolt by armed B Specials.[9]

Derry provided the venue for not one but three power struggles,
each with lasting significance. Firstly, there was the increased anger
within unionism, identified by Scarman, that the civil rights movement was aimed not at securing equality but at the destruction of the
state. Secondly, two distinct battles were occurring within nationalism.
The radicals, led by Eamonn McCann, had been progressively marginalised as more moderate spokespersons, such as John Hume and
Ivan Cooper, sought to find some sort of accommodation with the
Unionist establishment. The radicals were determined to use the
coming Apprentice Boys' march as a Trojan horse to smash the state
and usher in a socialist republic. This somewhat eulogistic account
captures the idealised hope:

> In the Bogside and elsewhere the rioting classes were not impressed [with
> James Chichester-Clark, the Prime Minister]. The unemployed youths
> of areas like the Bogside had, at the outset of the civil rights campaign,
> been regarded as marching fodder. Energetic and instinctively aggressive,
> they could be counted on to turn out for sit-downs, marches, pickets or
> any other protest activity which was organised. It was they who had
> turned out on 5 October [1968]. It was their energy and aggression
> which had powered the civil rights movement through its first frenetic
> months … The rage and frustration which lay just beneath the surface of
> life in the Bogside could no longer be contained within the thin shell of
> the CAC's [Citizens' Action Committee's] timid respectability. The
> 'hooligans' had taken over, and the stage was set for a decisive clash
> between them and the forces of the state.[10]

McCann and his coterie were not, however, the only revolutionaries in town. Seán Keenan, a close ally of Seán Mac Stiofáin, also viewed
the deteriorating situation as an opportunity to reassert the supremacy
of the republican vanguard and the position of militant republicanism
within it. Keenan was a long-standing member of the republican
movement and widely regarded as the leader of the IRA in Derry. His
influence within the movement was evidenced as early as 1962, when
he gave the oration at the republican plot in Milltown cemetery in
Belfast. 'One day,' he told the crowd, 'the appeal of those crying from
the grave [will] be heard not only by the faithful few but also by all
Ireland. Then Ireland, like a giant waking from its slumber, [will] throw

off the yoke of tyranny and wonder [why] it has borne it so long.'[11] Given the circumstance of the ending of an increasingly futile border campaign, the speech was simultaneously optimistic and prescient.

From early in 1969 Keenan had been manoeuvring to gain advantage within Derry Citizens' Action Committee, an umbrella grouping of those agitating for change. He was rebuffed after rioting in the city in April; however, by July he could not be ignored.[12] The Citizens' Action Committee met on 17 July to plan a strategy; its failure to agree provided Keenan with an opportunity. At the end of the month he formally established Derry Citizens' Defence Association.[13] The emphasis was on the creation of lines of defence. Petrol bombs were stockpiled and barricades were prepared. For public consumption a 'Peace Corps' was established to

> enrol stewards for order-keeping duties but it does not seem to have operated very efficiently. The director, a man of no previous experience, never received a list of those under his control.[14]

That, clearly, was the intention.

This was exactly the type of movement that Mac Stiofáin had unsuccessfully argued for at the IRA convention the previous autumn: under republican control but with representatives from disparate organisations allowed to join, giving the impression of wider support. With such a movement coming into existence just as Jimmy Steele was berating the IRA leadership in a Mullingar graveyard, it was apparent that militant republicanism saw in the Apprentice Boys' march an unmissable opportunity.[15]

Keenan was determined that the time had come to fight back. Derry would set an example. It not only represented the most flagrant example of the institutionalised discrimination in Northern Ireland but was also for that very reason the moral centre of the civil rights movement. Keenan would take opposition to the state to the next stage. The croppies would no longer lie down.

McCann and the moderate leadership of Derry Citizens' Action Committee had ceded control of the revolution they thought they could control. The only winner was Keenan, who saw in the coming conflagration Irish nationalism waking from slumber, as he had predicted seven years earlier.

As expected, the parade descended into chaos. Stewards from the Citizens' Defence Association were hopelessly overstretched as tension boiled over in Little James Street between Catholic demonstrators and

Protestant youths following the parade. The RUC's response was immediate: they charged down the network of small streets leading from the city centre into the Bogside.[16] Protestant civilians followed behind, smashing windows as they went along, unhindered by the police. The images of that night were to discolour still further the relations between the nationalist community and the RUC; from that moment onwards, the initiative fell into the hands of the Defence Committee.[17] In fact it fell into the hands of Seán Mac Stiofáin. Maurice Hayes recalls:

> The unionist government at Stormont had no contact with the nationalist community, did not listen to their spokesmen, and shared no confidences with them. Their main source of information was the police, filtered through an historically partisan ministry of Home Affairs. This convinced them that the Civil Rights Movement was a front for a republican rising backed by the Irish government and a cloak for the resurgent IRA. (The resurgent IRA bit came later, but that was effect rather than cause). In Dublin, where the thinking on the Northern Ireland problem had not moved since the Treaty Debates, it was all seen as a pogrom against Catholics which would require them, against their will, to do something. Nobody was quite sure what.[18]

The Bogside became engulfed in noxious clouds of CS gas as a tense confrontation between the RUC and nationalist demonstrators continued into the night. The Prime Minister, James Chichester-Clark, made a televised appeal for calm, telling the people of the Bogside: 'We want peace, not vengeance.'[19] It was too late, however, for rational discourse. The Battle of the Bogside amounted to nothing less than a unilateral declaration of independence. Not for the first time, Northern Ireland faced the threat of all-out civil war, forcing linked but subtly different concerns to the attention of reluctant governments in London and Dublin.

The Labour government in London saw in the mayhem the possibility of a quagmire like that created by the United States in Viet Nam. The most telling indication of Britain's primary concern comes from James Callaghan, who remarks in his autobiography: 'The advice came to me from all sides: on no account get sucked into the Irish bog.'[20] The British government had ordered the establishment of various commissions to investigate the alleged abuses inherent in the Stormont system but refused to allow the North to assert itself as the primary motor of British politics. Interesting new evidence provided by Peter Rose shows that John Chilcott, acting under Callaghan's direction, developed plans for military intervention. The full range of options was discussed, 'including troops in support of civil power and including direct rule but not immediately.'[21] This argument is confirmed by the recent release of the British Cabinet papers for 1969. As early as 13 February 1969 a draft bill suspending the Northern Ireland parliament and government was printed. Further contingency plans introduced that summer by the Ministry of Defence included five scenarios, ranging from sporadic civil disturbances to 'a situation of a Northern Ireland government which actively opposes the take-over of control by HMG [Her Majesty's Government].'[22] The plans were not adopted, nor was the threat explicitly put to Stormont. Instead, the British government took the somewhat naïve policy decision of hoping that if the Stormont government would change its priorities, the situation would resolve itself.[23]

The situation did not improve after the forced resignation of Terence O'Neill. London hoped Chichester-Clark would succeed where O'Neill failed, and believed assurances from the Northern Ireland Department of Home Affairs that the Apprentice Boys' parade could be successfully stewarded. The evidence suggests that the British government was simply preoccupied with more pressing matters— including internecine conflict within the Cabinet itself—to allow Northern Ireland to impinge until it was too late.[24] This is an assessment shared by Maurice Hayes.

> Northern Ireland was not high on the list of priorities and remained so throughout the period. I remember, after the fall of the first Wilson government, a former minister recounting with a sneer how surprised they were that Chichester-Clark and Co. seemed to think that the Home Office had nothing else to think about than Northern Ireland. Maybe if they had thought a bit more about it things might have been different. Then again they might have been worse.[25]

For Dublin, the threat posed by the violence in Northern Ireland also reopened internecine battles. The instability in the North was per-haps the most ideologically damaging. In a perceptive, if self-serving, contribution, Conor Cruise O'Brien noted that

> Fianna Fáil was a party, which exploited a Republican-revolutionary mystique, while practising very ordinary pragmatic middle-class politics. The effect of Bogside was to bring the mystique exploited into sharp collision with the pragmatism practised.[26]

Given the rhetoric of nationalism, a robust response was dictated; yet the violence underlined Dublin's powerlessness to influence Northern nationalism in either its constitutional or its militant form. Of even greater concern was the fact that the political spokesmen emerging from behind the barricades were equally contemptuous of the Southern state. Faced with the consequences of generations of empty rhetoric, and aware of the profound gap between ideological underpinning and contemporary reality, the leader of Fianna Fáil, Jack Lynch, moved first. He resolved to make a national address on television; but first he had to reach consensus with his Government about what exactly the message should entail. Blaney and Boland demanded that the Irish army should move across the border. Lynch, supported by Hillery, advised caution but agreed to ask the Irish embassy in London to 'request the immediate cessation of police attacks on the people of Derry.'[27]

Official papers reveal just how volatile the situation was. As the Government was meeting, progress reports were brought in. At 4:00 p.m. the Government was informed:

> There is a lull in the situation in Derry at the moment but further trouble is expected later tonight. Tear gas is being used on an extensive scale by the RUC. The Bishop of Derry is trying to arrange the evacuation of women and children and has asked Father O'Brien, the parish priest of Buncrana, to prepare the local hall to receive them.[28]

Official papers record that at 4:50 p.m. the ambassador to London was asked to 'request the British government to apply immediately to the United Nations for the urgent despatch of a peace-keeping force to the Six Counties.' An indication of the perceived threat to the stability of the Southern state created by the violence in Derry is apparent in the advice given by senior civil servants, who counselled against an Anglo-Irish summit meeting. They reasoned that the British government might

> manoeuvre the Taoiseach into appearing to have asked for, or approved of, the use of British troops in the North. This could lead to an adverse reaction from extremist groups in the south.[29]

A deliberate decision was taken, therefore, not to engage directly at the highest level, in order for Dublin to gain both time and consensus.

Against his instincts, Lynch agreed to harden the speech. He may have been one of the most popular leaders in the history of the state, but this stemmed more from his personality than from any political prowess, or indeed his ability to manage his Government.

A sense of Lynch's failure to control his Government was evident as early as 2 July 1969 in the Dáil debate on the nomination of his Government. Breaking with Dáil tradition, Kevin Boland spoke at length, denying allegations that he personally was involved in gerrymandering and in condemning the Labour Party as communists in the 1969 election. Despite repeated requests from the Ceann Comhairle, Boland continued with his speech. According to the Fine Gael TD Mark Clinton, Lynch sent a note to Boland, who responded by throwing it on the ground.

> He [Boland] says he is not arrogant. He got the Taoiseach's note; he twisted it up in his hand and banged it on the ground to show what he thought of the Taoiseach, the Ceann Comhairle and this House. This is the sort of treatment which Deputy Boland has been handing out to people outside this House and inside this House and he thinks he will get away with it again. He certainly will not and no threat of physical violence, which he has not been known to try to use inside the House as well as outside it, will deter me or any member of my party from expressing our view about Mr Boland's conduct.[30]

The incident was recalled years later by Conor Cruise O'Brien.

> Fianna Fáil is not a normal political party. It has many of the characteristics of a clan, and many of a Mafia. It feels that the State can derive its legitimacy only from Fianna Fáil and not from the democratic process, and is in consequence fully legitimate only when Fianna Fáil is in office. Co-opted outsiders like Jack Lynch can be very useful to Fianna Fáil in winning elections, but they have no real status within Fianna Fáil. As he came to realise this, Jack Lynch already felt insecure even in 1969.[31]

It was a measure of his relative weakness within Fianna Fáil that despite his winning a clear majority just two months earlier, hawks such as Blaney could in effect dictate policy.[32]

After a number of last-minute revisions to his speech, Lynch arrived at the RTE studios in Donnybrook on the evening of 13 August, aware that the speech could mark a defining moment. Desmond Fisher was the senior news representative on duty; he gave Lynch a bottle of whiskey to settle his nerves.

> I could not help noticing that his script was badly typed, with corrections in ink scrawled all over it. I said he could not possibly go on air with a

script in that state and immediately arranged to have it typed out in a large typeface with double spacing between the lines. He asked for a private telephone and I overheard him telephoning his wife, Máirín, to consult her on changes he proposed to make. At one point he asked me what I thought would happen if he were to order the Army into the North as some of his advisors counselled. I said I thought they would get about 20 miles into Down or Derry before they would be massacred in a fight with the British. He smiled wanly at my answer and said he had come to the same conclusion himself.[33]

Whether as a result of the fortitude offered by the whiskey or the telephone call to his wife, the speech made by Lynch that night ranks as one of the most important made by a Taoiseach since the formation of the state. He declared that only the ending of partition could provide a permanent solution, and accompanied this with an implicit threat.[34]

It is with deep sadness that you, Irishmen and women of good will, and I have learned of the tragic events which have been taking place in Derry and elsewhere in the North in recent days. Irishmen in every part of this island have made known their concern at these events. This concern is heightened by the realisation that the spirit of reform and intercommunal co-operation has given way to the forces of sectarianism and prejudice. All people of good will must feel saddened and disappointed at this backward turn in events and must be apprehensive for the future.

The Government fully share these feelings and I wish to repeat that we deplore sectarianism and intolerance in all their forms wherever they occur. The Government has been very patient and have acted with great restraint over several months past. While we made our views known to the British government on a number of occasions both by direct contact and through our diplomatic representative in London, we were careful to do nothing that would exacerbate the situation. But it is clear now that the present situation cannot be allowed to continue.

It is evident, also, that the Stormont government is no longer in control of the situation. Indeed the present situation is the inevitable outcome of the policies pursued for decades by successive Stormont Governments. It is clear, also, that the Irish Government can no longer stand by and see innocent people injured and perhaps worse.

It is obvious that the RUC is no longer accepted as an impartial police force. Neither would the employment of British troops be acceptable nor would they be likely to restore peaceful conditions—certainly not in the long term. The Irish Government has therefore requested the British Government to apply immediately to the United Nations for the urgent despatch of a peacekeeping Force to the Six Counties of Northern Ireland and have instructed the Irish Permanent Representative to the United Nations to inform the Secretary General of this request. We have also asked the British Government to see to it that police attacks on the people of Derry should cease immediately.

Very many people have been injured and some of them seriously. We know that many of these do not wish to be treated in Six-County hospitals. We have, therefore, directed the Irish Army authorities to have field hospitals established in County Donegal adjacent to Derry and at other points along the border where they may be necessary.

Recognising, however, that the re-unification of the national territory can provide the only permanent solution for the problem, it is our intention to request the British Government to enter into early negotiations with the Irish Government to review the present constitutional position of the 6 counties of Northern Ireland.

The measures which I have outlined to you seem to the Government to be those most immediately and urgently necessary.

All men and women of good will will hope and pray that the present deplorable and distressing situation will not further deteriorate but that it will soon be ended firstly by the granting of full equality of citizenship to every man and woman in the 6-County area regardless of class, creed or political persuasion and, eventually, by the restoration of the historic unity of our country.[35]

As a holding operation for a nationalism whose rhetoric was undermined by the action of those in the North determined to force the pace of change, the speech served its purpose. The hawks in the Government were temporarily mollified; the inability of the Government to make any real difference was masked by the appearance of a threat.[36]

The Stormont government was caught on the horns of a dilemma. The RUC was overstretched and clearly regarded in nationalist circles as having little or no credibility. If the administration called on the Special Constabulary, what was still a limited crisis could no longer be contained. Yet if it was to seek the help of the British army it would be ceding control over internal security, a threat it considered very real, given the exchange between the Cabinet Secretary and Sir Philip Allen on 3 August. Either way it spelt the effective end of untrammelled Unionist rule.

As a nationalist call went out for support to divert the authorities from the beleaguered residents of the Bogside, sectarian forces in Belfast began to stir. A group of protesters set out along the Falls Road to deliver a protest to the RUC station being built on the Springfield Road. The officer in charge refused to accept the petition and directed the organisers to the nearby Hastings Street station. An RUC patrol car came under grenade attack in the Lesson Street area off the Lower Falls Road, an attack that 'reinforced febrile RUC intelligence reports that the IRA were planning an uprising.'[37] Serious rioting broke out, and within minutes the Isaac Agnew car showroom was ablaze. The RUC station at Springfield was attacked, and the police responded with a baton charge down the Lower Falls Road. Barricades began to appear. The meta-conflict had begun.

For at least some of the new generation of political leaders in Northern Ireland the Lynch broadcast was evidence that after years of posturing, Dublin was prepared to guarantee the safety of Northern nationalists. Among those so persuaded was Paddy Kennedy, the Republican Socialist MP at Stormont for Belfast Central, who later became a central figure in the machinations surrounding Dublin's involvement in the pursuit of arms for Northern nationalists.

> When Jack Lynch made his speech I think there was a fair degree of satisfaction to this extent—that at least if things got out of control in Belfast we will always have Dublin to rely on. He was, as it were, implicitly giving us an undertaking that they would be the second guarantor, if you like: that they would come in to support and ensure that we weren't all massacred.[38]

This elation quickly turned to dread when the unrest spread to the working-class areas of Belfast. Within hours of the Lynch broadcast, Belfast was once more engulfed in flames, amid fears of a repeat of the pogroms of the nineteen-twenties. 'The broadcast of the Prime Minister of the Republic can have done nothing to lessen fears that a major challenge to the security of the state was developing' was the considered opinion of counsel for the RUC at the public inquiry into the political violence.[39]

The Lynch speech not only provided the context for the re-igniting of fears within loyalism about the threat of a military incursion from the South but also suggested to republican activists that the South could become embroiled, forcing a reluctant constitutional leadership to finish the national revolution.[40] The apparent monolith of Northern Ireland wilted in the white heat of the civil disturbances.

The sectarian interfaces of west and north Belfast once again became the scenes of pitched battles between nationalist demonstrators and the RUC and loyalist crowds. Barricades were strewn across the roads leading into Catholic enclaves. Stormont panicked and mobilised the B Specials. According to the RUC, there was no choice:

> The police took the view that much of the trouble had been caused by elements seeking to subvert and destroy the constitutional structure of the state, by force if necessary. It was considered that the Civil Rights Movement, though embracing many sincere and well-meaning people had been successfully infiltrated by the IRA for purposes wholly unconnected with reform or the removal of injustice, and that there existed a strategic plan which envisaged the ultimate destruction of the Government and Stormont by the employment of guerrilla tactics under arms.[41]

The mobilisation of the B Specials inflamed an already serious situation. Before it was stabilised with the arrival of the British army, eight people were to die as Belfast in particular witnessed the biggest forced population transfer in western Europe since the Second World War, a figure only surpassed since by the break-up of Yugoslavia.[42]

Particularly severe disturbances took place on the intersection between (Catholic) Divis Street and (Protestant) Dover Street in west Belfast. In an attempt to restore order the RUC launched a baton charge against Divis. As they advanced, loyalist crowds followed, setting homes and business premises ablaze. They were met with gunfire emanating from the Divis Street area. The first to die that night was Herbert Roy, a Protestant civilian hit in the chest by sniper fire. The RUC responded by sending in armoured cars, which came under sustained attack. The armoured cars responded by firing directly into Divis Flats. A bullet fired from one of these ricocheted off a water tank, killing a nine-year-old boy, Patrick Rooney, as he lay in his bed. Paddy Kennedy arrived on the scene moments later.

> It had blown away most of his skull as he lay in his bed and my only reaction at the time was to ask his father to go and get a saucer and a couple of spoons and we would try and clean the place up, scrape the cortex of this young boy off the walls ... There was a terrible sense of foreboding, a sense that a pogrom could start. I felt it myself. I felt that the RUC was out of control. I felt that if these mobs decided to systematically burn west Belfast ... there was absolutely nothing there to stop them doing it, absolutely nothing. There were no guns and you could not fight against guns.[43]

Father Paudge Egan watched the flames approach the Redemptorist monastery at Clonard as evening approached on 14 August. The monastery, built along the interface between the Falls and Shankill Roads, was a focal point for the Catholic community; in the circumstances of August 1969 it rapidly became the focal point for attack. Father Egan gave this account to a confraternity the following week, an account made all the more chilling for its measured delivery:

> We remember, my dearest men, I don't suppose we forget it easily, the night of Thursday the 14th of August. We remember this night when the Falls Road area was devastated by gunfire and by petrol bombs. In the early hours of the morning I was standing at the fourth-storey window of Clonard, looking out at a scene of desolation. And when I saw the leaping flames reddening the sky and the machine-gun fire breaking the silence of the night I found myself asking the question, is it possible that only three or four days ago we were assured by Stormont spokesmen that the forces of law and order had everything under control?[44]

This was just the beginning. During the night, west Belfast seemed to be ablaze. The situation was replicated in Ardoyne, a Catholic enclave in north Belfast. Rioting between rival groups engulfed the area. The public inquiry set up by the British government under the chairmanship of Lord Scarman concluded that both sides had been spoiling for a fight. The location was to be the interface between Ardoyne and Woodvale, across the network of streets leading from the Crumlin Road, the main thoroughfare of that part of the city.

> In the Crumlin Road and the side streets were to be found, and stumbled over, all the clutter of urban rioting—barricades, debris, flame, and liquid petrol. Normal traffic movement had stopped: the noise of hostile jeering crowds, the crackle and explosions of burning buildings, and the shattering of glass had enveloped the area. But save where the fighting was in progress, the streets were empty.[45]

An exchange of gunfire left Samuel McLernon, a bus conductor sitting in his front room, dead from a ricocheted bullet fired by the RUC. Michael Lynch, a bystander in Hooker Street, was killed by high-velocity bullets fired from an armoured car.

Rioting was not confined to Belfast. Outside the city John Gallagher was killed by a B Special patrol following a civil rights demonstration in Armagh. Rioting in other towns in an arc stretching from Enniskillen in the west to Strabane, Dungiven, Limavady,

Coalisland, Cookstown, Dungannon and Lurgan further stretched RUC resources away from the main urban centres.

For the first time since the formation of the state, Northern Ireland appeared vulnerable. Newspapers carried headlines proclaiming: 'Irish troops are on the border: army spokesman admits large forces of Irish troops are at the moment on manoeuvres in County Donegal and in the Cavan area.'[46] Field hospitals were set up along the border, and temporary camps opened at Finner in County Donegal and Gormanston in County Meath to house the refugees streaming out of Belfast. Northern Ireland appeared to be disintegrating, which heightened the sense of threat felt by the establishment.

According to the Scarman Report, counsel for the RUC made a strenuous defence of the police response.

> On the night of the 14th/15th August the situation in Belfast rapidly became critical. Gunfire was directed at police in both the Falls and Crumlin Road areas, and a number of senior officers formed the opinion that they faced an armed uprising, supported, if not led, by the IRA. That we suggest was a reasonable assessment of the situation having regard to the scale of the rioting, and the reports of the shooting which were being received.[47]

All along the sectarian interface, Catholics were on the move, retreating to the heart of the ghetto. People piled their belongings onto prams as their houses were burnt down behind them. In an interview published on the thirtieth anniversary of the events, Gerry Fitt told the *Irish News* that the atmosphere in Belfast was nothing short of hysterical.

> It was wild. You would have had to be there to see the emotion and hysteria that was there. Nobody could explain it to you; you couldn't read about it. You had to be there ... We were walking up the Falls Road, and all these people nearly had my coat torn off me. They were shouting, 'Gerry, get the army in, get the army in, they're going to murder us in our beds. We're going to be slaughtered.'

Surrounded by hundreds of people, Fitt telephoned the Home Secretary from a bookmaker's shop.

> There was something at the back of my mind saying, do you know what you're doing, you're asking for the British army to come in here. I don't know where it was coming from, but that's what it said. I said, 'I'm in a bookmaker's shop here and I'm ringing up to tell you there's a lot of very

hysterical, very frightened people here. There were five people killed here last night and unless something is done it could be absolutely terrible here.' He said, 'Gerry, I could get the army in. But it's going to be a devil of a job to get them out.'[48]

Emergency shelters were opened in schools and churches throughout west Belfast. Teachers and priests worked around the clock to provide solace and support to bewildered and terrified parishioners. Paddy Devlin, Northern Ireland Labour Party MP for the Falls, recalled entering one such shelter.

Old age pensioners sat about in terror, holding hands and saying the rosary. As the day wore on, with no respite from the sniping and the burning, other families from outlying mixed parts of the city converged on the Falls for safety. I rang the police several times throughout the day to ask for protection, only to be told by City Commissioner Graham Shillington that no men could be spared.[49]

No men could be spared the following afternoon either in what was one of the most psychologically important incidents of the August burnings. In the afternoon the streets surrounding Clonard monastery came under sustained attack. Priests from the monastery contacted the RUC for urgent protection. According to Father Egan, 'the call was received politely, but no help came.'[50] Teenagers hurled stones and petrol bombs to fend off further encroachment as the women of the parish retreated to the relative sanctuary of the monastery. As Bombay Street and Waterville Street were burnt, gunshots rang out. Prostrate on the ground lay Gerald McAuley, a fifteen-year-old schoolboy and member of Fianna Éireann, the IRA's youth wing.[51]

The descent into chaos witnessed by the burning of Catholic enclaves and in particular the attack on Clonard monastery, the symbol of the Catholic community in west Belfast, heightened the perceived threat of a pogrom and created consternation in nationalist circles far beyond the confines of the working-class ghettos.[52] The message was clear: the community needed more than rhetoric or even spiritual guidance, as Father Paudge Egan acknowledged.

They failed in their evil design that night. But their failure, my dearest men, was not due to any protection given by the forces of law and order. Let that be recorded. Let it also be recorded that they failed because of the bravery of the local lads, who, totally ill prepared and ill equipped, and comparatively speaking defenceless, fought against terrible odds, and saved this district from complete destruction.[53]

The Catholic hierarchy accepted this interpretation. As the situation deteriorated, its position hardened. On 14 August, Cardinal Conway appealed to Catholics

> not to allow themselves to be swept away by emotion—however natural and understandable such emotion may be—but to keep cool heads and realise that a general eruption of violence would seriously weaken the civil rights movement.[54]

Three days later he maintained that despite the 'terrible things done' in Armagh and Belfast

> we must remember that the great majority of Protestants in Northern Ireland are God-fearing people and a great deal of the tension on their part at the present time comes not from hatred but from fear. The fact that we regard these fears as groundless does not make them less real for them.[55]

But by the following week Cardinal Conway was complaining of biased news reports that had deliberately obscured the fact that

> the Catholic districts of Falls and Ardoyne were invaded by mobs equipped with machine guns and other firearms. A community, which was virtually defenceless, was swept by gunfire and streets of Catholic homes were systematically set on fire. We entirely reject the hypothesis that the origin of last week's tragedy was an armed insurrection.[56]

The bishops concluded that

> among Catholics belief in the impartiality of the Ulster Special Constabulary is virtually non-existent. The future can hold out no hope unless the whole community is able to trust the forces of law and order.[57]

It was a damning indictment and one that was repeated with forthrightness by H. G. McGrath QC, counsel for the Catholic residents, at the Scarman Inquiry. 'In the circumstances which pervaded on the night of 14/15 August those who used weapons on the Catholic side were legally and morally justified.'[58] It was a contention that the RUC's counsel took grave exception to.

> The events of the past two years, with their sorry catalogue of attacks on Army and Police personnel, must surely have convinced everyone that there are in Northern Ireland a number of people who regard murder as a legitimate means of achieving their political objectives. We submit that on the night of 14th/15th August 1969, such people were active in the disturbances in Belfast and that firearms were used against the police in circumstances which fully justified the return of fire.[59]

The Prime Minister of Northern Ireland was furious at what he saw as a deliberate attempt by the Irish Government to inflame the situation. His response was to do much to stoke up fears of an all-out invasion. 'We must and we will treat the government which seeks to wound us in our darkest hour as an unfriendly and implacable government, dedicated to the overthrow by any means of the statutes which enjoy the support of the majority of our electorate.'[60] Three days later, at a press conference at Stormont Castle, Chichester-Clark defended the calling out of the B Specials and repeated his claim that Northern Ireland faced a rebellion.

> The real cause of the disorder is to be found in the activities of extreme Republican elements and others determined to overthrow our state. That is why we have found it necessary to detain a considerable number of known and dangerous agitators … In this grave situation the behaviour of the Dublin government has been deplorable, and tailor made to inflame opinion on both sides. The moving of Army units, the calling up of reserves, the absurd approaches for United Nations intervention have all been moves of almost incredible clumsiness and ineptitude … I think that this is a very squalid business and all that the Dublin government has done is to convince us for all time that we must look elsewhere for our friends. We held out our hand to them as good neighbours. They have behaved much like those hooligans who have used the present troubles as an excuse to burn their neighbours out.[61]

Northern Ireland, however, was not the only state that perceived itself under threat. In O'Connell Street, Dublin, nightly rallies trundled out not only rhetoric but also concrete demands for guns. The British ambassador to Ireland, Sir Andrew Gilchrist, a veteran of the anti-communist putsch in Indonesia, noted the danger in a darkly sardonic note to the Foreign Office.

> All in all we are in for a fairly difficult time from the Irish. Someone said to me that I would soon have as many friends in Ireland as I had in Indonesia. I doubt if it will be quite so bad as that, but if I were a fire insurance company I would not like to have the British embassy on my books. (Fortunately, though highly flammable, it isn't ours.)[62]

The images of burning streets coupled with the presence of thousands of refugees brought the issue of Northern Ireland back to the top of the political agenda. An Ireland more concerned with relinquishing sovereign power by entry into the Europe Common Market than reasserting sovereignty over a part of the country whose very existence was an affront to the stated unity of the nation had a serious crisis on its hands.[63] Circumstances dictated that something had to be done, or, more importantly, seen to be done.

The Minister for External Affairs, Patrick Hillery, was sent to London to follow up the request made by the ambassador that the British government apply to the United Nations for an international peace-keeping force or, failing that, a force under joint British and Irish authority. Both requests were refused out of hand. Back in Dublin at a meeting of the Government, unable to secure a commitment to withdrawing Irish troops from Cyprus as a protest to the United Nations, Boland 'strode angrily from the room, throwing out as he went the threat of resignation.'[64] He returned to the Government only after the intervention of President Éamon de Valera, who warned him that his resignation would provoke a crisis that could lead to a Fine Gael administration.

Hillery proceeded to the United Nations the following day, calling for an urgent meeting of the Security Council to discuss the deteriorating situation. For the Security Council to accede to such a request would be an unprecedented development, as it would contravene article 2 of the Charter of the United Nations as an intervention in the internal affairs of a member-state. Hillery's expedition should therefore be seen as a public relation exercise for domestic political consumption.

The North was falling apart, and the Republic had no immediate answers beyond fear of contagion. The constitutional issue had mutated into providing nothing more than an ideological gloss; it was certainly not a policy imperative. Now the rhetoric of unfinished revolution reasserted itself. The Government decided to act quickly, without any unwelcome political contributions from the opposition. The Dáil was on summer recess and had the decorators in, and the official reason given for not recalling it was that there was nowhere to meet. The consequences of the August melee were not debated, therefore, until October. What is striking is the disparity between the publicly stated positions adopted in the Dáil that autumn and the altogether more secret and more destabilising agendas being followed both in relation to Northern Ireland and within Fianna Fáil.

The only minister with any real demonstrable interest in the issue was Neil Blaney. In the confused days of August 1969, Blaney's certainty in his dealings with the North was at a premium, especially in the highest echelons of government. The picture he painted at the

Government table determined that he would have a considerable say in future policy.

Neil Blaney had become by the late sixties one of the most powerful men in Ireland and was widely regarded as a king-maker within Fianna Fáil. His prestige rested on the relationship between the political machine he had created in County Donegal and the perception of power this gave him in his dealings with the electorate, with Fianna Fáil, and with the Government. As Paul Sacks notes in an astute analysis of the 'Donegal Mafia',

> each endeavour gained a measure of strength and influence from the other. The store of authority, prestige and power derived from his national position helped Blaney amalgamate control over his local party organisation and convert it into a smooth-running organisation, while the Donegal Mafia became an important resource to Blaney as a national politician.[65]

Blaney won his father's seat in Donegal North-East in 1948 and soon began his meteoric rise to the top of Fianna Fáil. The following year he became chairman of the organising committee of the National Executive; by 1956 he had become joint treasurer and was seen as a shrewd and capable administrator. De Valera appointed him Minister for Posts and Telegraphs in 1957 and promoted him again in 1959 to the Local Government portfolio. Blaney was above all a master strategist and recognised that to challenge Lemass's nomination of Lynch as a compromise candidate for the leadership in 1966 would be a tactical mistake. He was prepared to bide his time, building up his prestige in the party from the vantage point of the Department of Agriculture and Fisheries.

Blaney adopted a profoundly ambivalent position to the implications of the demise of economic nationalism. On the one hand he was instrumental in creating the dependence of the new economic elite on Fianna Fáil through Taca and in securing the success of the 1969 election on a 'red scare' platform. On the other hand he adopted an increasingly shrill formulation of the importance of the traditional goal of national unity. In the context of a searching debate over the ideological underpinnings of the country, Blaney adopted in public a fundamentalist position in the form of a commitment to the old certainties of territorial nationalism. A case in point was his intervention after the disturbances of 5 October 1968. While the Taoiseach restricted himself to condemning partition as the root cause, Blaney condemned the Northern Prime Minister as someone 'who tries to set himself up as the exclusive spokesman for the historic province of Ulster, when in fact he can only speak for a mere bigoted junta in six of its counties, a junta that has made his liberal image a shameful sham.'[66]

Blaney was keeping his options open and preparing the ground for his own accession to the top. In the immediate aftermath of the election Blaney and Boland represented a powerful axis, supported by Mícheál Ó Móráin, the Minister for Justice, who was regarded as something of a hate figure in the left-wing press.[67] As the current affairs magazine *Hibernia* pointed out,

> the intense personality conflicts which have marked the recent history of the party remain as explosive as ever—more explosive, perhaps, than the papering over of cracks in its monolithic facade may have led many to believe ... If he [Lynch] cannot face the prospect of a wrathful Blaney, an angry Boland or a sulphurous Ó Móráin then perhaps he should not be Taoiseach after all.[68]

But Blaney was quite simply too powerful for Lynch to dispense with. His power lay in the combination of his public and private attributes. As Sacks makes clear,

> on the public platform, he often projected the image of a hard headed and uncompromising republican, who regarded the political battle as something of a holy war. Privately, he seemed the sort of man to whom loyalty, respect and power were all-important.[69]

Blaney saw in the conflagration in the North an opportunity to create the conditions for transferring the loyalty, respect and power of the party from Lynch to himself. It was time to move.

Hibernia noted that it was 'not difficult to discern the influence of Neil Blaney behind the style and conduct of the Government's intervention,' an intervention it described as 'totally astute at home and almost totally inept abroad.' *Hibernia* was alone in the Irish media in condemning the 'sabre-rattling' whose 'only logical consequence is the incitement of subversion in the North and the adherents of this policy logically belong in the ranks of the IRA.' It concluded that

> the manner of Jack Lynch's intervention ... infused a completely new energy into the whole Republican movement ... a sobering consideration for the Southern government is the future effect, south of the border, of this replenished stream of Republican emotion and its new familiarisation with the rule of the gun.[70]

The Government meetings of 15 and 16 August 1969 were to be pivotal.[71] Its decisions set in motion the entire Arms Crisis. Four initiatives in particular were to have immense consequences. Firstly, the Minister for Defence and Minister for Finance were asked to investigate the state of preparedness of the Defence Forces and to make any arrangements necessary to augment their capabilities. Secondly, the Minister for Justice was asked to 'expand the intelligence service maintained by the Garda Síochána in the Six Counties.'[72] Thirdly, £100,000 was provided for the immediate relief of distress; this money was to be dispersed at the total discretion of the Minister for Finance. Fourthly, a newly formed four-member Government sub-committee was established, charged with overseeing all aspects of Northern policy, to be directed by Neil Blaney and Charles Haughey. The result of Lynch's decision was to cede control of the most important challenge faced by the state since partition to two of his greatest political rivals, in the process reopening the power struggle over control of the party. Tim Pat Coogan—then editor of the *Irish Press,* the pro-Fianna Fáil daily—recalls that the net effect of the emerging conflict was to provide the basis for schism.

> Fianna Fáil, the men in the mohair suits, the younger element the Charlie Haughey breed and the more traditional Fianna Fáil supporter and minister were like those Chinese dishes you get in which you have chicken and duck glazed together with sugar. Well, in the fires of the burnings of August the glaze came apart.[73]

This was indeed an apt metaphor for the power struggle for control over Fianna Fáil that the conflagration in Belfast opened up, yet one that Coogan himself is unwilling to follow up in his latest writings on the genesis of the Provisional IRA.[74] While two competing agendas were at work, each had the same primary goal: the maintenance of Fianna Fáil's hegemony.

Within Northern Ireland, however, the machiavellian undertones of the Government's deliberations were not considered to be of any great importance. Of much more significance was the fact that constitutional politicians were at one with the old-style militarists of the IRA: that guns were needed to defend Catholic areas from attack. At a crucial meeting at the Department of External Affairs in Dublin three independent nationalist MPs—Paddy Devlin, Paddy Kennedy, and Paddy O'Hanlon—demanded immediate access to the Taoiseach. According to Government records, Kennedy emerged as the main spokesman. He told the civil servants that if the Government was not prepared to send soldiers across the border, they wanted guns to defend themselves. When the delegation was told the Taoiseach was not available, tempers flared.

> Mr Devlin, who was more angry and emotional than the others, made for the door saying that he would see to it that he saw the Taoiseach before he left Dublin. He came back and muttered something abusive about the Government being responsible for deaths.[75]

It was this change in outlook, coupled with sympathetic hearings from sections of the Dublin establishment to these calls for arms, that was to open the way for a reassertion of the primacy of armed struggle. Following the failure of the border campaign, many members of the IRA had drifted away from the movement, among them John Kelly of Belfast, whose leaving was the result of his scepticism about the political path followed by the Goulding leadership. The cataclysmic events of August 1969 were to provide the grounds for the reappearance of Kelly and his colleagues in the movement.

> The IRA never did have great support within the nationalist community. The nationalist community had always an ambivalent attitude towards the IRA. While they would never support them in a forceful way, they always had at the back of their mind the notion that they were there in case they were needed, and on this occasion they weren't there. I think that struck at the very psyche of the republican ethos.[76]

With the arrival of British soldiers on the streets of Belfast the tension and fear of a pogrom receded in the wider community. Within the republican movement, however, the uneasy compromise over Goulding's choice of a political route because of the lack of an alternative was blown asunder. Goulding and Johnston had argued that the goals of the republican movement would be best served by ending not only the policy of abstention but the idea of a separate IRA. This would be done by the creation of a grand coalition of the revolutionary left, and this was due to be debated by the Army Council that autumn and again at the Sinn Féin ardfheis in January 1970.

At the heart of the strategy was the belief that through a campaign of civil disobedience ostensibly limited to the reform of Stormont, the stage would be set for a revolution. The Northern state would be provoked into over-reaction; in the ensuing period the false consciousness of the unionists of Northern Ireland would be exposed. The working class in the Republic would see that the political establishment in Dublin had a vested interest in partition and would join forces to transform the politics of the whole of Ireland.

Goulding saw in the immediate aftermath of the August violence that an explicit IRA intervention would be counter-productive, and he rescinded an order for the resumption of the 1956–62 campaign. A document entitled 'Fianna Fáil and the IRA' written by a source close to the political thinking of the Goulding wing attempts to provide a positive gloss to the policy. While attempting to demonstrate iron discipline, it inadvertently reveals the fragility of Goulding's control in the changed political circumstances of a Dundalk farmhouse in August 1969:

> The political education process of the IRA over the previous number of years stood by him, and the active service units kitted out in the kitchen remembering that war was but an extension of politics, laid down their equipment albeit grudgingly.[77]

The unease in the republican movement when the violence spread to Belfast had heightened when Goulding could not at first be found. He was filming in the Dublin Mountains with a British television crew. One activist who attended the meeting recalls that on the way he passed 'Free State army trucks stationed along the border, hundreds of trucks with fully armed troops in the back of them, up laneways and gateways.'[78]

The fatal flaw of the civil rights movement was the belief that the street protests it unleashed could be controlled. The moderates did not allow for the very different strategy followed by the radicals in Derry and in People's Democracy. The radicals did not allow for the hidden agenda of the republican movement; and the IRA leadership did not allow for the way in which the militarists in the movement saw in the upheaval the possibility of the resurrection of armed struggle. All under-estimated the impact that politics in the street would have on the psyche of unionism. The sheer scale of the violence stripped away the ambiguities at the heart of the IRA strategic view of the role of armed force in the politics of civil rights.[79]

NICRA was very much the creation of the republican movement; it was a creation that very quickly seeped out of its control. Tomás Mac Giolla later admitted:

> Of course it was [a republican front]. I mean we were organising it. Moreover, the funny thing about it was, the ones who were organising it were organising it in order to stop any further campaigns. One of our

purposes in all our agitation was to be using struggles without military activities and confrontation.[80]

From the beginning, republican activists were encouraged to pack meetings to decide who was elected and when. The scale of the infiltration is evidenced from the testimony of one senior south Derry activist.

> The IRA was involved in Civil Rights from the very start, from day one ... We knew who was going to be elected before we went to the meetings, that was all arranged beforehand ... they were all engineered well beforehand, although most of the people on some of the committees didn't know it.[81]

In the heat of the Belfast events of August 1969, it is clear now that those running Northern policies in Fianna Fáil viewed Goulding as perhaps the most serious threat. The cosy consensus that had dominated Northern politics since the twenties, during which Northern nationalist leaders were patronised by occasional audiences in Leinster House, was no longer a viable strategy. The nationalist electorate was under increasing threat from a loyalist backlash that the Stormont government was unable or unwilling to control; constitutional politicians were joining the clarion call for weapons; and there was a real fear that a republican movement with designs on the Southern state could fill the vacuum.

In such a volatile atmosphere People's Democracy sought to keep the tension high, and its policy of confrontation on the streets continued. Dublin—out of the picture through a policy of neglect—was determined to remedy matters as speedily as possible; but first it needed accurate local information. This was to be provided by significantly enhanced intelligence-gathering.

Soon after the formation of the Government sub-committee, Charles Haughey and Jim Gibbons, Minister for Defence, attended a meeting with senior military officers at McKee Barracks in Dublin. They wanted answers to several specific questions: what were the army's capabilities; what contingency plans could be made to ensure that weapons were made available; and whom should they be made available to.

The director of intelligence, Colonel Michael Hefferon, had just the person in mind for this mission: a young officer on his staff, Captain James Kelly. Kelly was well placed to provide Dublin with access to the new political forces in Belfast. His brother, Martin, was, and remains, a priest in the Falls Road. When the violence erupted Captain Kelly was visiting his brother; he had alerted Colonel Hefferon and was told to keep a close eye on the mood within republicanism in Belfast.

Kelly was on the scene when the militants took over by launching a coup against the Belfast leadership because of the failure to protect the community from loyalist attack in mid-August. His reports to Dublin provide compelling evidence of the extent to which the central goal of the Government sub-committee was to ensure that resources were directed to those it thought it could control.

Captain Kelly's first report to Hefferon was written on 23 August. In it he makes it clear that

> at present, the government has the support of the people largely because of its stand as publicly announced. In itself it finds acceptance even in the most extreme republican circles to the extent that there is some indication that extreme republicanism is willing to co-operate in achieving the unity ideal.[82]

Kelly makes it clear that recourse to the traditional policy of interning the IRA would be a 'catastrophe' that could lead to

> the possible situation where the authority would find itself taking coercive action against an increasing minority. If such a development were to take place it could only lead to a state of anarchy with the consequent discrediting of the country as a whole.

To avoid this Kelly proposes a radical move:

> It would seem to be now necessary to harness all opinion in the state in a concerted drive towards achieving the aim of unification. Unfortunately, this would mean accepting the possibility of armed action of some sort as the ultimate solution, but if civil war embracing this area, and civil war is not too strong a term, was to result because of unwillingness to accept that war is a continuation of politics by other means, it would be far the greater evil for the Irish nation.[83]

Kelly concludes that the only option open to the Government was to 'co-operate with the IRA and extreme republicanism generally' where they

> could be permitted to operate as covert nuisance squads in N.I., avoiding contact with the British forces, and supported by a psychological campaign from here.[84]

It is clear from this document that from the beginning Captain Kelly was acutely aware of how the volatile situation in the North could threaten the stability of the Southern state. It is through an examination of his further reports to Dublin that one can see that the underlying concern remains constant: how to avoid the threat of anarchy infecting the Southern body politic. It is questionable whether Captain Kelly would have remained in place if his analysis were out of kilter with at least some powerful figures in Dublin.

Kelly's was not a lone voice. Séamus Brady, a political adviser to Blaney seconded to the Government, was providing intelligence reports in which he warned openly that

> Belfast is a powder-keg. The feeling inside the barricades in Belfast with those with whom I spoke—and they are the people running the show—is that they are awaiting help from the south. By this I mean military help. They can see no going back to what was before ... [They] are completely committed to an end of the Stormont regime and a return to jurisdiction of an Irish government.[85]

Kelly's second report to Hefferon is equally revealing, in that it makes clear the need not only to harness the republican movement to its cause but also to counter what Dublin viewed as the threat of the radicals by involving the constitutional leaders. This would have the advantage of re-establishing control over nationalist politics. Kelly recounts a meeting held in Gerry Fitt's house on the Antrim Road, Belfast, on 13 September; those present included John Kelly and his brother Billy, leading figures in the Defence Committees springing up around Belfast (leading figures too in the sceptical wing of the IRA).[86] As loyalist rioting flared outside, Fitt is recorded as saying that 'it was of paramount importance to get in arms immediately.' John Kelly has confirmed this recollection.

> We were having this discussion about the necessity for weapons and Gerry was arguing the case, and just at that his wife Anne came bursting into the room and she shouted: Gerry, Gerry they're coming, they're coming and we could hear the noise out on the street as if a mob was coming. Gerry stood up and shouted: I told you, I fucking told you, there it is. Do you need any more proof?[87]

The document also shows that an Irish intelligence operative was intimately involved in attempts to create a new alignment of forces in Northern Ireland. The key to this strategy was the tacit approval of senior Northern politicians.[88] In recording that Jim Sullivan, the leader of the IRA in west Belfast, was a 'nut and a dangerous man,' under the influence of the radical left, Kelly clearly takes sides in the feud within republicanism.

> To date, arms and support seem to have got into the wrong hands in Belfast. This situation must be remedied. The republican movement on its part is capable of doing this at the moment, provided future support is properly channelled. It would seem that a modus operandi must be worked out with the IRA in the south and it seems this is possible of achievement, with left wing politics taking a back seat in both areas.[89]

The remedy for this, according to Captain Kelly, was for the Government to make a policy decision to finance the Kelly brothers, whose 'integrity' he underwrites. It is no coincidence that Captain Kelly should have included this proposal in a submission that implies that constitutional politicians were also in favour of such a move.

> The Kellys and their friends have no time for PD and for the new Sinn Féin policy in the South and arrangements are under way to re-establish control by pure republicanism which is concerned solely with a 32 county Ireland. In this connection they are willing to co-operate with the IRA in the South and would like to make arrangements with various people whom they see as Republican first and not true Sinn Féin socialists. In fact they see Sinn Féin politics as having disrupted the whole IRA/Republican movement.[90]

When the Dáil was eventually recalled, on 22 October, the Taoiseach made no reference to the intelligence provided by Kelly about divisions in the republican movement, or indeed to the workings of the Government sub-committee. Instead he used the occasion to attempt to convince the Stormont government that the Republic posed no threat. He restated Fianna Fáil policy as enunciated at a speech in Tralee the previous month; the core of this speech was that although partition was anathema to Fianna Fáil, there was no question of using force to bring about unity. This salient point was repeated in the Dáil on 22 October 1969.

> I want to assert again that it is Government policy that our legitimate desire for a united Ireland will be realised by peaceful means. First of all we want to see peace and tolerance restored in the Six Counties so that Catholics and Protestants, minority and majority, can live side by side with co-operation and in understanding based on equal citizenship ... [The] Government in this part of Ireland have no intention of mounting an armed invasion of the Six Counties. We could give a number of

reasons for this attitude but the most cogent, in our conviction, is that the use of force would not advance our long-term aim of a united Ireland. Nor will the Government connive at unofficial armed activity here directed at targets across the Border.[91]

The other party leaders, as evidence that a new consensus had emerged, broadly welcomed Lynch's comments in the Dáil. Liam Cosgrave concurred with what he took to be Fianna Fáil's stated policy that the consent of the majority in Northern Ireland was required for a united Ireland. He berated Northern unionism for living in the past, for failing to recognise that

> this is not 1912, 1914 or even 1920. Events have moved, circumstances have changed and things can never be the same again.[92]

The Labour Party, still smarting from the bruising 1969 election, was more forthright in its criticism of Fianna Fáil's handling of the August violence. In a perceptive intervention its leader, Brendan Corish, proclaimed:

> It is not good enough that when events such as those that have occurred in the Six Counties take place we should be blandly told that the Dáil is in recess, the people are on holidays, or worse, still, that the house is being decorated. Maybe the Government and the Taoiseach believed that some member of the house would run amok and further inflame an already inflamed situation.[93]

Given the propensity of Blaney and Boland in particular to comment on Northern affairs, affairs well outside their official remit, it was indeed striking that Fianna Fáil did not field any other ministers to support the Taoiseach's interpretation of party policy. In fact the supporting role fell on David Andrews, scion of one of the most influential figures produced by the national revolution. Andrews, who later became Minister for Foreign Affairs, commented:

> It is sometimes as well to say nothing in the context of a given situation. Words can be as damaging as bullets at a particular point of time. It might have been as well not to have reconvened the Dáil at that particular point.[94]

In general, however, there was a recognition that force was not an option, and the debate was restrained, concentrating on the need to assuage the real or imaginary fears of the Unionists. As Paddy Harte, Fine Gael TD for North-East Donegal and a bitter opponent of

Blaney, made clear, irredentist rhetoric had played its part in galvanising division in Ireland.

> What kind of picture have we been presenting to the Unionist, the Orangeman, the non-Catholic north of the border? What type of united Ireland have we been trying to sell him? Every time we opened our mouths it was: end partition; and when we talked about ending partition it had to be done today, tomorrow, next week or as soon as possible.[95]

In a riveting speech, Harte explained how he had gone to Derry in the midst of the Battle of the Bogside.

> I witnessed terror, revenge and hatred such as I never thought I would see from human beings. I asked myself why people lose their heads in such situations. Why do they want to throw petrol bombs? Why do they want to get guns to shoot others or to defend themselves? The answer, I decided, was 'fear, fear of each other.'[96]

Harte's party colleague Garret FitzGerald saw in the debate, and in particular in the contribution by Lynch, that the deliberations 'represented the first occasion in the history of the State in which we are seriously facing the problem of Partition.'[97] He suggested that the blame for the maintenance of partition lay primarily in the Republic, feeding into the siege mentality and drawing up a mental drawbridge to social, economic and political interchange.

> We did not create partition, but we maintained partition … Now we can make a fresh start … It requires an effort of imagination which we have not yet made. I hope that out of this debate that effort of imagination will come.[98]

The greatest feat of imagination, however, was the belief in the Dáil that what was publicly stated by Jack Lynch amounted to even an approximation of actual Government policy. Lynch did not tell the Dáil of the payments made to those who manned the barricades, of the financing of a newspaper that propagated the political views of Fianna Fáil—or, more accurately, the political views of Neil Blaney. He did not tell the Dáil of the training of activists from Derry in guerrilla warfare at an army camp in County Donegal. He did not tell the Dáil of the financing of a meeting in a Cavan hotel by the Minister for Justice at which the split within republicanism was fomented. And he did not tell the Dáil that some of his own ministers were deliberately using the Northern issue to destabilise his leadership by their ambivalence with regard to the use of force to solve the national question.[99]

The outbreak of violence in the North changed the balance of power within Fianna Fáil. Up to that point Lynch was in an almost unassailable position, despite the perception in the party that he was an interim figurehead. The former hurling and football champion was an electoral asset; but the changed circumstances of the time meant that a chief rather than a chairman was required. The ideological debates between Lynch and Blaney in particular in the coming months were to provide the only outward sign of the extent to which a shadow administration was plotting a board-room takeover.

The acceptance by at least parts of Fianna Fáil and by Military Intelligence of the analysis put forward by Captain Kelly—for whatever reason—was to have far-reaching implications. Kelly himself had no doubt that he was acting under orders. In a series of interviews for this book he never wavered in his assertion that he was made a scapegoat when he stood trial in September 1970 along with John Kelly, the Belgian-born businessman Albert Luykx, and the Minister for Finance, Charles Haughey.

> I certainly was the victim of a show trial, and it was a complete set-up from beginning to end. There is absolutely no doubt about that. The reason for it I can never understand, except that the viciousness went so deep in Fianna Fáil between various elements that they were willing to literally cut each other's throat and that the interests of Northern Ireland or the country at large didn't matter a damn to them.[100]

It is to a detailed investigation of the extent of Military Intelligence involvement in the murky world of paramilitary politics that we must now turn before assessing the truth of Kelly's assertion that he was indeed a victim of a Fianna Fáil show trial.

CHAPTER THREE

Reasserting Control

The Infiltration of the Defence Committees

THE barricades in Free Derry and west Belfast had a similar psychological effect on community relations in Northern Ireland to that of the economic boycott of the early nineteen-twenties. There were, however, two central and linked differences over tactics and general strategy. The first concerned control—or, more accurately, the lack of it—a situation Dublin sought to rectify with immediate effect. As Military Intelligence sought to infiltrate the republican movement, the money to be used in reasserting control over the forces of Northern nationalism was to be provided by the grant in aid now under the direct control of Charles Haughey and Neil Blaney. It was this combination of a hawkish policy of infiltration with attempts to outmanoeuvre Jack Lynch that was to give the subsequent crisis its potency.[1]

The divisions in the Belfast IRA were fast becoming unbridgeable. The split, which was to be formalised at a convention in December 1969 and confirmed at the Sinn Féin ardfheis in January 1970, occurred at a local level on 24 August at a meeting in Casement Park GAA Social Club, Belfast. Billy McKee, Joe Cahill and the Kelly brothers attended;[2] also present was Dáithí Ó Conaill, an essential ally of Seán Mac Stiofáin—an indication that the Belfast scheming had high-level support.

That support also extended to Military Intelligence. Captain James Kelly wrote to his superior:

Republicanism is well organised in Belfast, with 2,000 men plus, ready for action. They are being trained by ex-British Army personnel ... Arms are negligible apart from those under Sullivan/PD control. The Kellys' and their friends have no time for PD and for the new Sinn Féin policy in the South and arrangements are under way to re-establish control by 'pure republicanism', which is concerned solely with a 32 county Ireland ... The people concerned are so deeply involved in Belfast and certainly under observation that I would hesitate to arrange a meeting until a concrete offer of assistance emerges. If I had that, however, I could obtain the necessary details while making the arrangements for forwarding assistance. These details could then be checked before the assistance is actually on the way.

I feel it is incumbent to reiterate that urgency is of extreme importance in the situation as it now stands. Even with the British troops present, Catholics in many areas remain unprotected.[3]

The director of intelligence was not the only person to receive this briefing. Significantly, Captain Kelly also visited Neil Blaney and Charles Haughey to tell them of the information gathered in Belfast. It had come to his attention that these ministers were involved in a sub-committee dealing with Northern Ireland.[4] According to Haughey, Captain Kelly provided an important link between the Government and Northern nationalists, and such a development was in line with the policy adopted when the sub-committee was established.

We were given the instruction that we should develop the maximum possible contacts with persons inside the Six Counties and try and inform ourselves as fully as possible on events and on political and other developments in the Six County areas.

Was there any particular individual who was not in the Cabinet? I mean now any person who was concerned in creating a link between you and your fellow-members and the people in the North?

Yes, Captain Kelly.[5]

While Haughey provided the funds, it was to be Neil Blaney, Minister for Agriculture and Fisheries—and not Jim Gibbons, Minister for Defence—who became the main point of contact in the complex power relationship now being forged by Military Intelligence. The effect of this bypassing of established lines of authority was to bring into sharp focus the reality of two Government policies in relation to the Northern crisis. One was aimed at securing unity by consent; the other was prepared to cross the political Rubicon: the expression of mere vocal support to a besieged minority was to be replaced by a more hawkish policy of arming those who presented themselves as the defenders of the people. The stage was set for a coup in the Belfast IRA and for a political crisis in the Dublin establishment.

Garret FitzGerald pointed out in a savage indictment of Blaney after the acquittals in the arms trial a year later:

> When one reads this trial carefully, Deputy Blaney crops up time and time again and disappears again into the mist, covering his tracks so well that the District Justice refused information against him. How can we tolerate a position in which you have a senior minister, the Minister for Agriculture, running his own intelligence service in Northern Ireland, interfering in the Army, giving instruction to junior officers in the army in a matter of this kind and purporting, apparently, to instruct the Director of Intelligence, through his subordinates as to how he was to carry out his duties.[6]

On 22 September 1969 a group of armed men broke up a meeting of the Belfast Brigade of the IRA. The OC, Billy McMillen, was allowed to stay in nominal control, but only on condition that the Belfast Brigade break off contact with the Dublin leadership. According to Billy McKee, one of the main plotters,

> we weren't so much wanting to take over the IRA as determined to break from Dublin. We realised that the Dublin crowd and the Dublin leadership were nothing other than conmen. They were only using the North as a base, a springboard to help them in their left-wing political field. That was their intention—to use the IRA up here for that purpose. And they used it. So the Northern lads got together and we told them that we wouldn't have any more truck with the South and with the Dublin leadership.[7]

The main battleground for reasserting control was to be behind the barricades in Belfast. In such a febrile atmosphere, just as in Derry earlier in the month, the political leadership of Northern nationalism was again volatile. A Central Defence Committee was established, chaired by Jim Sullivan, with Paddy Devlin as secretary. This committee organised life behind the barricades, negotiating with the RUC and British army, briefing the media, and organising internal security. Control of the CDC meant control of the immediate future. As Paddy Devlin noted in his memoirs with remarkable understatement, 'I did suspect there was turmoil in the background from the way things were going inside the CDC.'[8]

The broadly based Defence Committees were in fact to provide the nucleus of the Provisional IRA. From the beginning the majority of the republican element in the CDC took its inspiration from what it considered to be a rejuvenated Dublin administration determined to reverse past injustices. It remained convinced that in its dealings with Captain Kelly in particular it was dealing with an officer who had the authority and the wherewithal to provide the necessary weapons. The apparent ease of access to, and support from, Government ministers, including Lynch himself, underlined these perceptions. John Kelly remembers the period as one in which the Northerners believed what they were being told by politicians in the Republic, whom he regarded as speaking with one voice.

> We assumed, being sort of innocents, if you like—lambs going into what turned out to be a wolves' den of politicians—[that we could] believe what we were being told by the leader of the state, by Jack Lynch, who didn't equivocate when we said we were looking for arms … It was always very definite—you know, that they understood that we were there in the pursuit of arms, that this had been put in place by Captain Jim Kelly, by Neil Blaney, by the other ministers that we had met. So there was never any doubt in our minds, you know, that there was any doubt in their minds as to what we were about.[9]

But there was considerable doubt and confusion within the Dublin establishment about what represented official Government policy. This was most clearly demonstrated in the handling of the media. Propaganda was an important facet of the conflict in the confused days of August and September 1969.[10] The Government redeployed public relations officials from state bodies, including five from Aer Lingus, to repackage news material and disseminate it throughout the world. The public relations consultants were then despatched to diplomatic missions in London, New York, Washington, Canberra, Stockholm, Copenhagen, Brussels, Bonn, and Paris. It was a costly initiative, based in large part 'on the assumption that the press in some countries, particularly Britain, would be unwilling, or unable, to interpret the situation fairly.'[11]

It quickly became apparent that two different agendas were being followed. The Government Information Bureau provided copies of Lynch's Tralee speech and reports collated from newspapers such as the *Irish Times*; the official line was that unity by consent was the only viable option considered by the Government. It also provided material printed and published by the civil rights movement, including Bowes Eagan's account of the People's Democracy march from Belfast to Derry at the beginning of the year. What was not made clear was that the Government Information Bureau itself had assumed editorial control of other texts disseminated.

The linchpin in the operation became Séamus Brady, a journalist and public relations consultant appointed by Charles Haughey to head a secret communications network.[12] Brady had considerable experience as a Fianna Fáil fixer and was at first employed by the Government Information Bureau to 'operate in the Six counties on a fulltime basis to collect information and data for the propaganda unit.'[13] It was his copy that formed the basis of the 'colourful adjectives' used to describe the situation on the ground. He also alerted Haughey to the need expressed by 'prominent members of various defence committees in the north' to counter 'the Stormont propaganda machine.'[14]

Following the presentation of a confidential report on that situation to his superiors, Brady was asked to meet the director of intelligence, Colonel Michael Hefferon, and his assistant, Captain James Kelly, at Army Headquarters. Brady agreed to introduce Kelly to associates in the North and became embroiled in a wider strategic plan, essential elements of which contradicted the official Government line. The first strategy pursued was to ensure that propaganda was made widely available, while not being traceable directly back to the Government.

Brady secured a commitment to publish two pamphlets—*Terror in Northern Ireland,* an anonymous account of the Belfast burnings, and *Eyewitness in Northern Ireland* by Aidan Corrigan, chairman of Dungannon Civil Rights Association. He also arranged for costing to be carried out for the establishment of a newspaper and a mobile radio station. Kelly and Brady held a further meeting with Haughey, together with Aidan Corrigan, at the minister's palatial home on the outskirts of Dublin. According to Brady, not only did Haughey look favourably on the idea of a newspaper but he also suggested the publication's name, *Voice of the North*.

In evidence to the Committee of Public Accounts, Brady declared that the director of the Government Information Bureau, Eoin Neeson, was instrumental in carrying out these plans.

> So far as I can recollect this discussion took place in Mr Neeson's office on Thursday, September 18, 1969. I have a clear recollection that my

involvement in both projects was discussed between us on the basis that, as was the case of the production of the two booklets, the Government and the Information Bureau would not be publicly connected with such projects but would privately support them, financially and otherwise.[15]

Three days later Brady resigned from the Government Information Bureau. He was to meet its director at the Royal Hibernian Hotel in Dublin on 25 September to discuss *Voice of the North*. According to Brady, it was agreed at this meeting that the Government Information Bureau would provide material for the paper as required.[16]

Brady organised a press conference in the Shelbourne Hotel, Dublin, on 5 October, ostensibly to launch Corrigan's *Eyewitness in Northern Ireland*. For Dublin a much more important sub-text was being promoted. Brady was accompanied by Paddy Kennedy, the Republican Labour MP, and Hugh Kennedy (no relation), press officer of the Citizens' Defence Committee.[17] The press conference was used to float the idea of reorganising NICRA. Corrigan described the association's constitution as 'a stumbling block, as it did not permit satisfactory representation from Civil Rights groups outside Belfast.' He suggested that 'a number of regional Civil Rights groups such as those in Fermanagh and Dungannon, had only tenuous affiliation with the NICRA, and an altered constitution would tighten the organisation and permit discipline and control to be maintained.'[18]

It was a busy weekend. As Brady was attempting to marginalise the left wing within NICRA, Kelly had secured the agreement of his superiors for the meeting, alluded to in his earlier intelligence report, to complete the distancing of the Belfast republicans now controlling life behind the barricades from the Dublin leadership. Along with attempts to change the direction of constitutional nationalism came a concern to minimise the power of the Marxist ideologists in Dublin.[19] In this the machinations in Dublin played into the hands of those in Belfast who, for their own reasons, were determined to move against Cathal Goulding. The power struggle had moved up a gear.[20]

The extent to which Military Intelligence sought to use the CDC as a device for manipulating the divisions in the republican movement into an overt split is evident from a further document Captain Kelly presented to his superiors, dated 6 October 1969. It concerns a meeting held in Bailieborough, County Cavan, on 4–5 October. Kelly now admits that this meeting was a cover for the arming of a Northern Command.[21] The document records what had been agreed at the meeting:

The NI Republican movement is now a six-county org. Its present first priority is the acquisition of arms for defensive purposes. It has the finance to accomplish this and it is the intention to import arms through the SOUTH.

The second priority of Northern Republicans is that of training and they see this as of extreme and immediate urgency. Training required could be classified under the following headings:

a. Weapon Training—an intensive one-week course.

b. INT [intelligence] Training—selected men—2 to each county— to undergo an intensive course of some days' duration.

c. Demolition Training—groups from each area to undergo a week's course.

d. Communications Training—selected men to train in RI [Republic of Ireland] primarily. Above Training is seen as given by the Defence Forces here.

It is realised; however, that there may be problems, in view of which it is accepted that a. [weapon training], as a reluctant alternative might be left in their own hands to take place in Southern camps.

The defensive aspects of operations is genuinely stressed but there is a definite feeling that in the final analysis the Defence forces will have to come to the rescue. In certain circumstances, Republicans see themselves holding such areas [as] Belfast, Derry, Coalisland and Dungannon, Armagh and Newry for a period, which would indicate that planning here would need to take into consideration a drive to consolidate these areas, with Belfast, the capital as the main objective.

Republicans are insistent that training if agreed to, must start immediately. Otherwise, events will overtake them.[22]

The meeting was arranged as a stock-taking exercise in which representatives of the Defence Committees could outline their concerns to the Irish military establishment. It took place against the backdrop of rising concern about the level of commitment the Government was actually prepared to offer.

The abrupt cancellation of training organised by the army at Fort Dunree, a barracks on the Inishowen Peninsula, served only to heighten this concern. Ten men from the Bogside had been inducted into the FCA to provide a cover for the training of Northern nationalists in guerrilla warfare. It was a pilot course, which was to be extended until the news leaked out. The director of intelligence, Colonel Hefferon, who had been instrumental in organising this operation, acted immediately: he issued an order cancelling any further overt involvement by the military and informed the Minister for Defence, Jim Gibbons, that this had been done.[23] The Bailieborough meeting was in large part an attempt to keep open the lines of communication, with Military Intelligence playing an important role.[24]

In a series of interviews for this book, Captain Kelly maintained that the money to finance this operation came from Charles Haughey.

> I was brought out to Haughey's house by the director of intelligence. Whether he was sent for by the minister or vice versa I do not know, I just went along. While there I mentioned about this meeting that was being arranged and that it should be financed in some way and I got £500 allotted to me, which I got the next morning from Colonel Hefferon.[25]

The willingness of the Government, through Captain Kelly, to further the aims of the Belfast republicans opposed to the Goulding leadership was to become apparent in the following months. This was to be arranged through intricate financial arrangements surrounding the dispersal of the grant in aid. The Government meeting on 16 August had decided that

> a sum of money—the amount and the channel of the disbursement of which would be determined by the Minister for Finance—should be made available from the Exchequer to provide aid for the victims of the current unrest in the Six Counties.[26]

Haughey authorised expenditure totalling £100,000. The vague terms gave considerable scope for creative accountancy. As early as 21 August the Government Information Bureau announced that the Irish Red Cross Society would be used for distributing funds to those most in need; in reality the Red Cross was itself used to disguise the scale of the Government's involvement.

Three days after the Bailieborough meeting Haughey held a meeting at the Department of Finance with the general secretary of the Red Cross Society, Mary Murphy. He had a problem. It had come to his attention that many deserving cases 'were not receiving any assistance.' He asked whether the society would make available a sum of £5,000 initially to be paid directly into an account in the Bank of Ireland in Clones held in the names of Paddy Devlin, Paddy Kennedy, and Paddy McGrory (a widely respected solicitor in west Belfast). According to Murphy, 'the Minister stated [that] these were reputable men and that a statement of expenditure would be submitted in due course.'[27]

Events were now moving quickly. The reliance on other media to propagate the message was about to end, as the printing presses of the *Anglo-Celt* in Cavan rolled off the first issue of the *Voice of the North*. The paper proclaimed its editorial independence; it called on supporters to send cheques to the popular West Belfast Stormont MP Paddy Devlin and to Aidan Corrigan, now described as a prominent civil rights leader, to help finance what was presented as a community newspaper.

> The *Voice of the North* is printed and published in the province of Ulster by a group of people who have decided that there is a need to speak out fearlessly for the Irish people of the Six Counties and to expose the propaganda of the Unionist regime which aims at covering up the truth and confusing the Catholic and liberal Protestant population of the North.[28]

Brady alleged that he found it difficult to get paid. Following representations to his ultimate paymaster, the Minister for Finance, he discovered from him that

> the Taoiseach had decided that no monies would be advanced from the Bureau propaganda unit for the newspaper.
>
> I felt very angered at the manner in which I was treated in this matter. I had organised distribution for the newspaper throughout the North, I had personally produced three issues of the newspaper to date; I had put my firm to the expense of paying £650 towards the project, apart from the loss of my own earnings in time, travel, etc. Moreover, a committee had been set up in the North, composed of prominent members of the Defence committees in Belfast, Derry and Tyrone, to run the newspaper and a managing editor had been appointed in the North.[29]

The reason for the reticence was clear. The intelligence picture had become more complicated, for two related reasons. Firstly, the military operation had come to the attention of Peter Berry, long-term Secretary of the Department of Justice. Berry's running of the anti-subversive unit had demonstrated to even his most ardent supporters an obsession with state security.[30] The Garda Special Branch had the Bailieborough meeting under observation, and the reports sent to Dublin of money changing hands and of heavy drinking painted a very different picture from Kelly's interpretation of 'the republican element of the defence committees only wanting weapons for defence.'[31]

Berry had taken a long and close interest in the ideological disputes within the republican movement. In 1969 he prepared two confidential memoranda for his minister. The first, dated 18 March, noted the elevation of Dr Roy Johnston and others; he warned that this 'facilitated them in indoctrinating the rank and file with the conviction that any occasions of social unrest could be harnessed to establish the IRA as a dynamic political force on whom workers and small farmers could alone depend for improved social conditions.'[32] Berry was in hospital undergoing tests on the day of the meeting. The head of the Special Branch, Chief Superintendent John Fleming, was so alarmed at the prospect of what he saw as a subversive plot that he called to Mount Carmel Nursing Home in Dublin to see him. Berry telephoned his minister, Mícheál Ó Móráin, and when he failed to establish contact with him he made contact with the Minister for Finance, unaware that it was Haughey himself who had provided the funds for the meeting. According to Berry's diaries, published in 1980 in the news magazine *Magill,* Haughey quizzed Berry about where he had got the information, without divulging his own involvement in the affair, a development that in retrospect 'dismayed' the department secretary.[33]

It is now clear that Haughey was playing an exceptionally complicated game, keeping open connections with both the militant republicans and those charged with limiting their influence. A third element was also added with the revelation that on the previous day he had requested the British ambassador, Sir Andrew Gilchrist, to come to his home in Kinsealy. Haughey had a proposal he wished London to consider. In return for British support for a united Ireland, he offered British access to the old treaty ports, or, alternatively, NATO access to them. According to Gilchrist, Haughey wanted a secret commitment that the border would be the subject of an intergovernmental review. Gilchrist told his superior that Haughey—whom he described as able, shrewd, and ruthless—was insistent that there was 'nothing he would not sacrifice, including the position of the Catholic church, to achieve a united Ireland.'[34]

The fact that the Minister for Finance was broaching diplomatic initiatives with the British ambassador raises serious questions about Haughey's loyalty to both Lynch and the principle of collective responsibility. That loyalty appears even more questionable in the light of the fact that the meeting took place after Haughey had authorised the spending for the Bailieborough convention, raising at least the possibility that he viewed the destabilisation of the North as something very much in his own personal interest and was using his interview with the British ambassador to sound out possible long-term solutions. There is no evidence in the Government papers to suggest that Haughey told any of his colleagues about his meeting with Gilchrist. This is not to suggest that he did not; but in the absence of an explanation by Haughey of his position it is hard to avoid the conclusion that he was much more involved in manufacturing the crisis than has previously been understood.

What was clear was that the implications of the two divergent strategies were now coming into sharp focus. Captain Kelly kept up the pressure for substantial training. By 16 October he surmised:

> One must reach the conclusion that the Republic must prepare to assist Northern Republicanism, which involves:
>
> Supporting Northern Republicanism in its preparation for Defence through arms and training.
>
> By being prepared to march into the North and retrieve the situation if circumstances warrant.[35]

On the same day, Chief Superintendent Fleming returned to the nursing home to see Berry with a full report on the Bailieborough meeting. Berry suggests that the situation was so grave that the Taoiseach had to be informed. A meeting was arranged for the following day; not for the last time in this crisis, Jack Lynch was to discuss the affairs of the nation in a hospital room. Nurses and doctors performing tests on Berry constantly interrupted the meeting—so much so that the Taoiseach declared that the situation was impossible.

According to Berry's account,

> no person with a scrap of intelligence could doubt that the Taoiseach was made aware by me on 17 October—the date of my medical tests is verifiable in the hospital records—of information of a most serious kind in relation to a plot to import arms and that he avoided making any more than a cursory inquiry. Indeed, I formed the impression from time to time that he was consulting me to find out how much I did not know and that he was not thankful to me for bringing awkward facts to his notice.[36]

Despite the fact that the meeting was conducted under trying conditions, it was an encounter of fundamental importance, in that it shows that Lynch was clearly aware of ministerial involvement with known republicans as early as October 1969. Kevin Boland alleges that the Bailieborough meeting was discussed by the Government in October; he refers to one meeting in which the Minister for Justice, Mícheál Ó Móráin, spoke of his department complaining that he [Captain Kelly] was meeting the wrong kind of people and this struck a sympathetic chord in the Taoiseach and some Ministers. The Minister for Defence always contended that it was what the besieged community were thinking and feeling we needed to know.[37]

Government papers released in January 2000 provide further evidence of both the essential veracity of Boland's testimony and the depth of Lynch's knowledge. The Government had decided on 14 August to establish a committee of senior civil servants from the Departments of Justice, External Affairs, Defence and Local Government 'to keep the situation under continuous review and to advise the Taoiseach on the matter.'[38] A further meeting on 21 August added civil servants from the Department of Finance to the committee. Given the existence of this committee, which reported directly to Lynch, the Taoiseach's claim to have been ignorant of the machinations of his ministers until 20 April 1970 is not credible.[39]

The Government files released in January 2000 raise more questions than they answer. Included are documents from Berry drawing attention to the role of Radio Free Belfast and expressing concern that it was broadcasting appeals 'for people of all walks of life in the Free State to force the 26 county government to further action in regards to the problem in the 6 Counties.'[40] The files also show that Berry was kept informed of the activities of the Northern delegations, in particular the outburst by Paddy Devlin at the Department of External Affairs.[41] This is evidence of the inter-departmental system working to disseminate information; yet there is no trace of any record showing the suspicions of the Special Branch about the activities of Military Intelligence.

Of equal importance is the fact that the IRA leadership in Dublin decided to expose the Military Intelligence operation. On 30 October the editor of the monthly newspaper *United Irishman*, Séamas Ó Tuathail, called a press conference at the Gresham Hotel. Ó Tuathail launched a scathing attack on Séamus Brady and three Government ministers, Neil Blaney, Kevin Boland, and Charles Haughey, accusing them of 'using Fianna Fáil gold to buy their way into the Civil Rights Association and other areas of influence in the North.'[42] The published account in the *United Irishman* went further, accusing Brady of being the public relations officer for Taca, the Fianna Fáil business support group. It suggested that 'the activity of Brady and a host of Fianna Fáil agents inside the North has involved the spending of thousands of pounds to harness Civil Rights workers so that the people so duped will look to Fianna Fáil for leadership in the impending crisis.'[43] As evidence it cited the establishment of a civil rights association in Monaghan within weeks of the August trouble.[44]

The paper concluded that 'all in all *The Voice of the North* sounds suspiciously like the voice of Fianna Fáil,' and that it stretched credibility to believe that

> Mr Jack Lynch is unaware of this cynical double dealing by his ministers. These Fianna Fáil ministers are doing their best to disrupt civil rights and anti-unionist forces which have been politically embarrassing to them.[45]

The *United Irishman's* criticism had little to do with the veracity of the accounts of the August burnings published in the *Voice of the North* or the two pamphlets paid for by the Government: it centred rather on what the Dublin republican leadership saw as the orchestrated attempt to 'restructure the civil rights movement.'[46] It is clear that the *Voice of the North* provided a covert opportunity for the Irish authorities to wrest control of the civil rights movement from those the Dublin military establishment viewed as irresponsible. The directors of the *Voice of the North* included those assembled by Captain Kelly and Military Intelligence as being more amenable to Dublin; they included Seán Keenan and John Kelly.[47]

The anger expressed by the *United Irishman* had also a lot to do with the use of the Bank of Ireland account in Clones. As we have seen, the account was ostensibly established to help 'people who were not receiving any assistance.' A total of £15,000 was transferred from the Red Cross Society to this account in three separate transactions, the first at the request of Haughey himself, the other two arranged by Anthony Fagan, personal secretary to the Minister for Finance, acting under the instructions of his minister.[48] Sums of £2,000 were withdrawn on 10, 17 and 24 October and again on 6 November.[49] While it is undoubtedly true that Paddy Devlin in particular contributed to legitimate relief operations, a significant proportion found its way into the hands of the IRA. Of even more significance is the fact that the barricades in Derry were taken down on 8 October and in Belfast two days later. There simply was no relief operation in Belfast to justify the scale and frequency of the withdrawals.

The dispute within the IRA centred not on the morality of taking 'Fianna Fáil gold' but on who was receiving it. As time went on it became apparent that the critics of Goulding were getting the bulk of the money, much to the chagrin of Jim Sullivan. Kennedy was then kidnapped.[50]

Captain Kelly argues that equal funding would not have made sense. Of the Goulding leadership he said:

> Basically their idea was—and it was told to me by one certain man who I met in the North who was quite clear about it—that he was aiming for a socialist republic that would overthrow both capitalist governments, north and south. And I remember that the obvious question that sprang to my mind was, well, how do you expect a government in the south to give you arms and support if you are going to overthrow it? It's just not on.[51]

Documents provided to the author make it clear that Military Intelligence itself viewed the displacement of the leading Belfast republican loyal to Goulding as the paramount objective. The message from Dublin was clear: there could be no truck with those regarded as subversive, whose agenda included the destabilisation of the Southern state. Kelly wrote to Colonel Hefferon that People's Democracy had

> gained control in the Lower Falls through Jim Sullivan. They are in a position to cause trouble at any stage. In line with their anarchical irresponsible policy, they are liable to do so without regard to the consequences to people or indeed to the ultimate republican objective of unity.[52]

Despite the disclosures in the *United Irishman,* publication of the *Voice of the North* continued, together with denials that the paper was in the pay of anyone. On 8 November, for example, it proclaimed: 'The *Voice of the North* is neither controlled nor influenced by any political party or any group north or south.'[53] By then it had a new paymaster: Military Intelligence.

Brady contacted Captain Kelly and told him that unless funds became available the paper could not continue. He told the publisher that his contacts thought the paper was performing a useful role and were prepared to subsidise it. He handed over £600 in cash. Over the next four months Kelly was to provide Brady with a total of £5,100, all ostensibly from his Northern contacts but in reality from the grant in aid administered by the Minister for Finance.[54] That Lynch was aware of the financial arrangements for the *Voice of the North* is clear from the testimony of his own director of information:

I felt I had no justification in passing these accounts for payment. Accordingly I reported the matter to the Taoiseach at the first opportunity and I told him of my concern regarding this publication. I recommended to the Taoiseach that neither the Government Information Bureau nor the Government should have anything to do with it. The Taoiseach agreed with this view and at his suggestion, I gave the Taoiseach the bills and invoices I had received and he said he would give them to Mr Haughey ... At a later date some of these bills were again sent to me. I gave these to the Taoiseach and again he said he would pass them to Mr Haughey. I am aware that he did so.[55]

At the beginning of November plans were made to transfer the operation of the Clones account to three separate accounts held in the Munster and Leinster Bank, Baggot Street, Dublin. All were under the direct control of Captain Kelly, and it was from these accounts that he financed the *Voice of the North*.

An analysis of its content reveals that the *Voice of the North* was not only used to change the direction of the civil rights movement along lines more amenable to the brand of majoritarian nationalism traditionally favoured by Fianna Fáil but that it became an important resource in the ideological power struggle operating at the highest echelons of Fianna Fáil itself. How payments continued to a newspaper openly hostile to the Taoiseach, with his tacit acceptance, remains a mystery.[56] Brady somewhat surprisingly contends in his memoirs that he accepted Lynch's interpretation in the Dáil debate in May 1970 that neither the Government nor Fianna Fáil had supported the *Voice of the North*.

> Looked at from hindsight now the Taoiseach could never have given his support, moral or financial. Its content from the start was anti-Unionist and overtly critical of his plan of trying to unite Ireland by appeasement. [The paper] was disposed towards the Blaney, Haughey, Boland side in Dáil Éireann and the Paddy Kennedy side in Stormont, critical of Jack Lynch's Government and sceptical about the John Humes, Gerry Fitts and Austin Curries of the North.[57]

From November onwards the focus of the paper changed as it became a policy vehicle for the increasingly obvious leadership ambitions of Blaney. Nowhere was this more apparent than in the public disagreements over what Blaney regarded as the Government's ideological retreat on partition. The debate centred on the efficacy of the use of force. Lynch had made it clear both at Tralee and subsequently during the Dáil debate on the upheavals in Northern Ireland that force was not an option. At stake was not simply the question of coercion, a mere tactical concern: much more fundamental was the question whether any section of the Irish people, defined in a territorial sense, had the right to opt out of the Irish nation. In his Tralee speech Lynch had put forward as party policy a pragmatic acceptance of contemporary reality. He suggested that it would

> remain our most earnest aim and hope to win the consent of the majority of the people in the Six Counties to means by which north and south can come together. We are seeking to win the agreement of a sufficient number in the North to an acceptable form of re-unification.[58]

Such a bald rejection of traditional policy opened a significant fault line within Fianna Fáil and undermined its central platform of having a distinct position on the national question. It was terrain that Blaney had shown considerable skill in navigating; it was terrain to which he returned in Letterkenny with devastating effect in a speech marking his twenty-first anniversary as a TD.

> What we are all being asked now is to forget the recent happenings, the murders of innocent people, the armed attacks by partisan police and Unionist gunmen, the hapless families burned out and forced out by threat from their homes—for all of which the Unionist version of justice has so far failed to produce a single culprit. We are being urged to get back to normality, in other words to permit the Stormont regime to return to business as usual. But normality is fraudulent and business as usual a myth while the Border is maintained. The people of free Ireland, and those who long for freedom in that portion of our country which is still fettered, are not prepared to accept another 1921 settlement from the British government. A united Ireland is the answer ...
>
> To say that the majority within the Six Counties should have the right to decide on Partition is to accept that Partition was in the first instance justified. Ireland was partitioned against the majority wishes of her people, and it is the majority of the people of all Ireland who alone have the right to decide this question. That is the primary civil right of all.

He agreed that peaceful means represented the best approach to ending partition. Then he launched a shot across the bows:

> But no one has the right to assert that force is irrevocably out. No political party or group at any time is entitled to pre-determine the right of the Irish people to decide what course of action on this question may be

justified in given circumstances. The Fianna Fáil party has never taken a decision to rule out the use of force if the circumstances in the Six Counties so demand ... If a situation were to arise in the Six Counties in which the people who do not subscribe to the Unionist regime were under sustained and murderous assault then as the Taoiseach said on August 13 we cannot stand idly [sic] by.

He concluded with what amounted to an overt call to arms:

The grave responsibility for the continuance of partition, and for the violence that flows inevitably from it, rests, as it has always done with the Government of Westminster. If they fall into the same error now as their predecessors in the past, allowing themselves to be persuaded that compromise will suffice for another fifty years, and that a rag-bag of reforms covering over the real problem will bring peace in our time in Ireland, then they are assuredly sowing the seeds of further violence and bloodshed for innocent people.[59]

The speech brought an immediate reaction. Lynch made it clear that the Minister for Agriculture was not in any way expressing Government policy: instead the speech, circulated in advance to the media (though not to the Taoiseach's office), was put down to a burst of intemperate impetuosity. 'While Mr Blaney's feelings on the Partition issue are very deeply felt, and he occasionally finds it difficult not to give expression to them, he knows and endorses Government policy on this issue as he did in Letterkenny,' was Jack Lynch's rather weak rejoinder.[60]

Blaney's speech was remarkable not just for its open criticism of the Taoiseach but also the timing of the intervention. Blaney was just about to go to London as part of a Government delegation that also included Haughey for crucial Anglo-Irish trade talks. Talking tough on Britain just before meeting its leaders always went down well in the Fianna Fáil heartland, particularly in the context of requiring agreement for common purposes on negotiations to enter the EEC. And other internal imperatives were at work. Lynch had quietly dropped plans for a Department of Economic Planning, which he had promised Blaney after the 1969 election.

Three Government ministers had attended the meeting at which the speech was made, including Boland and Ó Móráin.[61] Commenting on its significance, *Hibernia* noted the 'glaring divergences' within the Government on partition, which the Taoiseach was unable to manage. The fact that a member of his own Government dared to exploit that slender margin between honest intent and absolute pledge, reveals the weakness of his own command.

It concluded with a question.

> Neil Blaney evidently believes that his well-staged interventions on the subject of Partition arc conducive to his political advancement. But it is interesting to contrast this performance with that of a shrewd colleague in the cabinet who before, during or since the Northern Crisis, has uttered not a word in public or in private on any single aspect of the situation. His name? Charles J. Haughey.[62]

Haughey was playing a vital background role: sufficiently aware of the power of irredentist nationalism to privately support Blaney's crusade within the confines of Government secrecy, wily enough not to publicly move against Lynch unless the leader found himself exposed.[63]

The reaction in Northern Ireland to Blaney's rhetoric was more polarised. Paddy Kennedy was enthusiastic, saying it was 'reassuring to know that the Irish government is not going to stand idly by while their fellow Irish men are butchered in the North.'[64] Interviewed by RTE, John Hume, the independent MP for Foyle, squared up behind Lynch in attacking the futility of what he termed the divisiveness of Blaney's approach. He suggested that reality must be faced: breaking down the border by force in the absence of unionist consent would lead only to civil war. Speaking with what the television critic of the *Irish Times* described as his 'customary subdued strength,' Hume decried the logical outcome of Blaney's hawkish approach. 'It is not really Irish to be talking of shooting Protestant fellow-Irishmen.'[65]

Blaney received support from Eddie McAteer, who obliquely criticised his successor as MP for Foyle as a 'latecomer to the scene with a watchful eye for the TV camera.' He also hinted at the role Blaney had played in the early summer, saying that while it was 'not yet time to write the full story ... Neil Blaney was never far from our city in those fateful days of July and August.'[66]

Blaney himself entered the fray in a hard-hitting performance on RTE. 'I do not regard John Hume as any Solomon on this matter of partition,' he said. As he saw it, hoping for internal reform was simply not an option; promises had not been and could not be kept. 'It would appear that the bully boys of the Unionist Party may do as they wish, provided that they're able to block the minority up there: this is the only hurdle they have to cross to revert to their former status and former methods of operation.' He came close to breaking confidentiality by declaring that 'there had been hard words and plain speaking at the Cabinet meetings during August before decisions was made in the North.' He maintained that while there was at present no split in Government thinking, if there was a serious disagreement the 'extreme of going to the country in a general election' was an option to be considered. In that situation, with the party split, he was ready to declare himself a contender for the leadership.

> If there was a situation in which a Taoiseach was being sought for the party and that the party wished to consider me, well then in all probability, I would have to consider very seriously the implications of that and leave it to the party's best judgement, as has been done in the past in a fair selection, finally.[67]

The machinations of Southern politics were of little interest in Northern Ireland, even among the most politically aware. There was a recognition in the North, even among the most ardently nationalist, that the rhetoric of anti-partitionism had mutated into an ideological gloss to cover the perceived indecency of following the more mundane reality of governing the 26-county state.[68] What was significant about Blaney's interventions throughout this period was the attempt to inject some vitality into the debate. The general purpose may have been to gain power within Fianna Fáil, but that does not detract from the emotional power an appeal to old certainties had in the situation of a perception of threatened pogrom. It offered a possibility that the South would intervene if necessary; that Northern nationalism would not be betrayed; that something would be done. For those afraid of reprisals in Belfast, the Blaney approach provided much-needed comfort. For Fianna Fáil activists it demonstrated the vitality of the party, showed that it had an appointment with history; for the militant defenders of the Catholic ghettos here was proof that the 'slightly constitutional' party, in Seán Lemass's famous phrase, was going back to its roots. Taken together, this explosive combination had the potential to fundamentally threaten Lynch's leadership of the party and to plunge Ireland into civil war.[69]

One who clearly saw the danger was the Labour Party TD Conor Cruise O'Brien, who was in Belfast when reports came through of the Letterkenny speech. He called on Lynch to sack the Minister for Agriculture. He later argued that the 'risk of any condonation, from inside the Dublin government, of the use of force to end partition, could legitimise Catholic attacks on the British army, and build up towards various forms of war in Ireland.'[70]

Jack Lynch was a man under pressure. A lacklustre performance in the Dáil two days after the Blaney leadership challenge served only to heighten the perception that Lynch's stewardship was sailing into trouble. The parliamentary correspondent John Healy caught the mood when he commented that Lynch was

> less positive than he was a year ago when faced with exactly the same questions about exactly the same minister and dealing with the same issue—the use of force in the North. A year ago he simply rapped Mr Blaney's knuckles and there was no mistaking the firmness: yesterday it was a different performance as if in the intervening time the Blaney theme had struck a deeper response with the grassroots of the party and was gathering force and the Taoiseach, while upholding his own view, was less certain today than he was a year ago. He was under strain: Neil Blaney wasn't: that is the way it appeared yesterday.[71]

In the searing debate within Fianna Fáil it is clear that the *Voice of the North* subscribed totally to Blaney's interpretation of the role of ideology. His Letterkenny speech was extensively quoted, along with what was presented as an open warning to Fianna Fáil from Northern society.

> The Southern government had better sooner or later make up its mind whether or not Ireland is composed of 26 or 32 counties. If it accepts, as its constitution dictates, the authority of the Irish people to rule themselves, sovereign and independent over 32 counties, then should the tragic circumstances of August 1969 ever re-occur, where does it stand. What Southern politician or party has the right to sit in the safety of Stillorgan and tell the minority in the North that they have no moral right to possess a firearm with which to protect their lives and property.[72]

The paper agreed that force could be counter-productive but refused to rule it out as a tactic.

> But what of force itself? It has been used successfully in Aden, Cyprus, Kenya, Palestine and Algeria. Once it is mentioned in Ireland, however, almost everyone throws up their hands in horror and none more so than those who used force or the threat of force in 1912, 1920 and 1969.[73]

Of even more significance was the impact of the speech and its aftermath on the internal politics of republicanism. By design, Blaney appeared to be ensuring that the Republic would not stand by, that the Northern Command would not be isolated. It steeled the nerve of the Belfast leadership and convinced them that it was unnecessary to attempt to change the politics of the republican movement from within.[74] For the emerging Northern Command the promises of material support now appeared more than illusory. The reliance on republican unity could, it seemed, be jettisoned: the North could go it alone. For the republican movement it was a fateful decision.

The decision may have been rationally justified, given the circumstances of the time, where the policies adopted by the leadership were in sharp conflict with Northern realities. Its immediate consequence, however, was that once again Belfast simply opted out of the battle for the soul of the movement, a battle that was once again heating up with the decision by the leadership to press ahead with plans to end abstention at the 1969 IRA convention. Even those in the Southern leadership most attuned to the political implications of the August burnings and their potential impact on the IRA viewed the Northern emphasis on a localised agenda as a major tactical blunder.

> Mac Stiofáin and Ó Conaill were in constant contact with Belfast, but Belfast could not see its way. How did they get into the convention? Did they have to go to Goulding and give him their allegiance, which they had withdrawn in September, and what would the consequences of all that be? and so on. They were on what they regarded as a certain high ground; they weren't going to come down off it, so that was their position. They got themselves into a situation with regard to the convention that they couldn't get themselves out of. They felt that they were cornered, and any help that they could get from anyone they were going to take it. If people were offering them arms or money they were going to take it, because they were highly motivated on this community defence situation.[75]

The first attempt to provide arms for the Northern Command involved John Kelly and Pádraig (Jock) Haughey, brother of the Minister for Finance. The two travelled to London to arrange an arms deal. The money for the proposed shipment was to come from the George Dixon account in the Baggot Street branch of the Munster and Leinster Bank in Dublin; a request had been made on behalf of the fictitious George Dixon to arrange the drawing of cheques on a London bank. On 17 November the Munster and Leinster contacted the Piccadilly branch of the National Provincial Bank to provide advance clearance of cheques to a maximum value of £11,450. Further correspondence extended this facility.[76]

Kelly and Haughey arranged to meet an arms dealer at premises in Oxford Street. After a delay of eight hours they were introduced to Captain Markham Randall. Kelly remembers being suspicious of Randall, who described himself as a former officer in the British army who had extensive experience of arranging arms shipments in the Middle East. His suspicion heightened when the men arranged to go to another venue to conclude business. Kelly stayed back as Randall and Haughey walked along Oxford Street. He noticed that

> a woman was just in front of me. She was talking into her headscarf with a shopping bag. I knew then that the whole thing was rumbled and we had to get offside, which we did.[77]

Kelly rang Randall to tell him that he had been ordered back to Dublin. The gun-runners arranged a further meeting to arrange the shipment. According to Kelly,

> he had expressed an interest in visiting training camps in the 26 Counties, and so he arranged to come over to meet us in the Gresham. We had arranged for some people to meet him there as well, just to have a word with him, to find out exactly what he was at. But Jim Kelly intervened, and that was the end of that.[78]

Mac Stiofáin watched events unfold with increased interest. His particularly close relationship with the Kelly brothers gave him an unrivalled understanding of the politics of the republican movement north and south. He accepted in his memoirs that support had been forthcoming from Fianna Fáil. He claimed that it was

> cynically stumbling about trying to get in on the act in the North, but only to keep itself in power in the South. Fianna Fáil had been running a propaganda sheet called *Voice of the North*. It had been providing some degree of aid to the Citizens Action Committees. A few executives associated with it were willing to help these communities to get some arms. But all this was a very different matter from financing a split within the IRA.[79]

That interpretation is fine as far as it goes. On an all-Ireland perspective that contention can be sustained. However, the important factor that Mac Stiofáin does not allude to is the implication of the decision by the Belfast units to make a unilateral declaration of independence from the IRA command structure. The promises of support, financial and material, by Military Intelligence, acting on orders from sections of the Fianna Fáil Government, in many ways facilitated that decision.

In Dublin, Goulding continued with preparations for the convention. Unit conventions had been taking place throughout the year, but during the autumn not only did representation begin to change but, suspiciously, numbers began to be added. The first definite sign of a gerrymander came from a dispute over representation from County Tyrone. The leadership had been informed that a convention held in the early summer—before the August burnings—had selected one delegate; in November they were informed that a second convention was held and a further five delegates would be attending—all loyal to Goulding. The writing was on the wall. 'Goulding wouldn't have proceeded with the convention if he knew he wasn't going to get or manufacture enough support,' suggests Ó Brádaigh. 'He would have postponed the convention for some reason or another.'

There was recognition, however, that the differences were becoming unmanageable, with the dispute within the Army Council now turning on the inevitability rather than the possibility of a parting of the ways. According to Mac Stiofáin,

> six weeks before the split I was called to a meeting with Mac Giolla, Goulding, Garland. Garland did most of the talking. He said, 'Seán, it looks as if we're going to have a split.' I said, 'That's your problem. We have a crisis in the North and you persist to push through proposals which will split the movement.' I said, 'Cathal, you are the only one who could stop a split. Withdraw your support from the proposals. You ask me about my responsibilities. What about yours?' So after about twenty minutes I left.[80]

Goulding prepared a document on strategy that, he said, underwrote the policy of the movement, for distribution within Irish-American circles. In reality it was an attempt to discover just who was loyal. Even those totally opposed, like Mac Stiofáin and Ó Brádaigh, signed the document. According to Ó Brádaigh,

> my attitude was quite clear, because some of the delegates said to me afterwards, 'Why did you sign that document?' and that type of thing. I said, 'Well, the convention was fixed, it was taking place. Goulding was busy counting heads, figuring out whether he got a yes vote or a no vote.' My attitude was that if I didn't sign that document I wouldn't get

to the convention for some reason or another, that they would exclude me, and it was vital that I did get there. So that was accepted.[81]

Once again Blaney's hand can be detected in influencing the direction of the split. He was not content with providing mere rhetorical support to push through his agenda. In late November Captain Kelly arranged for John Kelly and Seán Keenan, by now the most influential republican go-betweens with Military Intelligence, to meet Blaney. The next stage in the operation was to take place in the United States. According to John Kelly, 'we were sent there on the express orders of Jim Kelly and Neil Blaney to ascertain how quickly arms would be available in New York from the Irish-American community.'[82]

America had long been an important source of finance for successive IRA campaigns, and as the political situation in Northern Ireland deteriorated it once again became a prize to control. Throughout 1969 significant divisions opened up between the main lobbying groups, specifically over the left-wing analysis put forward by leading figures in the republican movement, the civil rights movement and People's Democracy during speaking tours of the eastern United States.[83] Three separate relationships could be detected. The moderates in the civil rights movement allied themselves with the American Congress of Irish Freedom, a human rights lobby group run by James Heaney, which had proved its credentials by having the European Commission on Human Rights raise concerns about the Northern Ireland Special Powers Act in April 1968. A symbiotic relationship developed between the ideologists in Dublin and Belfast and the radical chic in New York and Berkeley, all of whom saw in Northern Ireland the possibility of linking the struggle to an international anti-capitalist movement. The National Association for Irish Justice, formed in New York in April by Brian Heron, a grandson of James Connolly, became closely aligned with People's Democracy and with Cathal Goulding.

In a much-publicised visit in August 1969, Bernadette Devlin completely alienated large swathes of Irish America by injudicious language.[84] She refused to meet the Mayor of Chicago, Richard Daley, because of his handling of the protests at the 1968 Democratic Convention. The revolutionary style may have caught the imagination of the radical left but it horrified opinion-formers. The *Chicago Tribune* commented: 'If this is the course to be followed by Catholics in Ulster, then the outlook is grim for everyone except Communists and other subversives who regard the religious conflict as a pretext for turning all of Ireland into Britain's Cuba.'[85] The prominent civil rights lawyer Frank Durkan remembers the impact such criticism had on attempts to mobilise opinion.

> It didn't go down at all well. In no time at all they had painted Bernadette as a communist advocate, and this idea of socialism and anything to do with left-wing politics was planted in the minds of the Irish-American conservative electorate, who would not have anything to do with it. It was a constant uphill battle to educate Irish America as to what was going on in the North.[86]

Goulding decided that such difficulties were unavoidable. He was determined to remain in the vanguard of world revolution, despite the potential political cost. In November 1969 he was the guest of honour at the convention of the National Association for Irish Justice, whose office in East 23rd Street, New York, appeared to a left-wing contributor to the *Irish Times* to be

> the office of Mr Cathal Goulding, Chief of Staff of the Irish Republican Army. When I drew his attention to this, Mr Heron said the office was available to all Irish Republican, radical, revolutionary and civil rights organisations that cared to make use of it. The IRA works closely with the NAIJ and the NAIJ officers think highly of Mr Goulding, of the IRA as it is now and of the IRA as they believe it will develop in the coming months. In short, the NAIJ exists to promote revolution in Ireland, north and south, by whatever means it can: for the moment its long-term faith is in the IRA.[87]

The third grouping, traditional Irish-American sympathisers who demonstrated their loyalty to the old country by membership of the Ancient Order of Hibernians and Clan na Gael—by far the most influential in numbers and financial clout—were either ignored or patronised. Their reliance on the language of physical force, of partition and of the British presence being the root cause of the problem was presented as evidence of their perceived ignorance or narrow-mindedness. They presented a rich vein for those who were to come to America preaching another message: determined to fight for Ireland and to fight against or at least not propagate what they saw as the scourge of world socialism and its corollary, anarchy.

It was to this market that Seán Keenan and John Kelly made their pitch. From Philadelphia to Boston they launched scathing attacks on the IRA leadership. They spoke of how the situation was desperate and how

Goulding and Johnston, for all their theoretical posturing, were unwilling or unable to provide weapons or planning. It was all very well to plan for a revolution, but revolutions involved dangerous consequences. Not arming the Catholics left them helpless victims. They claimed there was an urgent need for support, but first they needed weapons. They did not need to raise the money: they said they already had it.

A meeting was arranged in New York with five of the city's most important republicans, people who spanned the history of the movement from the glory days of the War of Independence, through the splits over the republican left in the thirties, to the futility of the 1956–62 border campaign. When they were told that the money to finance the operation was to come directly from the Fianna Fáil Government, there was incredulity. Michael Flannery was an IRA veteran from the twenties who had become a symbol of Irish resistance and a focus for the Irish-American community, together with the veterans Jack McCarthy from County Cork and Jack McGowan from County Clare, whose hatred of the Southern state came a close second to the struggle against Britain. Liam Kelly was an IRA veteran of the anti-partition campaign who had proclaimed from the hustings in Mid-Ulster in 1952 that constitutional methods were not going to solve the Irish question; what was required, he had famously proclaimed, was 'the use of force; the more the better, the sooner the better.'[88] Kelly had spent much of the border campaign interned in the Curragh. The fifth member of the group was Martin Lyons, an IRA member from the fifties and a man who was to become one of the most influential organisers of material support for the Provisionals within Irish America. All had every reason to doubt the sincerity of Fianna Fáil.

> We faced a great deal of criticism and a great deal of resentment and resistance from the more traditional older-generation Irish-Americans who had participated in the Civil War, who had been in the War of Independence and who said, 'How could you deal with a de Valera government? How could you deal with a Fianna Fáil government?' They were quite reluctant to enter into any deal with them. We had to sort of say, 'Look, do you have £100,000 to put at our disposal?' which was kind of the bottom line. They didn't have. So they went reluctantly with that idea, you know.[89]

This is a crucial admission. Most accounts of the trip suggest that it was a failure either because they did not raise the money or because Irish-

Americans refused to provide help for a plan financed by Fianna Fáil.[90] It was this coterie rather than Heron's NAIJ that was ultimately to provide the dynamic link between Irish America and the republican movement and to have a decisive influence over the direction of the 'armed struggle', a point now conceded for the first time by Seán Mac Stiofáin.

> The contacts that were made in December 1969 were the nucleus for Northern Irish Aid in America, and most of the arms and equipment for the IRA from the split until the summer of 1972 was from America. It was vital, vital. Without that I do not think it would have made the same effect and support. There were five people there, most good friends of mine afterwards, [who] organised [the] most successful gun operations in the history of the IRA.[91]

This too is a crucial admission. While Mac Stiofáin was always sceptical about Blaney's commitment to providing the goods, he was aware that if the dissidents were going to have to go it alone they would require support and weapons from the United States. The Keenan and Kelly adventure in December 1969 played a significant role in undermining the authority of Goulding and the established IRA leadership in the most lucrative market available for long-term fund-raising and arms.[92] In fact such was the anger at Keenan's involvement in particular that he was expelled from the movement specifically for undertaking the trip.[93]

The complex manoeuvring was reaching a conclusion, with prominent IRA contacts informing the Special Branch of the continuing involvement of Fianna Fáil ministers in attempts to import weapons. Further evidence of this comes obliquely from another entry in Peter Berry's diary, dated 10 December 1969. He records a meeting between Mícheál Ó Móráin and Commissioner Wymes and Chief Superintendent Fleming. According to Berry, the Garda officers gave him a complete run-down of the activities of Captain Kelly, his promises of arms, his offers of money, and his involvement over time with known subversives. They also told him that those two ministers, Haughey and Blaney, were involved in a plot to buy arms. Ó Móráin says he asked them to re-check their sources, as he continued to be unhappy with the information coming from one of the 'IRA Deep Throats'. However, despite his wariness of the source, he went and reported the information to the Taoiseach.[94]

If the IRA source sought to force Lynch's hand in dispensing with Blaney's services in advance of the IRA convention, he was to be disappointed. The dénouement came in a village in County Kildare in mid-December as delegates gathered to formalise the inevitable. Participants at the convention say the mood was sombre. Ruairí Ó Brádaigh remembers it chiefly as

> a case of the irresistible force and the immovable object … Everyone was quite philosophical, because if you like the fire had gone out of things and everyone knew where everyone else stood, and it was a question of formalising divisions which were already there.[95]

Seán Garland took the chair and began by pointing out that abstention was a mere tactic to be traded for immediate advantage. He told the delegates that while there was a risk that the revolutionary party could be co-opted into constitutional politics, the most pertinent example of potential success was that of Russia, where the Bolsheviks used the Duma to great effect between the February and October Revolutions. Ó Brádaigh, in particular, could not accept this interpretation, given that for him the national liberation struggle had yet to be completed. To the end, those opposed to the strategy thought they could make Goulding change direction. Even on the night there was an attempt to stave off the inevitable. The split itself could have been avoided if Belfast had tried to use its influence within the established structures; that it did not in many ways pre-ordained the split, which in the end centred neither on the August violence nor even on the creation of a national liberation front.

> It was just a practical thing that one could live with because it could be corrected in the future or amended or reshaped. All right, you could live with that. The other thing was so basic and had to do with the whole direction and, as you put it, the soul of the movement, it was so fundamental: this was the thing that people throughout history had divided on. This was what the Civil War was fought over—and a very nasty one at that.[96]

That other thing was abstention, the subject of searching debate in 1968 and the central tenet of the change of strategy throughout the sixties.

The final vote established the split. The official figures were 39 in favour and 12 against, a two-thirds majority; Ó Brádaigh claims that the vote in fact was 28 to 12. Four delegates from the South Clare, Tipperary and Limerick units failed to get collected at designated pick-up points; a further five delegates from County Tyrone could also be subtracted from the final total in favour of the proposals. If

Belfast had sent delegates to the convention, the future direction of the movement would have changed, and changed dramatically.

The vote was carried; then came a break in proceedings. As described by Ó Brádaigh:

> The people who thought like Mac Stiofáin and myself were all in a cluster somewhere in a corner, and somebody passed by and made a joke that there was going to be a putsch; and there it was. It was in its own way slightly embarrassing, if you understand me. We were on opposite sides. 'Where the hell is it going? What can be done about it? It has gone so far that I am not going to back down.' What was unspoken in its own way was that this was the parting of the ways. Nobody said it, but anyone who had any common sense would realise that.[97]

Immediately after the convention Mac Stiofáin travelled to Belfast to alert the new Northern Command to what was happening. There was recognition that Belfast had become crucial to the very existence of the IRA, but also a sense of foreboding that, according to Ó Brádaigh, a lack of strategic vision had blinded the Belfast leadership.

> This is vital. The world does not begin and end in Belfast, although it is a very, very important place and it is crucial. And I used to say, until 1969 Cork dominated the movement and from 1969 on Belfast dominated the movement; but what would follow from their line of going on, which was totally independent, was that they would be looking for support from all over the place. How do you do it—you know, organisation, all that type of thing. The logical and obvious way to do it was you went to the convention and you saw who, what representation was against— and you were in contact with them—who would provide the nucleus of what you were going to do, rather than jumping around the country hitting and missing.

Did Belfast then make a mistake and create the conditions for a sectarian war?

> That is stating it too far. How would I put it? They were in very great danger of isolation. They pre-empted the whole thing in September, and once you take these actions you have to live with them; and perhaps they weren't seeing down the road far enough, or things weren't happening quickly enough for them. But I would say that my perspective on these things would be a 32-county rather than straight in front of you, and each one is understandable in its own situation; but we could have done with Belfast representation at that convention.[98]

The first statement issued by the Provisional IRA, on 28 December 1969, referred specifically to the failure of the leadership in August, a failure put down to the single-minded pursuit of the ending of abstention.

> The adoption of the compromising policy referred to is the logical outcome of an obsession in recent years with parliamentary politics, with consequent undermining of the basic military role of the Irish Republican Army. The failure to provide the maximum defence possible of our people in Belfast and other parts of the Six Counties against the forces of British imperialism last August is ample evidence of this neglect.[99]

The phrasing is instructive, ranking in order the concerns of Ó Brádaigh, Mac Stiofáin, and the Belfast leadership. The traditional aims of the movement were left intact. The army would again be placed in the vanguard, and nationalism would be protected in the event of an increase in violence. As a combination it provided the Provisionals with a relevance with which Goulding could not even begin to compete.

The issue of funds, therefore, was a substantial one in speeding up the split in republican ranks. It is on these grounds that those determined to assert that Fianna Fáil set up the Provisional IRA find their strongest evidence; it is evidence seized upon by Tomás Mac Giolla, president of Sinn Féin at the time of the split.

> It will all come out, but I will be long in my grave at that time. But I can assure you that they did set up the Provisional IRA. They gave them money, they gave them guns to get started, and through that money and guns they were able to get their campaign off the ground by early 1970.[100]

The fact that money went to those who were later to become the Provisionals can no longer be in doubt. The payments from the grant in aid, and the involvement of Blaney, raise serious questions about the nature of Jack Lynch's control over his Government in the autumn of 1969. However, did the more traditional republicans who had 'missed out on the political education process of the middle and late sixties … who were politically uninterested and unaware,'[101] actually get any weapons from the Dublin operation? That is far from certain. At the time, Belfast was awash with rumours. What struck the experienced observer Michael McKeown was the constant and open talk about the flow of guns from the South provided from the Irish government. I was never quite sure what to make of all the stories I heard because on the one hand I couldn't believe people would be so indiscreet if there was such a flow, but against this, there was a fair amount of evidence of the availability of arms, particularly small arms and clearly the Pinheads—or the Provisionals as they gradually came to be called—were in receipt of funds from somewhere.[102]

Certainly a series of attempts was made to provide arms for the new Northern structure through contacts originated by Blaney and Captain Kelly. In addition, the emerging leadership seconded John Kelly, the Belfast republican, to work in tandem with his Military Intelligence namesake. 'I was seconded to go with Jim Kelly as, if you like, a representative of the broad-based defence committees, to oversee with him the importation of arms, to be the "good faith" factor.'[103]

When John Kelly came back from the United States he tried to see Mac Stiofáin. Mac Stiofáin was preoccupied with the organising of the Provisionals' convention and the creation of a new Army Council but arranged a meeting.

John came to me a few days before Christmas, a few days after the new convention for the Army Council, and told me about the arrangements made to bring in arms, and he told me that 'once they come in I will give them to you.' I said, 'John, I do not want any details. Give me a report now and again through your brother. Just give me a list of the weapons you ordered.'[104]

Kelly clearly believed that the Fianna Fáil connection was now bearing fruit. He was soon to be disappointed. A meeting was arranged with Captain Kelly and Neil Blaney to clarify the arrangements. Blaney suggested that it would take too long to get it through: in effect, he vetoed the deal and organised a Continental European deal instead.[105] John Kelly remembers that the meeting was exceptionally heated and believes now that Blaney wanted to make sure he retained control:

I think perhaps the feeling from the Government—which we presumed was still involved—was that they would have more control over weapons coming from the Continent than they would have had over a consignment coming from New York that was being organised by physical-force republicans.[106]

By the time of the American operation, preparations for the split were well advanced. Kelly and Keenan were determined to find weapons, and not just for defensive purposes. If they could have got the weapons from Blaney, then so be it; if not, then they were prepared to use the facilities provided to create their own network. Keenan felt his time had come. The combination of increased instability on the North and a virile debate over the meaning of nationalism in the South meant that the conditions existed for the completion of the national revolution. Northern Ireland was a society at the abyss, where the slightest provocation on either side could plunge it over the edge. A Belfast lawyer caught the mood when interviewed by Dick Walsh of the *Irish Times*. 'There are', he said, 'the hopeful and the informed.' Among the informed he saw 'little gain for anyone but arms dealers and a tiny manipulative minority in the present events.'[107]

The split in the IRA, and the apparent isolation of the left wing, clearly had important benefits for Fianna Fáil and for the maintenance of stability in the Southern state. Set against this, the increasingly shrill rhetoric touched a nerve in Southern society, providing the Provisional IRA with much-needed sustenance and providing Neil Blaney with a vehicle with which to continue with his leadership ambitions, whatever the political cost. 1970 was to be a crucial year for both jurisdictions in Ireland.

CHAPTER FOUR

Patriot Games

The Arms Crisis

THE operation to finance Northern nationalists took on a new perspective after the split in the IRA. The money transferred from the Department of Finance via the Irish Red Cross Society was no longer being used to protect refugees or to launch propaganda offensives: it was used to finance the emergence of the Provisional IRA, under carefully controlled circumstances.

Despite the acute disappointment felt over Neil Blaney's failure to release money for the New York operation, John Kelly was once again despatched by the Provisional Army Council to work alongside Captain James Kelly of Military Intelligence. In effect a covert foreign policy was also being prosecuted, as evidenced by the encounter with the British ambassador, Sir Anthony Gilchrist, at Charles Haughey's home in Kinsealy the previous October. The question is whether this properly reflected delegated authority or whether the Continental operation was a manifestation of dangerous delusions of power.

The internecine warfare within Fianna Fáil smouldered as the party prepared for its ardfheis in Dublin in late January. This was the first opportunity since the outbreak of violence for the party faithful to applaud—or denigrate—the Government's handling of the crisis. It also provided an opportunity for the hawks to push for a more active interventionist policy, in the process exposing the uneasy compromise at the highest levels of the party.

Neil Blaney was articulating a widely held sense within the party that national reunification was not only desirable but also the most important political issue facing the Government. An experienced observer has referred to Blaney's relationship with the Taoiseach in this period as one of 'insulting indifference'.[1] The fact that Lynch appeared powerless to stop Blaney's public outbursts served merely to strengthen Blaney's reputation and his resolve to stage a leadership challenge at the ardfheis. A circular was presented to delegates stating that the Donegal TD might make a bid for power.[2] This was accompanied by a number of speeches advocating the Blaney line on the involvement of the Irish army, providing further evidence of a concerted campaign. As in December, when he seemed in a radio interview to be reluctantly putting his name forward as a contender, Blaney was again using the profound questioning of the nature and extent of the state that the Northern question evinced to test the political waters. The correspondent of *Hibernia* noted that 'whether such emotional panegyrics were a source of satisfaction or embarrassment to the Minister could not be read in his rugged countenance but a well-organised section of the attendance greeted the exhortation with rapturous applause.'[3]

This ideological challenge was buttressed by the intervention of Kevin Boland, who used the ardfheis to outline a forceful rebuttal of 'unity by consent'. It was a clear attempt to use the party organisation as a lever to influence the ideological debate in the Government, made more potent given Boland's position as national secretary of Fianna Fáil. He argued that there could be no concession on the question of the intrinsic unity of the country, nor could the elevation to official status of a Unionist veto on self-determination be tolerated. 'There is not and never can be by a republican party,' he declared, 'any acceptance that any parliament or group of people—native or foreign—has the right to divide our country in this way.' To accept this state of affairs would be to negate the founding principles of Fianna Fáil. For Boland the fight was on to preserve what he regarded as the republican essence of the party. In his speech he gave tacit approval to the Blaney view that force could not be ruled out in pursuit of that objective—if circumstances warranted it.

> Our main objective must continue to be to secure the unity and Independence of Ireland as a Republic and every situation that arises in either part of the country must be assessed as to how it may affect this objective and must be handled accordingly—unhampered by preconceived ideas or predetermined conditions as to the methods to be used.[4]

Lynch was horrified at what he correctly interpreted as a sophisticated rejection of his leadership, and he began rewriting his address
while Boland was still at the podium. Lynch wrapped himself in the
rhetoric of de Valera and Lemass, pointing out that partition represented 'a deep, throbbing weal across the land, heart and soul of
Ireland'; at the same time he made it abundantly clear that he believed
coercion would lead only to civil war. He asked delegates to think with
their heads, not their hearts. 'The plain truth, the naked reality, is that
we do not possess the capacity to impose a solution by force.' And
even if the country had that capacity, such an approach would lead
only to a new dictatorship. 'The imposition by us on the subjugated
new minority of the Six Counties, and the whole country, of some of
the hateful, tyrannical practices that we and the world so recently
called an abomination—is this the Ireland we want?' What was
required was not an appeal to revolution but the evolution of better
relations between the two parts of the country, informed by mutual
respect and good will.

Lynch was asserting that the generational leadership change did not
represent discontinuity or the betrayal of core principles of the Irish
revolution but rather the pragmatic acceptance of new realities. In short,
his address entailed a restatement of the politics of accommodation
endorsed by Lemass. He concluded with a direct threat to those
determined to question his leadership.

> If anyone wants to change the policy that I have set out, this is the place
> to do it, and now is the time. If Fianna Fáil wants this traditional Fianna
> Fáil policy to be pursued by me as leader of the Government and the
> party, now is the time to say it.[5]

The speech received a ringing endorsement. It was indicative of
Lynch's leadership style. He made effective use of the most valuable
commodities in any political party—the twin issues of party unity and
loyalty to the leader—to cement his rule and outmanoeuvre his rivals.
The speech was also designed to solidify the process of redefining the
nature of Irish nationalism, begun at Tralee and fleshed out with
Lynch's appeal to a federal solution.

The importance of the speech rests on the evolution of a new political language designed to neutralise the power of rhetorical appeals to
irredentist logic. Its intellectual underpinnings can be traced to two
memorandums sent by the Tánaiste, Erskine Childers, to Lynch in the
confused days of August and September 1969. Childers warned that

in the Republic as well as the North 'there are people hoping chaos will reign because of a more satisfactory situation emerging, unification, dictatorship etc.' He argued that the Government must guard against the entry of the IRA and advocated a long-term strategy aimed at 'rethinking' partition policy based on 'securing unity by consent, no matter how grudgingly given.'[6] It was symptomatic of Lynch's political skill that a policy predicated on the acceptance of partition was dressed up and sold as the mechanism for ending it.[7]

As the delegates roared their approval of the Taoiseach and party leader, Blaney 'stared up studiously at the proscenium.'[8] Blaney and Boland may have been outsmarted at the ardfheis, but this was only a temporary defeat—and Lynch knew it. The very fact that Blaney could use the ardfheis to float policies that amounted to a public rebuke of the Taoiseach demonstrated his power within Fianna Fáil. As *Hibernia* noted, Blaney 'still remains the strongman of the party organisation and the force to be reckoned with after the heady excitement of the Ard-Fheis has evaporated.'[9] Equally, Boland's intervention demonstrated to Lynch—if not to the media, who misinterpreted the speech as constituting approval of the Taoiseach—that the hawks in the Government were gaining in strength and resolve.

The fact that the most pressing issue facing the state was no longer decided within the Office of the Taoiseach but was under the operational control of the Departments of Defence and Finance, along with the intelligence operation involving Blaney at the Department of Agriculture, gave considerable decision-making latitude to the hawks. Despite the commitment in the ardfheis speech to the pursuit of unity by consent and the abrogation of coercion, therefore, those directing Northern policy retained, in private, the option of military engagement as a matter of policy. Despite his increasingly shrill interventions, Blaney, with the tacit support of Haughey, was still in effect dictating a Government policy in which established lines of communication were blurred and departmental responsibilities ignored.

What remains unexplained is why Lynch did not move to censure his rivals in the aftermath of the ardfheis challenge.[10] The answer is to be found in the ideological dynamics of the nationalist political system, a system that received its legitimacy through the exposition of Fianna Fáil rhetorical republicanism. The violence changed the paradigm governing North-South relations; appeals to Lemass and de Valera had little relevance when the Irish question was on the move again after fifty years of Northern Catholic quiescence. The exposition of rhetoric alone served to underline how threadbare the ideological clothing on which the appeal of Fianna Fáil was predicated had become, while simultaneously inflaming an already dangerous situation. The Lemass policy of 'unity by peaceful evolution' lay in tatters, as also was any degree of influence over Northern nationalists, a fact clearly recognised by the most dangerous of the hawks, Charles Haughey.

A high-level Government source maintains that Haughey came to question whether Fianna Fáil was entitled to the sobriquet 'republican party' and increasingly regarded his father-in-law, Seán Lemass, as essentially 'a pragmatic nationalist rather than true republican.'[11] Haughey had close connections with the North: both his parents were born there, and his extended family retained a presence there long after his father took a position with the Garda Síochána in County Mayo. As a child in the strongly republican areas of south Derry he had personally witnessed the sectarian riots of 1935 in Maghera and the heavy-handed manner in which the B Specials had asserted Protestant domination in the hinterland. He regarded the border as anathema and felt personally aggrieved by the blatant discrimination and coat-trailing associated with Orange parades.[12] This background informed his political thinking as he chose a political party in which to advance his career.

> Fianna Fáil for a young person like me seemed to be identified with the Irish nation, with nationalism, with the programme of the development of the state and the country. It all fitted into an overall picture. I was a GAA person; I was an Irish-language enthusiast; and Fianna Fáil was a very natural way to go.[13]

But political exposure provided a harsh reality check for Haughey with the growing recognition that republicanism was little more than an aspirational cover for the Fianna Fáil leadership. For the ambitious young minister, as he ascended the ranks of party and government, there was little to be gained in emphasising the gap between rhetoric and reality. The disintegration of the North, however, offered the possibility of fundamental change and fundamental crisis. There was therefore an empathy with the demands by Northern nationalists for weapons in 1969 and 1970.

The use of majoritarian rule in Northern Ireland had made irrelevant the participation of the Catholic minority. Likewise, the political row over the abolition of the B Specials and the reform of the RUC reflected the Unionist sense of ownership of the forces of law and order. The identification of demands for civil rights with the destruction of the state demonstrated to many Catholics that they had no real place in Northern Ireland while Stormont retained power. This reflects more than a nationalist blind spot: it is an indicative, intractable feature of territorial disputes.[14] As Michael McKeown has noted,

> the possibility that the 'state' of Northern Ireland might have an identity which overrode these sectional considerations was never acknowledged. For the compliant Catholic then, those who were often stigmatised by their co-religionists as Castle Catholics, there could be no real focus for any loyalty they might wish to offer. If they wished to identify with Northern Ireland and regard themselves as citizens of Northern Ireland, they had to identify with a power system whose rationale demanded their own debasement.[15]

Accommodation, therefore, was inherently almost impossible to achieve. The more the minority pushed for equality, the more unstable the structure became. The application of further pressure by London to concede nationalist demands served only to undermine any attempt at selling compromise to the unionist grass roots as the elite was forced back into the atavistic defence of privilege.

The Government source suggests that central to Haughey's strategic considerations was this perception that Northern Ireland was incapable of reform. He saw no merit in an internal solution, a vital factor that was to continue to inform his political thinking in the seventies and eighties.[16] For Haughey, the new policy of 'unity by consent' was simply misguided, evidence of the continued inability of the Southern political elite to understand Northern realities. In the changed circumstances of 1969 and 1970 Haughey and his allies in the Government saw in the emerging conflict a historic opportunity that served a number of linked agendas, all designed to secure the leadership of Fianna Fáil. In an oblique reference, Haughey conceded as much by differentiating between the two wings of Fianna Fáil.

> One of the principal things that was always present in the minds of Fianna Fáil people, the republican Fianna Fáil party, was the Northern Ireland situation, so that naturally the whole Fianna Fáil organisation would have reacted, would have responded immediately to this … [The conflict] was new: this was a development that was tragic, cataclysmic, but one that we had to face up to, to take aboard.[17]

Crucial to the success of these strategies was the continued alienation of the Catholic minority in the North. It was not in the interests of the militants in the Government that an accommodation within Northern Ireland might be reached. This did not necessarily mean plotting violence: indeed Blaney and Boland were careful in their public utterances to abjure the use of force as a policy option. (Haughey simply did not make any comment whatever.) Rather, the destabilisation of Northern Ireland occasioned by the withdrawal of Catholic consent offered the means of recasting Fianna Fáil control over the political direction of the entire country. This was to be achieved essentially by revisiting the constitutional settlement that established partition in order to end it, with London and Dublin negotiating over the heads of the Northern population.

Haughey believed that only British acquiescence allowed Northern Ireland to remain in existence. What was required, he believed, was determined action to force a change in British policy. To a certain extent this was pushing at an open door. As early as 11 September 1969 the British Cabinet had come to the realisation that

> the whole Irish problem was once more on the move and there would be pressure for fundamental change going far beyond what was at present contemplated. In these circumstances, it was important to get a dialogue going with the Government of the Irish Republic ... If there were to be any prospect of a final solution relations between the North and South of Ireland, and between the South and the United Kingdom must be lifted to a different plane. As things stood at present this was likely to take a long time.[18]

The very possibility that violence could occur provided the potential for powerful leverage over the execution of British policy. It was an important distinction and one that served to demonstrate the power of militant republicanism as the legitimising ideology of the state.[19] In this there was a coalescing of interests between the hawks in Fianna Fáil and the Provisional IRA, both in the period 1969–70 and again in the late eighties. A document issued in the nineteen-eighties provides an interesting insight into the ideological underpinnings of armed struggle.

> Loyalism is not British. It is a distinctly Irish phenomenon and is not found in Britain itself, except as an Irish export ... The political/religious Orange leaders have hijacked the Protestant religion into a defence of imperialism ... Loyalism is an ideology and politics that can in no way be compromised with, short of the achievement of a united Ireland.[20]

The document is emphatic in its rejection of the idea of two traditions sharing a geographical area. What is remarkable is how closely this
corresponds to the view of unionism adopted by the highest echelons
of Fianna Fáil and, in particular, to the republicanism of Haughey and
Blaney. When Haughey eventually achieved his ambition to lead
Fianna Fáil in 1979, it was this belief that the Northern entity had no
legal or moral foundations that underpinned party policy.

> For over sixty years now the situation in Northern Ireland has been a
> source of instability, real or potential, in these islands. It has been so
> because the very entity itself is artificial. In these conditions, violence and
> repression were inevitable.[21]

At the same time, Haughey was profoundly aware of the dangers
posed to Southern stability if the Official IRA gained unfettered possession of the national question. He was determined that the Marxist-
Leninist policies of the republican movement under Cathal Goulding's
control had to be curtailed. Fianna Fáil had seen its support weaken as
a result of the abandoning of economic nationalism: while it may have
reflected economic realities, it destroyed a crucial ideological underpinning of the state and was one that had been ruthlessly exploited by
the republican movement throughout the late sixties. The perception
of corruption, endemic in the speculative culture of the 'mohair era'
that Haughey typified, served to further emasculate the national
credentials of the party. (With typical insouciance, Haughey told a
recent interviewer that he personally never owned the offending
fashion item, suggesting that he had 'far better taste than to ever wear
a mohair suit.') On a more serious note, Haughey maintained that on
economic matters he modelled himself on Lemass.

> We were fairly sincere people, we had confidence in ourselves, and we
> knew that things had to be done. We wanted to do the best we could for
> the people, and we set about doing it.[22]

The perceived threat to the stability of the Southern state posed by
an alliance of the radical left and the Goulding IRA was therefore the
second major factor governing strategy—a strategy accepted by
Colonel Michael Hefferon and many in the Government and civil
service, including the Department of Justice.[23] It was therefore very
much in the interests of Charles Haughey—as the embodiment of
Irish capitalist culture he did much to foster—to curtail any attempt
by the republican movement to use the national question to challenge
the economic or social basis of the state.[24]

In a crucial policy document published in the *United Irishman* in January 1970 to accompany the formal split in Sinn Féin, the Official IRA announced that it had not given up the right to wage armed struggle: indeed it regarded it as

> inevitable that before the 70s ends, Britain's claim to a right to interfere in Ireland's affairs will again be challenged in arms. This time we must win. This time we can win because it will be a revolutionary struggle of the Irish people and not a military challenge by a small heroic section.

The key to the success of that strategy lay in accepting the ending of the self-imposed marginalisation occasioned by the policy of abstention. For Goulding this was the key challenge of the decade and the reason the IRA had temporarily accepted its own secondary role the previous month.

> A democratically elected Army Convention decided by a large majority to remove all restrictions on the leadership in regard to electoral policy so that they could use the tactics best suited to the occasion to smash the power of the Establishment, North and South.

The strategy of subsuming the IRA within a grand revolutionary alliance in such conditions was for many Northern activists the ultimate evidence of Goulding's commitment to dogma over reality. His revolutionary strategy had pushed Northern Ireland to the edge; when it teetered, a showdown between theory and practice became inevitable.[25] Attempting to further non-sectarian aims in the midst of tribal warfare was always going to be a difficult proposition; it offered the opportunity for the hawks in Fianna Fáil to split the movement with promises of immediate unity. The Northern conflict, therefore, and control over the direction of the republican movement, the main agents who would prosecute that conflict, became a crucial factor in the machinations surrounding the attempts by Haughey and Blaney to reposition Fianna Fáil in Irish politics.

Haughey met Goulding in September 1969 in an attempt to get him to redirect the thrust of the IRA. An arms deal was arranged between the minister's brother, Pádraig (Jock) Haughey, and Goulding. Goulding received £2,500 from Haughey but was not prepared to shift political strategy.[26] It was at this point that Haughey decided to kill off two irritants at the one time. The IRA had to be split; and Lynch had to be removed. The Northern republicans offered him the perfect opportunity to achieve both objectives. If Northern Ireland was to collapse, the political prize was worth the risk: not only would the central goal of Fianna Fáil policy be achieved but, crucially, the political judgment of Lynch would be seriously undermined, paving the way for his dismissal. Those determined to limit the political contagion were helped considerably by the belief among many in the republican movement in the North that conditions offered the best opportunity in a generation for furthering the aims of unity.

On 10 January 1970 Sinn Féin delegates had gathered from throughout the country to formally endorse the change in policy. Goulding left little to chance. A statement was issued by the Army Council demanding that the proposed changes be ratified, an indication of the continuing primacy of the military instrument, even among those determined to end it. The statement also contained a warning to the dissidents: 'if they persisted in error, then all sentiment must be put aside in dealing with them.'[27] (It is ironic that when the Provisionals themselves ushered in the ending of abstention in 1986, Martin McGuinness used a similar veiled threat when he announced from the podium that the only place the dissidents were going was home. Central to his calculations was the fact that the Provisionals retained control of the Northern arena, control they had wrenched from the hands of the Goulding element in 1969–70, with the help of the hawks in the Fianna Fáil Government.)

Delegates to the 1970 ardfheis known to be opposed to the changes were denied access to the venue or told they could not vote because their subscription had not been paid. Among those refused entry was the young Gerry Adams, an IRA volunteer from Ballymurphy, who later became the most influential Provisional of his generation, leading the movement into the partitionist structures he decried in 1970.[28] Then he was at one with Ruairí Ó Brádaigh and Seán Mac Stiofáin, with their appeal to republican doctrine.

> We find it absolutely incomprehensible from any republican standpoint the campaigning in favour of Stormont parliament in August, September and October last year when it was in danger of being abolished altogether by the British government. In any future struggle for freedom it would surely be preferable to have a direct confrontation with the British government on Irish soil without the Stormont junta being interposed. In any event, the taking away of the Orange Order's power bloc would surely be a step forward rather than backward.[29]

The innate conservatism of Irish political life, coupled with the active support of important sections in Fianna Fáil and the unease of the Catholic Church at left-wing politics, provided the opportunity for the Provisionals to make inroads in Northern society.[30] The Northern arena had become the battleground, and the terms of the debate, insinuated by Fianna Fáil mandarins, created a domino effect from which there could be no turning back. The Officials viewed the Provisionals with disdain, a view endorsed by their followers in the media, including Rosita Sweetman: she concluded that the fundamental problem with the Provisionals was that 'they haven't educated the people as to what they are fighting for, because they are still clinging to romantic nationalism, the Establishment can buy them off.'[31]

The Goulding wing had recognised as early as October 1969 the purpose of the strategic manoeuvrings taking place, with the revelations in the *United Irishman* that elements in Fianna Fáil had decided to destroy its support base.[32] The offensive continued into December, with the *United Irishman* making veiled references to the role of Fianna Fáil in demonising the left in the United States. It bitterly resented the criticism of the National Association for Irish Justice as communist extremists in NICRA and warned:

> Let those who contemplate a witch-hunt think again. They will be starting something they will be unable to finish.

The paper attempted to dissociate the republican movement from the 'instant revolutionaries of the ultra-left' and vowed to uphold NICRA from the bigoted reactionaries of the ultra-right.[33] It bitterly complained that 'failing the unlikely event of unionism being blown away by a blast of sham nationalist rhetoric, the total performance of Fianna Fáil [after August 1969] was worse than useless.'[34] A sense of the exasperation felt by the proto-revolutionaries is evident from Michael Farrell's plaintive analysis of the split. 'Angry militants blamed the August debacle on the new emphasis on politics, forgetting that the civil rights movement had shaken the Northern State to its core, forced direct British intervention for the first time since 1922 and secured the disbandment of the B-Specials.'[35]

Ó Brádaigh and Mac Stiofáin recognised this but recognised too that power and control were ultimately slipping into the hands of those who controlled the North. Appeals to republican certainty on their own provided little or no basis for support in 1969–70 (or indeed in 1986, with the ending of abstention, or more recently with the republican movement's formal acceptance of unity by consent through its acceptance of the Belfast Agreement). Equally, appeals to left-wing agendas without taking cognisance of sectarianism provided a blueprint for oblivion.

Increasingly the ideological split centred not on abstention but on the fear of communism. The campaign against the totalitarianism of the left became a significant element in the attempt to win broad support in the Republic while simultaneously weakening the power of the Officials. In many ways it was redolent of the 1969 general election, when Haughey's skilful manipulation of the 'red scare' put paid to the Labour Party's hopes of a breakthrough. A telling example is to be found in the 'Republican Lecture Series'.

> While we who went to Parnell Square [after withdrawing from the Sinn Féin ardfheis], believe in a Democratic Socialist Republic for all Ireland, it seems certain that the ultimate objective of the leadership which remained at the Intercontinental Hotel is nothing but a totalitarian dictatorship of the Left.[36]

The republican women's organisation, Cumann na mBan—which had angered Goulding by refusing to march in a parade in Sligo the previous year alongside representatives of the Connolly Youth Movement—issued a statement on 25 January pledging support for the Provisional Army Council.

> An Army Council which advocated entry into Leinster House, Stormont and Westminster and promoted an extreme form of socialism, forfeited the right to speak for the Republican movement. Therefore we consider the Provisional Army Council to be the true voice of Republicanism.[37]

The Provisionals began setting up a new organisation and distributing a new newspaper under the control of Ó Brádaigh. Seán Keenan had established a North-West Republican Executive, taking in Counties Derry, Tyrone, Fermanagh, and Donegal, the republican heartland, where a visceral sense of 'nationhood denied' stemming from the failure to implement the findings of the Boundary Commission continues to inform political thinking. Keenan told the meeting: 'All the signs are that the bigoted elements which wrought havoc and destruction last August are again gaining momentum.'[38] This provided the opportunity for concerted action. Ó Brádaigh made it clear that the Provisionals now had an appointment with destiny. 'Nothing short of the full implementation of the aims of the 1916 proclamation would ensure a just and lasting peace in Ireland.'[39]

This return to republican first principles was clearly in evidence at the Easter commemorations, which were increasingly militaristic in tone, as were announcements by the Provisional Army Council and its political wing, Provisional Sinn Féin. The Provisional Army Council's Easter statement warned that its full resources would be used 'to protect our people against attack from both Crown forces and sectarian bigots.'[40] On 19 April 1970 Ó Brádaigh, speaking as president of Provisional Sinn Féin, told a group in Cavan:

> It appears that a supreme crisis in the North is imminent. Republicans must be ready to play their part to the full in whatever way is necessary.[41]

Firstly, they needed arms, and the section of Fianna Fáil running Northern policy was prepared to give them that material support. But it was the equivalent for Fianna Fáil of a nuclear option: it could be used only once and had the capacity to destroy everybody. Haughey and Blaney were playing for high stakes. Blaney's views became indistinguishable from Ó Brádaigh's in April 1970; he gave an infamous interview to the *Irish Independent* in which he called in effect for war.

> I do not think that we can ever have lasting peace while we do not have governmental control over the entire island. In fact, I don't think there can ever be lasting peace while foreign forces occupy part of the territory.[42]

Lynch's failure to assert control over Northern policy from January 1970 onwards, despite the intelligence reports compiled by the secretary of the Department of Justice, Peter Berry, and the open militarism of the Provisionals, demonstrated an incredible lack of party control. It also reflected a misunderstanding of the symbiotic relationship now emerging between high politics in Dublin and the political manipulation of events in Belfast, which in turn affected the direction of Government policy and in particular control over the Department of Defence. Tracing the relationship between Gibbons, Haughey and Blaney throughout the Arms Crisis reveals the extent to which an indecisive and weak Government as a whole was implicated in a policy far removed from its stated objectives.[43]

In the immediate aftermath of the August violence, Haughey and Gibbons were given instructions by Lynch to ascertain what measures could be undertaken to enhance the effectiveness of the Defence Forces. An indication of the poor state of affairs was the fact that when Lynch ordered the army to set up field hospitals in August 1969, lorries took two days to reach the border from Cork. A recruitment drive was ordered to bring the permanent strength up by 3,500, but senior officers admitted that even with this increase, if extreme circumstances warranted it the army could only hope to put up 'a brief but gallant defence.'[44] It was clearly not in a position to provide sustenance to the nationalist minority in the North.

An alternative strategy was fashioned with, at the very least, the tacit support of the Minister for Defence. Boland has argued that Gibbons supported the suggestion that military help should be given to the nationalists in the event of a 'doomsday scenario'. This was never adequately defined, but Boland suggests that throughout the autumn of 1969 Gibbons was quite insistent within the Government that nationalists should be able to defend themselves. Boland regarded the delegation of authority to Gibbons and Haughey as particularly staggering, a development that could be understood only in the context of Lynch believing that nothing would be done. 'He did not want anything done; he would have disagreed with any specific proposal to do anything; but he gambled on his belief that nothing would be done and he was wrong.'[45]

Blaney, for example, was instrumental in persuading Northern nationalists to continue sending delegations to Government Buildings in Dublin to meet ministers and to press their demands for weapons. This provided political cover for the imperative of changing Government policy, keeping up the pressure on Lynch and justifying the need to provide arms to a group now openly stating in its official publication the need to prosecute the war against the British.[46] In the shadows, the final preparations were being made to provide untraceable weapons.

Again it was Blaney who set the agenda, becoming in effect an unofficial quartermaster for the Provisional IRA, as he admitted in an interview in 1993. 'We didn't help to create them but we certainly would have accelerated, by whatever assistance we could have given, their emergence as a force.'[47]

Captain Kelly had been summoned to see Blaney in early January. Blaney had what Kelly now describes as something of a 'brainwave':[48] to use a Continental arms dealer to bring in weapons. Kelly argues that he was not kept fully informed about the American connection, or the reasons for Blaney's refusal to use it; he suggests that dealing with a professional arms dealer, though in a secret manner, is further evidence of the authorisation from the highest levels of Government. The point of contact was an arms dealer in Hamburg, Otto Schleuter. Blaney not only provided the name of the dealer but also later suggested that

Kelly use the services of Albert Luykx, a Belgian-born business associate of Blaney's who ran a restaurant in Sutton, County Dublin.[49] Of even more significance was the fact that the importing was to be carried out by Military Intelligence, with the knowledge and consent of the director of intelligence, who reported all activity directly to the minister, Jim Gibbons.[50]

Under Irish law, only the Department of Defence and the Department of Justice can sanction the importing of weapons. The wide-ranging directive that ordered Haughey to release funds for the Defence Forces, coupled with Blaney's role in the sub-committee directing Northern policy, provided a powerful nexus of control over Gibbons, essentially a junior member of the Government. Military Intelligence was clearly working under orders from the Government sub-committee or, more accurately, from Blaney and Haughey, a development that raised eyebrows in the Special Branch of the Garda Síochána.[51] A crucial manifestation of that power emerged in February with the decision by the Government to establish concrete contingency plans in the event of the North disintegrating. On 6 February the Minister for Defence met the chief of staff, Lieutenant-General Seán Mac Eoin, and the director of intelligence, Colonel Michael Hefferon, to discuss the Government decision.[52]

The directive suggested that the army prepare for incursions into the North and make weapons and gas masks available, all of which were mentioned as imperatives in Captain's Kelly's report on Bailieborough that was presented to the Government by Gibbons. In sworn evidence to the first arms trial, Mícheál Ó Móráin confirmed that Haughey and Gibbons were given explicit instructions to do whatever was required to prepare contingency plans for the North. When asked whether that included getting guns, Ó Móráin replied simply, 'Oh, yes.'[53]

According to Hefferon, the directive formed the basis for military strategy, providing the justification for supplying weapons to the Northern Defence Committees.[54] For Captain Kelly too it was evidence of the official nature of the enterprise and made him question whether his eventual arrest and prosecution reflected political rather than criminal considerations. On 19 February, Kelly arranged to go to the Continent to inspect an arms shipment, carrying with him £10,000 drawn from the George Dixon account in the Munster and Leinster Bank, Baggot Street. The deal was to consist of '200 sub machine guns, 84 light machine guns, 50 general purpose machine guns, 50 rifles, 200 grenades, 70 flak jackets and 250,000 rounds of ammunition and 200 pistols.'[55] This is hardly the equipment required for the defence of localities but rather the kind of armoury associated with a total breakdown of security in Northern Ireland, which was precisely the defence used in the subsequent arms trials.[56] That Military Intelligence was prepared to run such an operation, which owed its genesis to a plan hatched by the Minister for Agriculture and paid for by the Minister for Finance, provides a telling insight into the wider purpose of the operation.[57]

Kelly informed Hefferon of his plans, and he in turn briefed the Minister for Defence. According to Hefferon, Gibbons was clearly aware that the weapons 'were to be for the Northern Defence Committees, in the event that a situation would arise where the Government would agree to them going to them.'[58] The weapons were to be held under Kelly's control as an army officer. The plan was to store them in a monastery in County Cavan. At no stage did Gibbons insist that the plan be called off or at least put on hold until the Government could discuss the matter.

Back in Germany, Kelly was finding it difficult to inspect the cargo and returned to Dublin to arrange the final payments from the Baggot Street account. On his return he was determined that the operation should have the open support of the Minister for Defence and committed Blaney to arranging a meeting with Gibbons. Blaney acquiesced, and a meeting was arranged at the Department of Defence.

> I was reporting direct to Colonel Hefferon, and because I realised the seriousness of what was taking place I decided—and wrongly, maybe: maybe I shouldn't have done it, and I don't think Colonel Hefferon was very happy that I did it—but I met Blaney one day, and Blaney was into it again, but I said I want to speak to the minister myself personally about what is going on.[59]

The significance of this encounter is that it took place before any attempt to bring in weapons and shortly after Gibbons met a delegation from the North, including John Kelly and Seán Keenan, arranged at the behest of Blaney. According to John Kelly, once again there was no equivocation.

> It was always very definite. The response was definite that they understood we were there in pursuit of arms, that this had been put in place by Captain Kelly, by Neil Blaney, by the various other ministers that we met. So there was never any doubt in our minds that there was any doubt in their minds as to what we were about.[60]

Captain Kelly alleges that he told Gibbons precisely what was going on in great detail, including his reservations about not being able to inspect the cargo and his belief that he would have to return to the Continent.[61] It is certainly unusual for a relatively junior military officer to have direct access to a Government minister, a fact that Gibbons admitted in court. He denied, however, any detailed knowledge of the operation, or of Kelly's plan to return to the Continent.

> Captain Kelly informed me that the people who had come previously in the month of March—a deputation to visit various members of [the] Government—that they had a proposal to import weapons from the Continent. That was put in a very general way and I assumed it to mean there was a general intention.[62]

The following week Kelly met the arms dealer Otto Schleuter in Antwerp and arranged for the cargo to be shipped into Dublin. With everything in place, he held a meeting with Hefferon, who, aware of the restrictions on the importing of arms, advised Kelly to report the matter directly to Haughey. This was a crucial move. While only the Department of Defence or Department of Justice could authorise the importing of weapons, the Department of Finance could exempt goods from customs inspection.

Kelly went to the Department of Finance on 19 March to get the clearance. Haughey was engaged, and the request was transmitted to the minister's personal secretary, Anthony Fagan. The civil servant, who had been involved in the transfer of funds to the Baggot Street account and dealt with Kelly on routine matters relating to the operation of the relief fund, contacted the Revenue Commissioners. It was confirmed that the Department of Finance had the power to exempt from examination any goods coming into the country. According to testimony in court, Fagan was told by Haughey to 'see that it is done.'[63] Haughey's counsel saw nothing sinister in this.

> As far as Mr Haughey is concerned … he did not, when he was giving that particular direction, know what the consignment was. But even if he had known he would still have given the direction, because as far as he was concerned it was an Army Intelligence request and he was giving them the facilities which he, as minister, was entitled to give, and was doing it officially.[64]

In evidence, Haughey himself testified:

> My instructions were that the Army Intelligence were to be facilitated by the guns being cleared through customs without being opened, whether

there was a licence for them or not. My instructions had nothing to do with a licence—they may well have been licensed, but I would still wish them to go through without being opened: this was the point.[65]

On 25 March all the plans seemed to be coming together as the *City of Dublin* edged up towards the quays. Captain Kelly, accompanied by John Kelly, watched the ship berth, believing that all the paperwork had been cleared and that the guns would be aboard. They even contacted the Customs Surveyor, Diarmuid Ó Ríordáin, to explain that they were waiting for a secret consignment—not exactly the behaviour one would associate with conspirators having no support from the Government. By coincidence, a standard arms shipment was also due to arrive in Dublin that morning and Captain Kelly, recognising the officer in charge of the receiving party, went over to talk to him. Again this does not point to a perception of illegality, though it is questionable why Kelly should make his presence felt in the middle of a covert operation if security was the main priority.

The presence of the military party did, however, unnerve the IRA men waiting with a lorry to offload the weapons destined for the covert operation. These included John Kelly's brother, Billy, a senior Provisional commander in Belfast, and Seán Keenan, the veteran Derry republican. The decision to involve the IRA personnel was made after consultations with the director of intelligence, Colonel Hefferon. He had informed Kelly that if the arms were transported to an army barracks 'it would attract tremendous attention, and once the arms were got into army custody, it might be difficult to get them out again.'[66]

In the event the guns were not on the ship: they had been impounded in Antwerp because of the lack of an 'end user's certificate', the procedural formality that could only be supplied by the Department of Defence or Justice. All that was aboard was a number of flak jackets, described on the ship's manifest as 'cotton'. The depleted stock was brought to Captain Kelly's house in south Dublin, where Seán Mac Stiofáin, chief of staff of the Provisional IRA, collected it.[67] Unknown to Captain Kelly, the Provisional IRA had other ideas: they themselves wanted to make the decision about when doomsday arrived.[68]

Kelly realised there was a serious problem, and he arranged a further meeting with Gibbons. Unknown to Kelly, Blaney had already apprised Gibbons in considerable detail of the fiasco. Gibbons appeared to be more concerned about whether Kelly had informed the other military officers at the port of the true purpose of his mission on the docks.

> I said to Captain Kelly, I presume that at that stage you disappeared into the shadows and from recollection again, he appeared to assent to this. I said I presume that's the end of that lot anyway, and Captain Kelly said no, it's not, and indicated that by some means or other it would be possible to retrieve them.[69]

Again there was no attempt to admonish Captain Kelly, or to tell him to desist. It seems clear that by this time Gibbons had more than a 'vestigial knowledge' of the planned importing and did nothing to stop it. Gibbons's relationship with Blaney and Haughey entered a different level as a consequence of the rioting in Belfast in April 1970, making it exceptionally difficult to disentangle the Minister for Defence from what became known as the 'arms conspiracy'. The rioting was sparked by the decision to permit an Orange parade to pass by the Catholic housing estates of Ballymurphy. A local agreement was arrived at between the organisers and the residents that no music would be played as the parade passed the Springfield Road. Gerry Adams alleges that the organisers broke this agreement by playing sectarian tunes, prompting a change in the community's relations with the British army. The entire area was saturated with CS gas as fighting intensified, marking the beginning of a sustained and inevitable process of Catholic alienation as grievances took on a nationalist character. The military response to the activities of stone-throwing gangs served to strengthen support for the republican movement. The perception took hold of an army of occupation supporting the triumphalist sectarian practices associated with the Orange Order. For both wings of the republican movement it offered the first real potential to capitalise on the alienation of the Catholic community.[70] According to Adams,

> there was an instant resurgence of national consciousness and an almost immediate politicisation of the local populace … The relatively sophisticated organisational structure in Ballymurphy welded the population of the estate into a formidable body of insurrectionaries.[71]

Jack Lynch was on holiday in County Cork at the height of the Ballymurphy disturbances and could not be contacted. Blaney spotted an opportunity to make a move. He informed Gibbons that he had in his possession evidence of the direst kind, a suggestion that implied that the doomsday scenario had begun. This evidence had been provided to him by none other than John Kelly, the Belfast republican delegated by the Provisional IRA to liaise with Fianna Fáil.[72] Blaney requested Gibbons to send weapons and respirators north. Significantly, he told him he was making the request after consultation with Haughey, a further indication of the formal delegation of authority on Northern issues to the two hawks, notwithstanding their disagreement over policy with the Taoiseach. Gibbons acquiesced, agreeing to move five hundred army weapons to a base in Dundalk.

Gibbons later suggested that he agreed to move the weapons only because of a fear that Blaney himself would take the matter further, embroiling the state potentially in a civil war. It was a startling admission, indicating not only the mesmeric hold that Blaney apparently had over Gibbons but also inadvertently revealing that the Minister for Agriculture had operational control over military decision-making in relation to Northern policy. Gibbons contacted the chief of staff, telling him that

> I had this request from Mr Blaney, and it might be better to comply with it and to make sure that the strictest security was observed at all stages. I think I recall saying something to the effect that 'if I don't do this, he may do something rash himself.'[73]

Gibbons further stressed that there was never any possibility that the weapons would leave military control, and defiantly defended in court his right, as Minister for Defence, to move weapons inside the jurisdiction. That right is not disputed; there is clear evidence, however, that the purpose of the transfer of weapons was to arm Northern nationalists.

At the first arms trial the testimony of the director of intelligence, Colonel Hefferon, destroyed the credibility of his minister's account. Hefferon had attempted to make contact with Captain Kelly in Hamburg, giving an added air of authority to the plan. He testified that he wanted Kelly to supervise distribution 'should it be necessary to distribute the arms. I rang his wife and asked her to get in touch with him and have him return immediately.'[74] There was, according to Kelly, an element of farce about the proceedings.

> Word came down to Clancy Barracks to pile all the stuff onto trucks, and they drove off down the road helter-skelter for Dundalk, and I think for weeks afterwards people were handing in gas masks that they found on the road that had fallen off one of the trucks. They weren't too well packed, it seems.[75]

Blaney himself admitted the purpose in an interview with the BBC in 1993: they were to go directly into the hands of the Provisional IRA.

> They would have gone into Ballymurphy and whoever was capable of handling, using and directing their organisation without name—not because I have the name but because I just do not know.
>
> *But presumably they would have gone to the newly emergent Provisional IRA?*
> Probably.
> *Because you say they wouldn't have gone to the Officials?*
> No way, no way.[76]

The plan was aborted. Lynch was eventually contacted and countermanded the order. The Ballymurphy incident indicated just how centrally involved certain elements of Fianna Fáil were in the descent into chaos north of the border.[77] Still, Lynch did nothing. There was no investigation, no dismissal, and no change in the prosecution of policy; he simply countermanded the order.

In the immediate aftermath of the rioting in Ballymurphy, Gibbons held a meeting with Haughey. He wanted to know if Haughey was aware of any conspiracy to import weapons. 'I said there is something going on about guns and I think I told him about the incident at Dublin docks, the attempt to import weapons.' He also told Haughey about Blaney's account of the planned importing through Dublin port. Haughey said he was not aware of any 'conspiracy to import weapons,' and both agreed that collective Government action was the only way to deal with such matters. The phrasing is instructive: for Haughey there could be no 'conspiracy' if what he was attempting to do was to accede to a legitimate request to help Military Intelligence, which was under Gibbons's nominal, if not actual, control.

Colonel Hefferon retired from Military Intelligence on 9 April but, significantly, made a decision not to inform his successor of the covert operation. This he justified on the grounds that 'the whole project of importing arms was of very great secrecy, in which some Government ministers—to my mind acting for the Government— were involved, and I felt that it should more properly be communicated to him by the Minister for Defence.'[78]

But Hefferon's retirement meant that Captain Kelly had lost influential cover for his operation as he prepared for what became the final attempt to import the weapons paid for out of the public purse. When he returned to Hamburg to find out what had happened to the consignment he was accompanied by Albert Luykx, the restaurateur suggested by Blaney, to act as an interpreter. Otto Schleuter told the two men that the weapons had been transferred to Trieste but that it would be possible to intercept them in Vienna and transfer them by air to Dublin. Schleuter then suggested that a further four hundred machine-guns could be made available, and Kelly arranged to buy them as well. Luykx, seeing the possibility of acting as a business agent for the arms dealer, made arrangements to act as the company representative in Ireland. Schleuter's agent in Vienna made arrangements to bring the consignment in on scheduled Aer Lingus flights, prompting John Kelly to visit Dublin Airport, introducing himself as 'an assistant to Mr Haughey's assistant.'[79] When it became clear that international regulations prohibited the transport of firearms, negotiations opened with John Squires, managing director of a charter subsidiary of Aer Lingus. Again the operation fell foul of the requirement to produce the end user's certificate. What was remarkable was the fact that Captain Kelly did not appear to know what it was, though this was apparently the reason the Belgian authorities had given for allowing the shipment to leave Antwerp the previous month. Squires became suspicious, and his suspicions were heightened when he was told that the operation involved a secret attempt to import weapons for the army and Gardaí. He checked with the Department of Transport and Power, which in turn informed the Department of Justice. The report landed on Peter Berry's desk.[80]

Berry told Ó Móráin that 'there's a ring of steel around Dublin Airport.' Ó Móráin was entertained by the drama and afterwards remarked, 'You'd think we were in fucking Casablanca or somewhere.'[81] The trap was about to be sprung.

Two arms of Government were in effect working at cross-purposes. On the one hand, Military Intelligence was cooking up schemes for arming insurgents in line with sub-committee orders; on the other hand, the Department of Justice was getting alarming reports from the Special Branch that Government ministers were conspiring with known members of the republican movement to import arms. Just what was Government policy, and who was running it—Lynch, Ó Móráin, or Blaney and Haughey?

The presence of the Special Branch in large numbers alerted the customs officer who had been in negotiations with the Kellys, and he rang Anthony Fagan to ask what was going on at the airport. Fagan immediately telephoned Hefferon and Haughey, telling the minister that unless someone rang the head of the Special Branch, Chief Superintendent Fleming, the cargo would' be seized. Once again Haughey found himself trying to smooth the entry of weapons for the North; this time, however, he found himself up against a formidable adversary in Peter Berry.

> I am quite certain that the question of some minister, not necessarily me, some minister telephoning Chief Superintendent Fleming to give clear-ance for the consignment was inherent in what Mr Fagan said to me …
> Mr Fagan told me he had already been in touch with Colonel Hefferon. I had no doubt in my mind that this was a consignment which was coming in as a result of the direction which we had given in pursuance of the Contingency Plans.
>
> *Did you appreciate that it was arms and ammunition?*
> No, I did not appreciate or know at that point of time, and even when I spoke to Mr Berry the words 'arms' and 'ammunition' were never used.[82]

Berry's recollection of the telephone call was very different. He recorded that Haughey had offered a guarantee that the consignment would be shipped directly to the North, in return for the withdrawal of the security operation at the airport.

> Mr Haughey then said, 'I think that is a bad decision.' I made no com-ment. He then said, 'Does the man from Mayo [Ó Móráin] know?' I said, 'Yes.' He then said, 'What will happen to it when it arrives?' and I said, 'It will be grabbed.' He then said, 'I had better have it called off.'[83]

Haughey's counsel vigorously disputed this interpretation, insist-ing instead that the former minister had finished the conversation saying, 'Well, it had better be called off, whatever it is.' This was the centrepiece of his defence,[84] a strategy designed to downgrade his client's involvement, to depict a minister determined to facilitate Military Intelligence, a loyal servant committed to avoiding govern-mental embarrassment. Haughey himself used the same phrase in his testimony.

> The Taoiseach was not in Dublin at the time, and I regarded it as my first duty to see that there was no adverse publicity, no seizure of an arms cargo or anything like that occurring. That is why I said, 'It had better be called off—whatever it is.'[85]

While the machinations were going on in Dublin, Captain Kelly remained in Vienna, seeking final clearance to put the weapons on board a plane to Dublin. It is significant that the person he rang for instructions was the private secretary to the Minister for Finance. The following day Fagan rang Kelly to say that his minister had instructed him that the operation was cancelled.

Haughey denied that he even knew Kelly was in Vienna; he also denied that he knew Colonel Hefferon had retired from the army, and argued that he assumed that because Military Intelligence had first asked for clearance from Finance, his refusal to grant it meant the end of his involvement. He further testified that he agreed to meet the Minister for Defence on 20 April to ensure that there was no possibility that the operation—whatever it was—could be resurrected, because security had been compromised. Gibbons, by contrast, had earlier told the court:

> I asked Charles Haughey if he could stop the operation, and he said, 'I'll stop it for a month.' I said, 'For God's sake stop it altogether.'[86]

Haughey's counsel suggested that Haughey did not say, 'I'll stop it for a month,' but agreed that the whole thing should be called off, because everybody knew about it. Counsel contended that the true state of affairs at that meeting was that Gibbons—alone—was in on the arms plan, and Haughey knew he was in on it.

The centrepiece of Lynch's position on the crisis in the North was that his Government was fully committed to unity by consent, a view enunciated at Tralee and reinforced at the showdown with the proponents of Blaneyism at the ardfheis. This allowed Lynch to claim not only that he knew nothing about attempts to import weapons but that such a policy ran counter to everything he believed in. When the entire edifice began to crumble, between April and May 1970, it was this defence that Lynch used to justify the subsequent sacking of Blaney and Haughey. But it simply does not stand up to scrutiny.[87]

As the Kellys continued with their attempts to get the weapons in, Berry had arranged a meeting with Lynch on 13 April, at Lynch's request, to pass on the names of two IRA men to a clergyman who wanted to make a personal appeal for peace. According to Berry's account, which forms the basis of the seminal *Magill* series on the Arms Crisis, Ó Móráin told him to tell Lynch 'anything he felt he should.'[88] Berry asked him whether Ó Móráin had reported the allegations against two Government ministers made by the Garda Commissioner and the head of the Special Branch the previous December. Lynch said he had not been informed and, according to

Magill, asked Berry if Ó Móráin would even remember the present meeting—an indication of the potential embarrassment if the story came out. As *Magill* pointed out, this meeting was significant because 'it suggests that the Taoiseach did not take action on the first hearing of the arms plot even if he had misunderstood Berry's information at Mount Carmel [nursing home] in October 1969.'[89] Still, Lynch did nothing.

On 20 April 1970 Berry went to see President de Valera to force Lynch to stop what Berry perceived to be a threat to the state. This is a crucial encounter, for a number of reasons. There is the overt questioning of executive authority in a civil servant going to the President rather than accepting the decision of the Taoiseach. Lynch's stated view is that the first he heard of attempts to import weapons was when Berry came to see him on 20 April 1970, after the failure to get the weapons in. This sits uneasily with the highly unusual decision by the secretary of the department to flout constitutional convention. This was done because of Berry's perception that it was a last resort, a wake-up call on the threat posed to democracy by the arming of what he regarded as dangerous subversive organisations.

While it is true that the two ministers had considerable latitude in the prosecution of Northern policy, it was on the basis of delegated authority. Others in the Government outside the sub-committee were kept informed of all developments. Captain Kelly maintains that Colonel Hefferon passed all his reports to Gibbons for Government discussion.[90] Kevin Boland confirms this interpretation; he asserts that the Bailieborough meeting was presented to the Government for discussion within days of it happening; he also alleges that after that meeting the Minister for Justice, Mícheál Ó Móráin, was also told to initiate his own set of contacts within the republican movement.[91] Looking back on events now, Boland believes that Lynch had delegated authority to the sub-committee to establish what support could be given to Northern nationalists in the belief that nothing could be done. If that was the case, then it was an enormous tactical mistake.[92] At the same time, Lynch consistently failed to bring the matter to the Government so as to ascertain what exactly was going on. The Government was quite simply not under his—or anyone's—control.

Lynch had recognised that the feuding factions were determined to stop at nothing to realise their ambition of acceding to the leadership of Fianna Fáil. His failure to intervene reflected not only the power of appeals to irredentism: it also reflected the political skill of the plotters. Lynch also recognised that a confrontation was inevitable and that he was the main target of the ambitions of the Boland-Blaney-Haughey caucus.[93]

The smouldering antagonism between the warring ministers, despite the apparent rapprochement on the Northern issue, had continued to make good political copy for the newspapers and the opposition alike. Blaney's attempt to raise farming subsidies by publicly declaring his hand in demanding an increase in milk quota prices in the weeks before the budget was a case in point.[94] The judgment of Mícheál Ó Móráin was also being called into question with increasing regularity. Journalistic exposés of his contempt for the law he was meant to uphold as Minister for Justice and his allegedly drunken behaviour at a judicial function in Dublin in April were steadily eroding his political standing as Garda morale collapsed.[95]

By 29 April, Lynch had begun the process of reasserting his position, whatever the political cost to his leadership of Fianna Fáil. Even then it was an aspiration more easily decided than acted upon. Lynch recognised that he needed firm evidence if he was going to catch them out; acting on suspicion alone had the potential to destroy his credibility.

Blaney was summoned to see the Taoiseach in his office. Lynch made it clear that he knew all about the planned importing of arms and was determined to stop it; he wanted Blaney's resignation there and then. Blaney protested his innocence, and was allowed to continue the Government's defence of the budget. This provided the first direct hint of the trouble that lay ahead. Blaney maintained to the Dáil that the Government was united and made short work of opposition taunts by telling them to stop looking for spies under the bed. He did, however, make one telling comment.

> We should also keep in mind that this Government will be here, bar some strange and extraordinary happening—and there could be one that comes to mind—but bar that—
> *O'Leary:* An earthquake.
> *Blaney:* No, but the next thing to it.[96]

Lynch then went to see Haughey at Mount Carmel nursing home—the same hospital where Berry had provided him with evidence of an arms plot the previous autumn. Haughey too protested his innocence. The two most powerful barons in Fianna Fáil were contemptuous of Lynch's ability to assert his will, each daring him to act. It was to be a serious miscalculation. Two days later Lynch held a crucial Government meeting; he told his assembled ministers that under no circumstances should they engage in Northern affairs without his explicit approval. The doomsday scenario was now closed.

It was an indication of his isolation that Lynch did not reveal to his Government his doubts about loyalty—theirs or his. On the same day, Captain Kelly was brought to a prison in Dublin and questioned by Chief Superintendent Fleming of the Special Branch. Kelly remembers that Fleming's sole line of questioning was on which ministers were involved. But Fleming was to do more than simply question Captain Kelly: he brought him to see Jack Lynch himself in Government Buildings.

> What Jack Lynch was doing was creating a situation where he could disgrace and eliminate elements of his Government. He wasn't man enough to face up to them in cabinet. He wasn't big enough, strong enough to say to them: 'No, listen, fellows, cop yourselves on here.' He thought he could use me; he thought he could use Colonel Hefferon. Well, he used Gibbons to do his dirty work for him.[97]

For a prosecution to stick, Lynch had to ensure that the Minister for Defence was not in any way implicated in the scandal. He was already sure that Berry would testify that Haughey was trying to authorise the importing of weapons for the Provisional IRA. Extricating Gibbons was both essential and high-risk. Gibbons was well aware of Kelly's exploits on the Continent: when the fiasco at the airport marked the end of the attempts, Kelly held a further meeting with Gibbons, this time in Blaney's office.

> We just chatted about what had taken place and what was going on and what the hell was happening really. Then Gibbons made some remark to me like 'You'll be in the hot seat now,' or words to that effect. I said, 'If I am in the hot seat so are you: you are the name who authorised it.' And he said something about me being 'a brazen bastard.' From then on my antennae were out.[98]

The meeting in Blaney's office was called in part to discuss investigations by the Special Branch into the arms importing and the reasons behind its failure. As we have seen, Captain Kelly told Gibbons in March not only of the failure of the Dublin port operation but of the subsequent plans to use the airport to bring in the shipment. If Kelly was acting illegally, it is simply inconceivable that he should go and see the Minister for Defence in his office in March and again meet him with Blaney on 23 April. Blaney assured those present that nothing could be done about the matter, because nothing had been imported. He gave Gibbons a letter indicating that a representative of Schleuter's would come to Dublin on 3 May to lay on a demonstration of military equipment for Weluks, Albert Luykx's firm.

> He told me it was a copy of a letter which had been sent officially to the Minister for Defence and had gone to the ministry rather than the minister, in the ordinary way, and I gave this letter to my private secretary and I said, 'Destroy that thing.'
>
> *Why?*
>
> It was now apparent to me that they were in some way involved in this affair, and the giving of the letter to me by Mr Blaney was in some way very suspicious to me.
>
> *Was there anything in the letter of which you were afraid?*
>
> Yes.
>
> *What?*
>
> I was afraid that the letter for some reason or another was a plant.
>
> *Was a plant?*
>
> Yes.[99]

In this exchange one comes to the nub of the Arms Crisis. Gibbons in effect was suggesting that Blaney was involved in treason and was trying to implicate him. In fact Gibbons was a pawn in a much more dangerous game, a game that had profound implications for the nature of Irish democracy, not once but twice: firstly by Haughey and Blaney, and secondly by Lynch. This is a view shared by Seán Mac Stiofáin, the first chief of staff of the Provisional IRA.

> They [Haughey and Blaney] wanted to criticise Jack Lynch's policies, and secondly they wanted to have the republican movement in the North nothing here [in the Republic] and under their control. It ended as a political show trial. It started to help the people in the North. All the reports from [Captain] Kelly and others were, we wanted arms to defend ourselves; then Lynch knew that if the thing blew up there was an opportunity to destroy his main opponents in the political party.[100]

The attempts to keep the story out of the public arena had become impossible by this time. The *Sunday Independent* had been given a copy of a document naming the alleged conspirators and pointing out in an oblique manner the role of Peter Berry in going to the President. It decided not to publish the story. The note then came to the attention of the leader of Fine Gael, Liam Cosgrave.[101] Again the Dáil was to see the momentary surfacing of the subterranean power struggle going on inside Fianna Fáil as the Taoiseach announced the resignation of the Minister for Justice.

> I should like to announce, for the information of the Dáil, that Deputy Michael Moran [*sic*] yesterday tendered his resignation to me as a member of the Government. I have advised the President and he has accepted the resignation with effect from today. It was my hope to introduce a consequential motion for the appointment of another member of the Government today. This is not possible and I will do so tomorrow at 11.30 a.m.
>
> *Mr Cosgrave:* Can the Taoiseach say if this is the only ministerial resignation we can expect?
>
> *The Taoiseach:* I do not know what the Deputy is referring to.
>
> *Mr Cosgrave:* Is it only the tip of the iceberg?
>
> *The Taoiseach:* Would the Deputy like to enlarge on what he has in mind?
>
> *Mr L'Estrange:* What did Mr Blaney say last week when he threatened the Taoiseach in public?
>
> *Interruptions.*
>
> *Mr Cosgrave:* The Taoiseach can deal with the situation.
>
> *The Taoiseach:* I can assure the Deputy I am in complete control of whatever situation may arise.
>
> *Mr Cosgrave:* But smiles are very noticeable by their absence.[102]

Lynch had carefully prepared his ground. The head of the Government Information Bureau, Eoin Neeson, rang the *Irish Times* to ask how long the paper could be held for a story; he did not say what the story would be. When it came it was political dynamite. In the early hours of 6 May 1970 a press statement signalled the collapse of attempts to keep the feuding factions within one administration.

> I have requested the resignations as members of the Government of Mr Neil T. Blaney, Minister for Agriculture and Fisheries, and Mr Charles J. Haughey, Minister for Finance, because I am satisfied that they do not subscribe fully to Government policy in relation to the present situation in the Six Counties as stated by me at the Fianna Fáil Ard-Fheis in January last. Caoimhghin Ó Beoláin [Kevin Boland], Minister for Local

Government and Social Welfare, has tendered his resignation as a member of the Government and I propose to advise the President to accept it. A special meeting of Fianna Fáil deputies will take place at Leinster House at 6 p.m. today to consider the position that has arisen.[103]

CHAPTER FIVE

Debating Treason

Closing the Net

I T was ironic that the crisis broke on the day of the official commemoration of the 1916 Rising. A military band played rousing airs before officials including the President, Éamon de Valera, and Frank Aiken, a former chief of staff of the IRA. Seán Lemass stood shoulder to shoulder with the Taoiseach, Jack Lynch, flanked by the Minister for Defence, Jim Gibbons, and the leader of the opposition, Liam Cosgrave.

Force and legitimacy, unquestioningly accepted in the context of the 1916 Rising, were seen to be propelling the nation once more into conflict. Were all the gains of the state, so jealously protected, at risk from such adventurism? Rumours swept the city. Just how feverish the mood had become is clear from the reporting of the magazine *This Week*. While there was never any possibility of a military coup, the parallels with Fianna Fáil's entry into government in 1932 were pronounced.

On Wednesday morning a reporter, Tony Gallagher, visited Captain Kelly, who

> expressed surprise but did not display open astonishment that his name had been mentioned in connection with the Cabinet crisis. He would not comment further.[1]

According to Kelly's published account, the reporter cited a ministerial source for 'the real Gibbons story.'[2] Kevin Boland fuelled the speculation by telling reporters that Lynch was 'very definitely wrong' to sack the two ministers.[3]

At 11:30 Lynch entered the Dáil, looking 'drawn and even haggard.'[4] The search for political advantage began immediately. Cosgrave had earlier agreed to Lynch's request to adjourn proceedings to facilitate the Fianna Fáil meeting. When Lynch moved to adjourn, Cosgrave departed from his script. 'I do not wish to be unreasonable, but the business of the Dáil and of the country is entitled to precedence over a Fianna Fáil party meeting.'[5] Lynch was asked to clarify the position. Had the ministers submitted to his will? His reply was nothing short of staggering. 'I have not yet received the resignations, but the constitutional position is that I am entitled to act on my request.'[6]

What was clear was that Haughey and Blaney had not surrendered their seals of office; they would fight, and that fight would be at the Fianna Fáil party meeting. While Lynch believed he could force through his agenda in the Government—ditching his three most powerful rivals and in the process losing a fourth—it was quite another matter to ensure that the parliamentary party would support his decision. The party meeting was to be crucial: it had indeed what the *Irish Times* regarded as the potential to be 'the most decisive of any similar gathering held since the end of the Civil War.'[7]

The parliamentary sketch-writer John Healy captured the feverish mood nicely in his review of the day's events.

> Fianna Fáil politicians are suspicious and worried and uncertain. In a quieter corner I stumble across an old hand in the party: he is crying quietly to himself: he has given his life to the party and he cannot accept what he has heard in this house of rumour, and innuendo.

By mid-afternoon Healy detected a change in emphasis, a recognition that the 'Party of Reality is going to be the party of reality.'[8] Lynch, it was believed, must have had enough evidence to push his recalcitrant ministers to the outer reaches of political power—the back benches. Haughey, recuperating from a riding accident, left his sick-bed to attend the meeting.

The party managers decided to place before the meeting a positive resolution affirming the right of the Taoiseach to make whatever appointments he desired. Blaney, Haughey and Boland supported the motion.[9] Faced with a choice between a damaging split and a general election, which could not possibly be won in the circumstances, the party closed ranks. Sources quoted in *Hibernia* suggested that no-one opposed the motion or asked any serious questions, proving the parliamentary party 'to be as useless as the Party managers cleverly estimated it to be.'[10] Fianna Fáil was not to split—at least in public; at least for now. After fifty-five minutes the deputies trooped out, some to the bar, others to restaurants around Government Buildings.

Kevin Boland and Neil Blaney nonchalantly walked into the Dáil chamber just before the debate was due to begin, their relaxed mood in stark contrast to the feverish speculation. The Dáil was packed to capacity as Lynch entered the chamber. He began by nominating Desmond O'Malley as Ó Móráin's successor at the Department of Justice. He told the Dáil he had tried to secure the resignation of Blaney and Haughey, but

> as neither would comply with my request, accordingly on my advice the President has terminated their appointments with effect from the 7th May, 1970 … On my advice also, the President has today accepted the resignation of Caoimhghin Ó Beoláin, Minister for Local Government and for Social Welfare, as a member of the Government with effect from the same date.[11]

Even after the press statement, even after the parliamentary party meeting, neither was prepared to go voluntarily or to admit that they had done anything wrong. Yet both were now in the Dáil about to vote for the Government.

Lynch then outlined the case against the two ministers.

> On Monday 20th April and Tuesday 21st April, the security forces of the country at my disposal brought me information about an alleged attempt to unlawfully import arms from the Continent. *Prima facie,* these reports involved two members of the Government.

He suggested that the reason for the delay in bringing the matter to a conclusion was that Haughey had been in hospital, having fallen from his horse on the morning of the budget; medical consultants would not allow an interview until 29 April. Blaney was interviewed on the same day; Lynch gave no indication of why he delayed the interview with him.

> Each of them denied he instigated in any way the attempted importation of arms. They asked me for time to consider their position. I agreed to do so. In the meantime I authorised the continuation of investigations and I made personal investigations myself, following which I decided to approach the two Ministers again and to repeat my request that they tender to me their resignations as members of the Government. I did so

on the basis that I was convinced that not even the slightest suspicion should attach to any member of the Government in a matter of this urgency.[12]

The members of the Dáil listened to this in stunned silence. John Healy noted that the chamber was

so hushed that the thump thump of an engine in the bowels of the building reached into the Chamber and sounded like the communal heartbeat of the crowded Chamber. He had finished in ten minutes and the political reputations of two Ministers lay in shreds on the floor. He sat down in silence.[13]

The intrigue deepened when the leader of the opposition, Liam Cosgrave, revealed that he had had a private meeting with the Taoiseach the night before. He said he was in possession of information that

indicated a situation of such gravity for the nation that it is without parallel in this country since the formation of the state. By approximately 10 p.m. two Ministers had been dismissed and a third had resigned.[14]

Cosgrave told the Dáil he had evidence of an attempt to import weapons for use by 'an illegal organisation', and that an army officer was involved. He quoted from a document allegedly written on Garda stationery—the same source presented to the *Sunday Independent* the previous week. He went on: 'This is a situation without parallel in this country, that not merely involved here is the security of the state but that those who were drawing public money were, in fact, attempting to undermine it, and that there was a failure to deal with this situation by the Taoiseach.'[15] According to Cosgrave, those involved included 'Captain Kelly, the former Minister for Finance, the former Minister for Agriculture, and two associates of the ministers.'[16] This paraphrasing was crucial. Cosgrave did not list all the names on the document. He omitted the name of Colonel Michael Hefferon, the director of Military Intelligence, and that of Jim Gibbons, the Minister for Defence. Both were named in the document from which he was quoting but he made no reference to them.

Why? The entire Crisis boiled down to whether the attempt to import arms was legal or not. Since the only person who could authorise the importation was the Minister for Defence, it was crucial that Gibbons appear in any subsequent trial as a prosecution witness. Clearly, this would be impossible if it could be established that he had prior knowledge of the operation. Lynch gave Cosgrave an assurance that Gibbons had no part in the affair and Cosgrave took him at his word.[17]

The exchanges became more and more bad-tempered as Cosgrave told the Dáil that

> the people of this country can now, tonight and not for the first time in our history, be grateful to this party for the selfless dedication to the service of the nation—
>
> *Mr J. Lenehan:* Ah, shut up. Your father sold the North, and damn well you know it.
>
> *Mr Cosgrave:* … that it has discharged without regard to personal interest or party consideration. The position that has now arisen is that this country is drifting into anarchy. This is a situation that those whom we commemorated at Arbour Hill today could never have visualised.[18]

The massed ranks of Fine Gael gave Cosgrave a standing ovation.

The Labour Party leader, Brendan Corish, embarked on a different tack, seeing in the crisis the ultimate failure of the Government to either enunciate or prosecute a viable policy. The political and moral bankruptcy of Fianna Fáil was on display; the only rational approach was to 'resolutely exclude from the national consensus those who encourage and condone violence and especially those who engage in surreptitious collusion with violence practised by others.'[19]

As the debate continued, the political temperature soared. Thomas O'Higgins of Fine Gael was prompted to ask,

> Are we going to permit this country to be turned into a banana republic? Are we going to have our institutions, our code of conduct and our conventions whittled away by cynical ambitious men who respect no law except the law of the jungle?[20]

Logic dictated that if one accepted the Taoiseach's account, then the Minister for Finance was presiding over a budget while under suspicion. The state was faced with the intolerable situation of having its finances 'under the control of a member of [the] Government actively conspiring to arm an illegal army inside this state to subvert the policy of his own colleagues and his own leader.'[21]

There was recognition of how the debate in the Dáil fed into the wider picture with the consequent risk of instability spreading southwards. This was expressed with clarity by Conor Cruise O'Brien, the Labour Party spokesman on Northern Ireland: he told the Dáil that growing polarisation in the North convinced him of 'a most earnest sense of impending national tragedy, with a festival of destruction in prospect for the marching season,' which in his view had the very real possibility of engulfing the entire country.

> This is the fire that those people are playing with. I do not think honestly that they understand. I do not think the Taoiseach understands. I do not think the gentlemen he depends on know anything more about it than that which they read about when they were twelve years of age. This is a party of ignorance and fanaticism and this has led to this folly which has fallen on their heads and, unfortunately, on the heads of all the people.[22]

Fianna Fáil was undergoing the most sustained character assassination since the nineteen-thirties; there appeared to be no respite as opposition deputies combined in an attempt to share in its destruction. The Labour Party was particularly effective, seeing in the debate an opportunity to settle old scores. Justin Keating, another of the party's intellectual firebrands elected in 1969 despite the 'red scare' tactics of Fianna Fáil, launched into a savage indictment.

> Not a single one who had an honourable trade and could make his living and save his soul in another way had the moral fibre to sacrifice his own political career to honour and truth and dignity. Not one. They are unified indeed, but unified with loss of all stature, of all validity, of all honour in the eyes of this country.[23]

And still the onslaught went on, greatly augmented by the media, which fed the crisis. How long could the crumbling façade be maintained? The *Irish Times* editorial was typical.

> Mr Lynch has paid the price for assuming that a problem would go away if he pretended that it was not there. His vapid protestation on more than one occasion that Mr Blaney and he really thought on the same lines about the North is seen as nonsense. It remains to be seen if those who are of a like mind with Mr Blaney throughout the country can similarly be contained or won over.[24]

Lynch made another intervention to shore up this constituency, in the process making a number of telling observations about the strength of nationalist ideology and its failure to provide an adequate response to the conflict in the North. He proclaimed his loyalty to the founding principles of Fianna Fáil and the republican ideal and referred to the strength of popular feeling caused by the outbreak of violence in the North. He reflected on the decisions made in August 1969 and in the process addressed directly the continuing power of irredentist rhetoric.

> I was accused of sabre-rattling in having sent certain units of the army for ambulance purposes near to the border. I will readily admit that there was another reason why I did so. It was not so much to look towards the border as to look south, because there were decent people in this part of the country who felt incensed at what was happening in Derry and what ultimately happened in Belfast. It was important that we had then at strategic points along the border army units and Garda units, not just to help refugees, to help people injured in the troubles in the North, but to ensure that we knew what was happening from the South. That was one of the reasons that action was taken. I believe that action prevented a great deal of bloodshed which might otherwise have occurred.[25]

Lynch was careful in his choice of language, judging that there was little to be gained by providing the Dáil with a detailed explanation. He expressed his unease at having to take this action, a recognition of the former ministers' pedigree. There was also what *Hibernia* termed the 'magnificently hypocritical tribute' to their ability, brilliance, and dedication. Lynch was doing enough to destroy any potential challenge without giving them the opportunity to stage a come-back. For *Hibernia* 'the whole performance was conducted with the discipline and stylized ritual of a tribal sacrifice.'[26]

If Lynch thought such an approach would take the sting out of the situation, he was to be disappointed. Kevin Boland, speaking to the *Irish Independent,* accused the Government of employing 'Gestapo tactics', tapping politicians' phone lines and behaving like a dictatorship.[27] The gloves were well and truly off. The protestations of unity in the party were clearly revealed to be a sham even before Boland rose to speak in the Dáil; by the time he had finished many wondered if the Government could survive.

Boland declared that the Taoiseach had the right, of course, to order his Government in whatever way he saw fit. He, however, was not prepared to serve in a Government that, as he saw it, trampled on the principles of natural justice. His critique was devastating.

He recalled his days as a young recruit in the FCA. An officer told the recruits that getting drunk was conduct prejudicial to good order and military discipline. According to the officer, he alone would decide on what amounted to drunkenness.

While it might be all right to expect soldiers to serve under the condition that if an army NCO says you are drunk you are drunk, I do not expect ministers of a Government to serve under the condition that if Mr Peter Berry says you did a thing, you did it.[28]

Boland moved to deny the vision of republicanism enunciated by Lynch. It was a direct challenge to his leader. He declared that partition was totally unacceptable, as was the question of the Southern Government itself using force to impose its will. There was, however, a crucial caveat: no section of the Irish people had the right

to opt out of the Irish nation. It certainly does not mean there is any acceptance of the right of any foreign country to divide our country, to maintain an army in it, or to legislate for any part of it.[29]

Boland was taking irredentist rhetoric to its logical conclusion. He maintained that the ultimate goal for Irish society was to get rid of both states: the Republic and everything it stood for was now on the altar of Irish nationalism, a sacrifice in the hope of achieving the final solution to the nation's ills. For Boland, the commemoration at Arbour Hill two days earlier was not merely window-dressing: it was the most pressing issue facing the state and had to be acted upon. If that meant the possibility of embroiling the country in a bloodbath, then so be it.

There is no doubt that the people in the Six Counties are, in fact, in the same position as the people in the whole country were in before 1916, and they are entitled to make their own decisions ... It would be presumptuous for us to attempt from the smugness of this 26-County state to dictate to our fellow-countrymen who are suffering under British imperialism, because that is what they are suffering under. It would be unpardonable for us to take any action to frustrate the efforts of our people in the Six Counties to protect their lives and property.[30]

And if the only organisation to secure that was the IRA, then Boland was content to allow it to secure its objectives.

There is here in this part of our country an established situation of a democratically elected Government operating under a democratically adopted constitution, and no such Government could tolerate the existence of an armed organisation not under the Government's control. No such Government could permit the importation of arms into this country for such an organisation. I am absolutely certain that no-one who was a colleague of mine in the Government believes otherwise. However, while such an organisation is clearly illegal here, the position in the Six Counties is clearly different.[31]

Boland appeared oblivious to the contradictions in his speech. On the one hand he was advocating the destruction of both states, yet simultaneously he was arguing that it would not be justifiable to tolerate an IRA campaign to advance change within the Republic. He concluded with what amounted to an open invitation to the IRA.

Arms importation into this part of our country by any agency other than the state is illegal and should not be permitted, but arms importation into the part of the country in which the writ of this Government does not run is not illegal as far as I am concerned. It is our duty to advise against it, but it is not our business to interfere, and any co-operation with the security forces of the country that continues to occupy six of our counties is, in my opinion, intolerable.[32]

For John Healy this was an

astonishing single-handed explosion from within the citadel itself ... a speech, which rocked Fianna Fáil to its foundations and planted a hatchet in the back of his leader, Jack Lynch. When Mr Boland finished about forty backbenchers clapped him. The front bench kept solidly quiet.[33]

Michael O'Higgins was next to speak, capturing in a particularly timely and graphic metaphor from the conflict in Viet Nam the magnitude of what was happening.

There is a dreadful fascination for all of us when we hear stories of self-immolation. The absolutely horrifying picture of a Buddhist monk or some other persons of that kind who lies down on the ground, empties a tin of petrol over himself, applies a match and burns himself to death is a fearful, fascinating, morbid picture. I do not know whether today we are witnessing the self-immolation of Fianna Fáil.[34]

A more devious game was being played. Outside the Dáil the Government strategy was coming under sustained attack. Central to this was the calculated destruction of the credibility of Jim Gibbons, and in the process the credibility of the Government.[35] The question was, who was using who, and for what purpose?

The Stormont MP Paddy Kennedy was in town. He told a press conference that he knew Captain Kelly and could vouch for his integrity. 'I would be extremely surprised if any action he had taken was taken without the full knowledge of his superior officers and the Minister for Defence.' When asked why Kelly left the army, Kennedy suggested that 'he possibly resigned to be able to tell what happened, rather than be muzzled by not being able to comment.'[36]

Gibbons was furious. He took to the floor of the Dáil and renounced the captain and any suggestion that he had given implicit or explicit consent to arms importing for Northern nationalists.

> I wish emphatically to deny any such knowledge or consent. I was aware through the Director of Intelligence that attempts to smuggle arms were a constant danger, and these attempts were kept under surveillance at all times. I wish to say that I discharged my duty to the full extent of my knowledge of the situation. I want to say also that in recent times I formed the opinion that Captain Kelly was becoming unsuitable for the type of work that he was employed in. I want to say that certain suspicions were forming in my mind. I was kept informed by the Director of Intelligence, but nothing concrete emerged. I am satisfied that at all times I honoured the obligation that was placed in me by the Taoiseach when he made me Minister for Defence.[37]

Gibbons also used the occasion to specifically deny that the Government had in any way agreed to help train civilians. It was a breathtaking deceit.

> There was some reference to the training of civilians in Donegal. I want to point out the position of the Defence Forces in this regard. The Defence Forces train only members of their own ranks, whether they be FCA or army or navy personnel. That is the extent of their training.[38]

Kelly was incensed at what he saw as the final betrayal. He arranged for Dick Walsh of the *Irish Times* and a reporter from the BBC to come to his house.

> Under privilege of the Dáil, Mr Gibbons has attacked me. All he has said is a tissue of lies. Any work which I did I brought to the knowledge of Mr Gibbons at any and every opportunity. He is completely aware of anything I did prior to my leaving the army.

Referring directly to the Minister for Defence, Kelly declared:

> This man is an unmitigated scoundrel, and I say this not under the privilege of Dáil Éireann. I met him at his office in Leinster House on April 29th and I gave him a full account of my work. We parted on amiable

terms. Mr Gibbons has often indicated that I was doing an excellent job for the country as an intelligence officer.[39]

This was a crucial admission and cast serious doubts on both Gibbons's and Lynch's credibility. Why was Gibbons, on whom 'not the slightest suspicion' had arisen, meeting a Military Intelligence captain whose allegedly nefarious activities had already come to the Taoiseach's attention? Either Lynch had totally failed to protect his minister or he had become so paranoid that he could no longer trust anyone. Either way, his judgment in this matter was undermined from this intervention onwards.

As Kelly was dictating his statement to the BBC, Neil Blaney took centre stage in the Dáil. He went on the offensive from the beginning, accusing the opposition of attempting to create a constitutional crisis. 'I have run no guns, I have procured no guns, I have paid for no guns, I have provided no money to buy guns, and anybody who says otherwise is not telling the truth.'[40] The speech amounted to a personal leadership manifesto, rebuking Lynch's policy of consent and rehearsing the Tralee and Letterkenny arguments of the previous year. It was also a speech designed to reopen the scars of the Civil War.

> I could not but be Fianna Fáil and republican unless I was to renege the heritage of my parents before me. I was born while my late father was under sentence of death. He was again on the run. A few years later, as a child, I was kicked out of the cot I lay in by one of the forces of the then alleged nation, the people who would now decry what republicans stand for and what they then stood for. These are the sort of things that at this time come back to me.[41]

He reiterated his suspicion of the Special Branch in the nineteen-twenties and the Blueshirts in the thirties. The Special Branch men were 'as often drunk as sober when they came on these raids, perhaps because having sold out their republican principles they had to drown their shame in liquor.'[42]

> I apologise to no-one for my views and the views I hold in regard to the reunification of Ireland, but I do think it is necessary at this particular moment to restate my position. I have been misrepresented, grossly misrepresented, by the architects of partition both in this house and in Stormont on the question of force. I have never advocated the use of force as a means of bringing about unity of this land—never. Those who say otherwise are liars ...

Believing, as I do, that violence and perhaps bloodshed may not be far away in the Six Counties, I charge the leaders of Fine Gael for the disreputable role they have been playing during the past few days to bring down this Government by attempting to provoke a constitutional crisis. They are simply following in the footsteps of their predecessors who sold out in 1925, sold out on the border question and handed over almost half a million of our people against those people's expressed wish and against the expressed wish of the majority of all of the people of this island, this land, this country of ours, the thirty-two counties—sold them out and handed them over to the domination of the Orange junta in Stormont, handed them over to discrimination in jobs and in housing.[43]

He regarded the posturing of the opposition as a nauseating but not surprising development, given the fact that 'Ireland has always had its British lackeys: you can pick them out in every generation, those hypocrites, those who for their own ends are always ready to play Britain's game in this country.'[44] That being said, Blaney concluded that there was no question of a split. Fianna Fáil still held to the principles of the revolution; only Fianna Fáil could be the moral guardian of the nation's destiny. According to Blaney, it was this higher calling that motivated his action.

I want to say that Fianna Fáil is not split. It is not even splintered. I say this as one of the people who is no longer in government, who is gone from the Government, who refused to resign from the Government. I want the house to know why. With no disrespect to the Taoiseach or to the Government, and with sadness so far as the President of the country is concerned, I refused to resign because I believe that by so doing in view of the extremely delicate situation in the Six Counties I would be aiding, perhaps causing, something that would result in some explosion about which we might be very sorry in the future.[45]

It was a declaration of loyalty to the party that Lynch could do without. According to John Healy,

to say the Fianna Fáil deputies—the new still to be ratified Ministers included looked grim is an understatement. Mr Colley, Mr Gibbons and Mr Lynch kept their heads buried in their hands or otherwise masked for most of the Boland and Blaney speeches. The smiles of satisfaction, which should be on the faces of the promoted did not appear.[46]

It was also, as Conor Cruise O'Brien remarked, a remarkable piece of 'political theatre, touching the chords of passion and appealing for unity.' He noted that while Blaney had disavowed the activities of Saor Éire (the group responsible for the killing of a garda during a botched armed robbery on the Dublin quays two weeks earlier) he did not specifically disavow the IRA. He called on Lynch to repudiate 'not merely the language but the tone and the whole style of the speech, which was pouring petrol onto flames.'[47] Fianna Fáil, he concluded, had a 'dangerous and infectious sickness. It is incubating the germs of a possible civil war.'[48]

Blaney's speech was carefully designed to be read as an overt attack on Fine Gael, the subliminal message being that if the circumstances warranted armed intervention in the North, then for the Government not to supply help and encouragement amounted to the same thing. Taken together with the Boland intervention it represented what the *Irish Times* called the 'national schizophrenia, which commits us all to achieving our aims by peaceful means yet urges us to applaud violence or at least sympathise with it.'[49]

The dressing up of the intrigue as supporting the legitimate right of Northern nationalists to request and receive help from the Southern government was buttressed on two further fronts outside the Dáil. Eddie McAteer, a long-standing ally of Blaney, issued an ambivalent statement.

> My party is committed to the Lynch peace line, but this does not mean that we are to meekly bow down like sheep for summer slaughter. The screeching dove might well remember that Neil Blaney stood beside us in our hour of need and is still willing to sacrifice a bright political future to help his fellow-Ulstermen. And if the midnight knock comes to our door, would not the gentlest of us love the feeling of security that a pike in the thatch can bring.[50]

Of more critical importance was a press conference organised in Dublin that evening, a development that had the potential to make Lynch's position all but untenable. Blaney's personal adviser, Séamus Brady, who had been at Captain Kelly's house in the afternoon, arranged a spontaneous press conference by the Kelly brothers of Belfast to declare just how closely involved the Dublin Government had been in arming the Northern Command. Billy Kelly was introduced as chairman of St Patrick's Parish Citizens' Defence Committee, John Kelly as a member of a delegation that regularly met senior Southern politicians. In reality, both were leading figures in the Provisional IRA.

Billy Kelly revealed that discussions with Government ministers, Lynch, Blaney, Haughey, and Gibbons, had taken place as recently as a month beforehand. The delegation received no publicity at the time, because of a request by the Taoiseach. However, it was clear that the delegation saw that the purpose of the press conference was as much to undermine the credibility of the Minister for Defence as to embarrass his leader.

> I asked the Minister [Gibbons] what sort of guarantee he could give us if our minority were attacked like last year ... We discussed the amount of protection the British army could afford to give, and I pointed out that the British army were not in a position to protect all of the minority population in the Six Counties. I told him it was a physical impossibility.

According to Kelly, one of Gibbons's final assurances was that 'if the worst came to the worst, there is no need to fear.'[51]

The manoeuvrings of Séamus Brady came to the attention of Garret FitzGerald. In what was arguably the most incisive contribution of the 36-hour debate, FitzGerald outlined Brady's role in organising the interventions of Captain Kelly, Paddy Kennedy, and the Kelly brothers. He detected a pattern.

> We are not in the High Court trying this case, but it is clear that Deputy Blaney is out to get Deputy Gibbons. It is also clear that Mr Séamus Brady is Deputy Blaney's PRO. It is evident that Deputy Blaney's attitude is that if he is going out of Government, Deputy Gibbons is going too. We may ask why. The most probable explanation is that Deputy Gibbons was not, as Deputies Blaney and Haughey thought, working for them but that all the time he was informing on them to the Taoiseach. Deputy Blaney will not forgive that particular betrayal.[52]

FitzGerald was in no doubt about the risks that lay ahead, and who constituted the most serious risk.

> Deputy Blaney [is] a ruthless and unscrupulous man, feared by so many members of his party, the Paisley of the Republic, with the Hitler-like ability to stir up a mob, determined to oust the Taoiseach, working away now at this through his agents, seeking to bring down the Government while at the same time mouthing sycophantic platitudes, a man of civil war, a man exploiting divisions of the past with a view to deriving vicious benefit from them in the future, a man who could well capture power in Fianna Fáil.[53]

Ironically, the story in *This Week,* designed in large part to shore up the position of Gibbons, served only to make the Government more unsteady. *This Week* alleged that some time in August or September Lynch had been informed that Blaney was in contact with the Northern Command of the IRA. It reported that Blaney and Haughey had held meetings together and separately

> on several occasions with high ranking members of the IRA in Dublin ... The reports were vague: there were no times, places or hard and fast details to back them up. Unverified the information they brought could not be acted upon immediately. Lynch was left in a lonely dilemma of doubt, which he had no clear way of resolving.[54]

This, for the Fine Gael prosecutors, was evidence of serious duplicity. As John Bruton pointed out,

> either Deputy Gibbons did tell the Taoiseach at the end of last year, as in the *This Week* story, that he knew of the plot, in which case the Taoiseach did nothing about it and has misled this house in saying that the first knowledge that he, the Taoiseach, had of this affair was on the 20th April, or—the alternative—the Minister for Defence himself was involved in the plot behind the Taoiseach's back and did not go to the Taoiseach.[55]

The explanation for Haughey's involvement was, for many, the great unanswered question of the scandal. Haughey issued a statement through his solicitor, again denying involvement but prepared to put his ministerial career on the line to defend Fianna Fáil.

> The Taoiseach informed the Dáil that he requested my resignation on the grounds that he was convinced that not even a slightest suspicion should attach to any member of the Government. I fully subscribe to that view, as I have been able to gather the Taoiseach received information of a nature which in his opinion cast some suspicion on me. I have not had the opportunity to examine or test such information or the quality of its source or sources. In the meantime however I now categorically state that at no time have I taken part in any illegal importation or attempted importation of arms into this country. At present I do not propose to say anything further except that I fully accepted the Taoiseach's decision as I believe the unity of the Fianna Fáil party is of greater importance to the welfare of the nation than to my political career.[56]

For FitzGerald, Haughey was

a man of great ability. He was betrayed, I think, by a curious casual arrogance of power. I do not understand it. I do not understand how a man who had so much power could still be ambitious for more in such a way as to betray and undermine his own Government. He is an enigma in this.[57]

As the Dáil debate ended, the obvious and naked pursuit of power perplexed the Dublin media. Blaney and Haughey had both in effect denied the charges, and Lynch not only spoke of his disgraced ministers' brilliance and dedication but also held open in Haughey's case the possibility of once again returning to the front bench. The ministers stood accused in Dáil Éireann, but their vote and those of their supporters had the potential to keep Fianna Fáil in power. Everyone appeared to be amazed at the blatant contradiction—everyone, that is, except Fianna Fáil itself. The criticism was overwhelming. *This Week* claimed that Irish democracy 'began to die a slow death of shame as the great cover-up got under way.'[58] The answer lay in the power struggle that was now erupting on the streets of Belfast as well as in the corridors of Dáil Éireann.

Lynch announced that he had turned over all the papers in his possession to the Attorney-General and that it was for him to take whatever action was justified. As Haughey continued his recuperation at his mansion, Blaney embarked on a victory cavalcade from Monaghan to Letterkenny. A hundred cars crossed the border at Aughnacloy, County Tyrone, where an RUC guard accompanied it through volatile areas. Blaney crossed the border again at Lifford, and a pipe band heralded his arrival to a crowd of seven thousand people assembled in the market square in Letterkenny.[59] Blaney in particular had attached himself to a form of action in which the only way back from the political wilderness was conflagration. He said the five people involved had no regrets—a reference that implies that, contrary to Lynch's protestations, Mícheál Ó Móráin's resignation was connected to the scandal.

In Belfast, the uneasy peace began to break down. Trouble flared when a bomb exploded in a bar in the dock area. Rival gangs began gathering along Lepper Street, which separates the (Catholic) New Lodge and (Protestant) Tiger's Bay, one of the sectarian interfaces that crisscross north Belfast. It stretches credibility to believe that the first outbreak of sustained violence in Belfast since August 1969 was not connected to the ministerial scandal taking place in Dublin. The centre of the violence was St Patrick's parish in the New Lodge; the central figures in the Citizens' Defence Committee there were John

Kelly and his brother Billy. The rioting around the New Lodge was the most serious outbreak of disturbances since the previous August. Youths fought running battles with soldiers, who responded with tear gas. The Bishop of Down and Connor, Dr William Philbin, appealed for calm. The television pictures, he said, were shocking: 'youths were depicted firing stones and other missiles at the military, who refrained from using the weapons they held in their hands.' The community, he said, had a responsibility.

> Conscientious and mature persons should come together and act as vigilante committees and stewards, asserting the will and the authority of all of the people in the district ... The vigilantes were to be required, not just for the coming nights but in all probability for the entire summer. Failure to maintain preventive measures may have consequences for the whole of this city which are too horrible to contemplate.[60]

While the bishop did not know it, he was giving a green light to the Provisionals in their battle with the Official IRA.[61] The propaganda battle within the republican movement heated up as the inexorable descent into violence continued, in large part sustained by the disclosures made by both sides in the continuing dispute. The Sinn Féin leadership in Dublin issued a statement:

> Six 26 County Army Intelligence officers were sent to the six counties to report on the personalities and characters of the leading members of the civil rights movement and the political philosophies and ideologies which they represented. Their task initially was to sort out the right-wing people who could be supported for a take-over of the NICRA. These moves had the full backing of the Dublin government but were mainly under the direction of Mr Blaney.[62]

The editor of the *United Irishman,* Séamas Ó Tuathail, spoke on television, making it clear that Captain Kelly was not the only intelligence officer working in the North: he named two others, Captains Duggan and Drohan.[63] Not to be outdone, Seán Keenan led a delegation to Dublin and told a press conference organised by the Northern Defence Association that he had information that suggested there would be an imminent attack by the main loyalist paramilitary group, the Ulster Volunteer Force, on Catholic areas of Pomeroy, Dungannon, Maghera, and Dungiven. The Northern Defence Association maintained that it was not advocating violence, but it wanted answers to five important questions.

Seán Lemass, Jack Lynch and Charles Haughey in 1965.
(The Irish Times)

Captain Terence O'Neill and Jack Lynch at Stormont in December 1967.
(Belfast Telegraph)

October 1968: confrontation between civil rights marchers and the RUC in Derry.

Bernadette Devlin in the early days of the civil rights campaign.

A loyalist march in Armagh, with Rev. Ian Paisley to the fore.
(The Irish Times)

Eddie McAteer, leader of the Nationalist Party, makes his concession speech following the loss of his Westminster seat to John Hume in the 1970 general election.

Ballymurphy, June 1970: burnt out buses. (Victor Patterson Archive/Linen Hall Library)

Eamonn McCann in 1970.

Troops enter the Lower Falls Road in Belfast to impose the curfew, July 1970. (Victor Patterson Archive/Linen Hall Library)

Falls Road curfew. (Victor Patterson Archive/Linen Hall Library)

Rev. Ian Paisley.
(Lensmen)

Members of the SDLP arrive at Stormont, October 1970.
(Victor Patterson Archive/Linen Hall Library)

Neil Blaney being shouldered by supporters after his acquittal in the Four Courts, Dublin, July 1970. (The Irish Times)

Martin McGuinness, Dáithí Ó Conaill, Seán Mac Stíofáin and Séamus Twomey at an IRA meeting in Derry in 1972. (Victor Patterson Archive/Linen Hall Library)

Brian Faulkner.
(Belfast Telegraph)

Paddy Kennedy.
(Victor Patterson Archive/
Linen Hall Library)

Loyalists attack civil rights marchers in Derry. (Victor Patterson Archive/Linen Hall Library)

Hooker Street, Belfast, 1969.
(Victor Patterson Archive/Linen Hall Library)

Kevin Boland.
(Victor Patterson Archive/
Linen Hall Library)

Jim Gibbons.
(Victor Patterson Archive/
Linen Hall Library)

Dáithí Ó Conaill.
(Victor Patterson Archive/
Linen Hall Library)

*Charles Haughey, Minister
for Finance.*
(Victor Patterson Archive/
Linen Hall Library)

1. What will Mr Lynch's policy be in the event of further outbreaks of trouble on a greater scale, perhaps, than last year?
2. Will Mr Lynch and his government stand idly by and see people slaughtered and their homes destroyed?
3. What alternative to defensive measures does Mr Lynch have to offer?
4. Will Mr Lynch now tell us that he will accept full responsibility for any loss of life or damage to property?
5. Will Mr Lynch tell the Irish people, plainly and clearly, that he is abandoning the people of the North to the violence from sectarian bigots and the berserk attacks of crown forces?[64]

The statement concluded with a reminder that 'the people of the North have always played their part in the national struggle … Are we to be abandoned now?'[65] The timing was crucial. The story hit the headlines just as Lynch was seeking a renewed vote of confidence in the Dáil. While there was never any question that the intervention would in any way change the vote, it did underline the strength of irredentism in the Republic, a strength that Blaney, in particular, was quite prepared to be associated with. The passing of time has obscured just how powerful an impulse this was in Irish society, particularly in Fianna Fáil.[66] While there is no doubt that Lynch played his cards exceptionally well, it was by no means a foregone conclusion that he was going to triumph.

Conor Cruise O'Brien remarked in the confidence debate that there appeared to be a failure within Fianna Fáil to recognise the significance of Boland's assertion that the present situation in Northern Ireland could be compared to 1916.

> The unmistakable corollary of this is that the Government should go to the help of those men who would have been encouraged by this collusion to start such a rising. If that is not a corollary, then the policy is as contemptible as it is insane. I will make the charitable assumption that the policy is just insane.[67]

The Tánaiste, Erskine Childers, agreed with much of what Cruise O'Brien had to say. To his colleagues in Fianna Fáil he spelt it out clearly. 'Nobody in the Fianna Fáil party who wishes to remain a member of Fianna Fáil can directly or indirectly, privately or publicly or otherwise, engage in the importation of arms into the North, go into the North and inspire activity or the use of arms by any of the groups there.'[68] Military intervention without taking cognisance of the position of the British army was simply political and military suicide.

The Minister for External Affairs, Dr Patrick Hillery, used his speech to flesh out the alternative to arming the North. He asked a simple but profound question:

> Who do we mean when we speak of 'our people' in the North ... It is not possible or desirable that one sole tradition in Irish history should make an attempt to dominate another. We saw how that failed utterly in Northern Ireland. Shall we, for our part, attempt to transfer that failure in reverse to the whole country, or shall we take the alternative and try to understand that the only solution to the Irish question is the solution that recognises the value of all our Irish traditions. Starting from this recognition we could work to bring them together peacefully.[69]

Hillery accepted the real fears expressed by the Northern Defence Committees but felt them to be exaggerated. There was an approximation to what Lynch had in fact meant by his television speech of August 1969 when he suggested that the Government could provide safeguards. These safeguards, 'which I am mentioning but not describing, are more reliable than anything which could be achieved by yielding to the demands for guns.'[70]

The illusion of action would in itself provide the buttress to stability. This recasting of the nature of republicanism found tangible expression with the intervention of George Colley, Lynch's chief rival in the 1966 leadership contest, now in effect his chief lieutenant. Colley declared that it was

> intolerable that men should try to cover with the cloak of republicanism their base aims of sectarianism and the imposition on the people of an unfree workers' socialist republic. Reunification could only occur by peaceful means, and the breaking of the connection with England was a separate matter.

He hinted at the depths of division within Fianna Fáil when he made it clear that the commitment of the Taoiseach and the Government to the non-use of force was so strong that they risked an enormous amount and placed the national importance of that policy before party affairs. They had been prepared to dissolve themselves rather than give way on principle.

Fine Gael and the Labour Party were not concerned with ideologies of republicanism or of which brand name was sacred but continued with the job of probing the weak spot in the Fianna Fáil façade: the credibility of Lynch. With their concentration on the unanswered questions in the Gibbons-Kelly dispute, any attempt by Fianna Fáil to attempt a redefinition of republicanism in the short term was doomed to failure. Recognising this, Lynch determined that any further information could not be divulged without the risk of prejudicing the case, prejudicing any possible prosecution and ultimately frustrating justice. He did, however, make three important admissions. Firstly, he again distanced Ó Móráin from the scandal by saying that he secured the written resignation of the Minister for Justice 'to dissociate him from the action I was subsequently going to take.'[71] In other words, Lynch was admitting taking over the functions of the Department of Justice for a particular reason. Secondly, he provided the opposition with a promise and his own party with an explicit threat.

> If the Attorney-General takes no action, that will not be the end of the matter. I am not afraid to give to the country what evidence I have and the information I have about this whole transaction, but not at this time.[72]

Most importantly, he told the Dáil that he was satisfied that there was no possibility that any money could have been taken out of public funds for consignments of arms of the size they were dealing with.[73]

It was clear that the new Government, which Colley defined as the most dynamic in the party's history, was determined to make a stand on the issue and did have an acute understanding of the implications of the spreading of the Northern contagion. The problem was that it was too late to stop the slide towards anarchy in Northern Ireland, a point that Lynch himself implicitly accepted. He concluded with a plaintive appeal to the forces of Northern nationalism. He rebutted the challenge of the Central Citizens' Defence Fund by arguing that making firearms available would result in

> throwing the minority to the wolves, to a state torn by strife and civil war ... I appeal to those militantly minded to pull back from this precipice and instead of pursuing this suicidal course of destruction to try to listen to the voices of moderation and tolerance so that mutual trust and understanding can lead them to take the first halting steps away from that precipice and lead them to the only future that can bring peace and happiness to this island of ours.

Following the admission by Lynch that Military Intelligence officers had been operating in the North, Ian Paisley submitted a motion to the Stormont parliament calling for arms searches in the Falls Road and the Bogside.[74] This view extended beyond the realms of evangelicalism and into the right wing of the Ulster Unionist Party. At a Unionist Party meeting in Fivemiletown, County Tyrone, John Taylor called on the Republic to 'withdraw its spies and end collusion with rioters.'[75] Here was evidence to the right wing that the civil rights movement was really just a plot. There was a need to batten down the hatches, refuse any more concessions to a rabble determined to destroy the Protestant people—the mirror image of what Blaney had termed 'our people'. The result was an increase in the already dangerous tension in the North. The efforts of Lynch, Childers and Colley to fashion a new language of republicanism had come too late. The genie was out of the bottle.

The Northern correspondent of the *Sunday Independent* noted the exasperation and the danger by declaring that

> there are more self-appointed (indeed even rejected by the voters) humbugs, theorists, rabble-rousers, publicity-seeking tub-thumpers per square mile in the Six Counties than ever before in its history. The political scene is one of confusion. The people are bewildered and alarmed. They feel like passengers in an express train from which the driver has fallen. Who can take control to prevent disaster? Is history going to record that at the critical moment in 1970 there was no leadership, just a feuding rabble too busy making ideological and party war on each other to see the national danger?[76]

The most immediate problem, however, was within Fianna Fáil. If the Attorney-General issued proceedings against the dismissed ministers, the party could split. However, if there were no charges, the ex-ministers could clearly adopt an uncompromising position and claw their way back to office on the grounds that they had been unfairly dismissed in the first place. The Attorney-General would make his decision on legal grounds alone. For the moment, therefore, the politics of the crisis was hostage to the law.

In the end, the Attorney-General issued proceedings. From the government's point of view, this at least clarified the matter. The political fallout from the decision to prosecute meant that Fianna Fáil had a chance to rid itself of the 'turbulent priests' on its ultra-national wing. Party dissidents unhappy with the decision to prosecute had enough support to topple the government but were loath to do so, not least since the prosecutions were a matter of legal process rather than political decision. The reasoning was clear. While Boland, Blaney and Haughey had significant control over the levers of party power,

Lynch's acknowledged strength—demonstrated as recently as the 1969 election—was with the electorate.[77]

On 27 May the Special Branch acted. John Kelly, who had arrived in Dublin the previous evening, was arrested as he left Captain Kelly's house in Terenure. Later that afternoon Captain Kelly himself was arrested. Albert Luykx was picked up at Dublin Airport as he arrived back from Brussels.[78] The three were charged that they had attempted, 'with persons unknown, to import weapons and ammunition into the State in a manner such as to contravene section 17 of the Firearms Act (1925) as amended by section 21 of the Firearms Act (1964) and thereby committed an offence contrary to common law.'[79]

Captain Kelly repeated that his fate was linked with that of Gibbons. As related by his solicitor, he wrote on the charge sheet: 'I plead not guilty as charged and I wish to state further that anything I did while as a serving officer I did with the knowledge and approval of the then Minister for Defence, James Gibbons.'[80]

The following morning Haughey and Blaney were arrested in their homes and held at the Bridewell for an hour before their court appearance. As the former ministers sat in a Garda cell, Kevin Boland invited the media to his house on the outskirts of the city. He accused Lynch of felon-setting, of following a Fine Gael policy in recent weeks, and of reneging on Fianna Fáil policy. In case there was any doubt about his position, he declared open war on the party leader.

> Under no circumstances would I be prepared to continue under the leadership of a man who had committed an act of unparalleled treachery against the people of the Six Counties … As far as I am concerned the Taoiseach has got to go.[81]

Boland was clear, however, that there was no need for a general election, with the uncertainty that such a campaign would produce: a palace revolution would suffice. True republicanism, he held, would not close down the option of force as a defence option. The issue needed to be debated, but only within Fianna Fáil. A special ardfheis would provide the mechanism for a 'slightly constitutional' coup.

The intervention had crucial implications, not only for the stability of the Lynch Government but more importantly for the stability of democratic rule in the Republic. By using the most extreme language in the Irish political vocabulary, the accusation of treachery, Boland raised the stakes dramatically, calling into question the potential discarding of the rule of law. As John Healy remarked with incredulity,

Boland 'has chosen very dangerous ground and is putting further into jeopardy two basic institutions—the Executive and the judiciary—while employing ideological emotionalism in the process.'[82]

The issue of the ardfheis was neatly sidestepped when the new Minister for Justice, Des O'Malley, issued a statement saying that the Attorney-General had acted according to the Constitution and that as the matter was now before the court, he was precluded from further comment. This raises an interesting question. Would the paranoia and hysteria generated by the crisis have been avoided if Lynch had used the institutional route from the beginning?

In one sense, this gets to the kernel of intra-Fianna Fáil politics. Lynch was clearly not in control of his own Government nor of the party as a whole. He simply had not got the power to jettison his ministers on his own. This explains why he did not sack them either at the private meetings on 29 April or at the Government meeting on 1 May. To a large extent, the opposition's handling of the initial crisis gave the party a reason to unify. To a large extent this is also why Haughey, Boland and Blaney voted in favour of the confidence motion at the parliamentary party meeting before Lynch addressed the Dáil. This too was the reasoning behind Boland's call for a special ardfheis. Each faction wanted control of the entire organisation, not just of part of it. And this is why there was no possibility of a Fianna Fáil split but every possibility that Lynch could lose the battle for the soul of the party.

As Boland was playing with jettisoning not only Lynch but also the independence of the judiciary, the alleged conspirators—Neil Blaney, Charles Haughey, James Kelly, John Kelly, and Albert Luykx—faced charges in the Central Criminal Court. All except John Kelly were given bail. Blaney returned to County Donegal, where, in a 'tough emotional speech' to five hundred people at a dinner of the Milford Comhairle Ceantair of Fianna Fáil in Portnablahy, he questioned the republicanism of some members of the Government.

> Don't let those who are not republican take it over for their own gain or gratification. It can happen and at no time more likely than when a party has been a long time in government. Over the years in government we attract people we would prefer to be without. It is hard to identify them until the crunch comes and then it is too late.[83]

The complex relationship between Northern and Southern politics in this volatile period is further evident from the interventions of the *Voice of the North,* which became a vital resource in the Blaney and Boland campaign. From the arrests onwards it directed its attention to discrediting the opponents of the Provisional IRA in Belfast and the opponents of Blaney and Haughey in Dublin. It made it clear that 'it was now reasonable for the Catholic minority to look elsewhere for defence given the fact that Mr Lynch has told the minority that he has washed his hands of them.' The paper saw in the arrests of Haughey and Blaney and in the interventions of Boland evidence that

> the republican flame has not been extinguished in the South ... The rank and file of [Fianna Fáil] must now decide whether or not it is a Republican party.[84]

Turning its attention northwards, *Voice of the North* declared that the 'fearless young people of Burntollet'[85] had transmuted into 'talking revolutionaries, extreme Socialists, Trotskyites, Maoists, [and] petticoat revolutionaries like Bernadette Devlin, Máirín de Búrca, Farrell, McCann etc.'[86] 'It has fought Unionism tooth and nail, it has fought communism, the Reds, it has fought the phoneys known as the Peoples Democracy.'[87] The paper maintained that it would fight against slander and vilification from whatever quarter. The main source of discontent was the *United Irishman* and the Goulding leadership in Dublin. The Provisionals were determined to make their ideological presence felt.

An indication of the Provisional IRA's growing sense of political power came on 14 June when it made its pilgrimage to Wolfe Tone's grave in Bodenstown, County Kildare, under the thinly disguised cloak of the Defence Committees. The gathering was organised by Jimmy Steele, the veteran republican who had given the first indication of a split in the movement in a Mullingar cemetery the previous summer. Ten bands took part in the parade to the cemetery. John Kelly, now released on bail, led a sizeable contingent from Belfast. Wreaths were placed on the grave by representatives from Belfast and the United States, an indication of the importance the Provisionals placed on Irish America as a source of material and ideological support.

Dáithí Ó Conaill, a senior figure in the IRA now euphemistically described as chairman of the North-West Republican Executive, gave the oration. The message was at once uncompromising and defiant. Following the burnings of the previous August, 'a grim determination arose that never again would the forces of the British crown run riot with impunity through any Irish city.' Ó Conaill castigated Lynch's suggestion that the British army could provide adequate defence as

> a most shameful abdication of responsibility ... You preach about law and order, forgetting that law is not stronger than life or man's desire to be free. You can no longer contain the spirit which arose from the ashes of Bombay Street, and you could never understand it either.[88]

The speech gave a clear sense of the Provisional IRA's agenda in the summer of 1970 and the relationship between the politics of the republican movement and of Fianna Fáil. Ruairí Ó Brádaigh argues that Fianna Fáil's interest—or that of a section within it—was purely selfish, in that it wanted to advance its political power and the power of certain individuals. For Ó Brádaigh the Arms Crisis was prompted by

> the revelation that certain elements of the establishment were working outside it. The prosecutions were an attempt to right the system.

The establishment, however, failed to take into account the fact that

> the critical decision taken by the first Provisional Army Council was when it decided on a policy of defence, defence and retaliation, then defence, retaliation, and offence. That was the really big decision.[89]

The republican movement remembered the way in which Michael Collins was galvanised by the threat of pogroms in the nineteen-twenties into temporarily providing defensive capabilities for the Belfast IRA but did not allow the conflict to destabilise the Free State. There was anger that once again the Northern question was going to be forfeited for the sake of stability in the South. The Provisional IRA was now giving notice that the new vanguard of the revolution was not prepared to allow anything to stand in the way of its objectives. To Britain the message from the Bodenstown cemetery was unambiguous:

> You sent your troops to keep what you call the peace. You forgot that peace must be based on justice and cannot be imposed by British bayonets. The more your troops impose their will, the nearer you bring the day of open and direct confrontation.[90]

For the second summer in a row, the marching season had the potential to smash the fragile construct of 1920–22. When Ó Conaill addressed the faithful in Bodenstown, unknown to most present he had secured the funds for persevering, whatever the consequences.

The internal power struggle in Fianna Fáil had served to provide the touch-paper for a more explosive conflict, one from which there would be no return for a generation.[91]

CHAPTER SIX

Northern Realities

The Rise of the Provisional IRA

British general election in June 1970 brought in a Conservative government under Edward Heath, whose minimalist approach to Northern Ireland was accompanied by an assertion, in response to Unionist demands, of the primacy of military containment as the determinant of British policy. The fear of involvement, combined with the fear of rebellion and loss of power, stymied any possibility of compromise. Despite the phased introduction of the reforms begun by Terence O'Neill and continued by James Chichester-Clark, the Northern conflict was mutating like an untreatable cancer, changing direction, unresponsive to treatment, causing rising frustration and anger in Belfast, London, and Dublin. The hope that the civil rights campaign could act as a palliative was revealed to be a chimera. The fight for equality had turned into a pivotal national cleavage, heightening sectarianism and rendering irrelevant the alternative strategy put forward by the Official IRA in the Northern arena. Britain's reliance on the military instrument completed the alienation of a nationalist minority and denied an effective political alternative to the Provisional IRA.

Behind the appearance of chaos, certain groups and individuals saw in the deterioration the possibility of historical and political advancement. For the Provisional IRA the diagnosis was disarmingly simple: if the problem was untreatable, the kindest course of action was to root out the cancer of Stormont by forcing direct rule. But first what was required was an injection of financial, military and ideological support. The United States provided the Provisional IRA with reserves of money and arms.

There was also a previously unacknowledged symbiotic relationship between the ideological power struggle at the highest levels of Fianna Fáil and the descent into chaos in Northern Ireland. It is through deconstructing the competing agendas of those outside forces, which manipulated the inherent contradictions in the Northern state during the summer of 1970, that one can trace the reasons for the rise of the Provisional IRA. This also reveals how the SDLP, formed in inauspicious circumstances in August 1970, was also in part a creature of Southern elite political infighting, designed to provide an alternative buttress.

Each faction in Fianna Fáil used the changing nature of the conflict in the North to solidify its position. With Haughey and Blaney gagged by the pending court case, Boland began a sustained but ill-considered campaign of questioning Lynch's judgment. Blaney's acquittal on 2 July came too late to save Boland, who had by then resigned from the parliamentary party and the National Executive, but it did convince the Government to give sustained consideration to Northern policy. To transform the battleground on which the militant aspirants within Fianna Fáil chose to fight, the Lynch Government fashioned an ideological response that was to create a constitutional nationalist alternative based on the reform of the Northern state, which in turn minimised the destabilisation of the Republic.

Despite the sacking of the feuding ministers, there remained considerable doubt whether the mild-mannered Taoiseach could retain power in the midst of rising tension north of the border and the simmering of an increasingly bitter recidivist ideological dispute in the Republic. Lynch may have survived the immediate crisis, but in one sense he was never so isolated. In the summer of 1970 even his staunchest supporters saw in the Northern crisis the possibility for political advancement.[1] This owed less to the personalities at work than to the implications of questioning ideological certainties at a time of turmoil.

There were considerable ironies at work. The eventual forced removal of Kevin Boland prompted the resignation from Fianna Fáil of his father, Gerry Boland, the former hard-line Minister for Justice who had allowed IRA internees during the Second World War to die on hunger strike. He had famously told the Dáil that the IRA was dead and that he had killed it. Now, for the IRA's erstwhile executioner the threat to the stability of the state—or, more accurately, to Fianna Fáil—emanated not from the subversives of the IRA but from the Taoiseach. 'If he does not want the Fianna Fáil organisation to crumble about his ears he had better go to the back benches, and the sooner the better.' By the weekend, however, the focus of change turned inexorably northwards.[2]

The heavy-handed arrest of Bernadette Devlin on the outskirts of Derry on 26 June, coupled with the refusal of Belfast Orangemen to reroute the controversial 'Tour of the North' parade, sparked serious disturbances in both cities, in which ninety-six people were injured. The contrast in the security response to the Catholic and Protestant communities tainted perceptions, reinforcing fears about the threats emanating from each and severely damaging the credibility of the British army as an impartial force. Its ultimate effect was to arrest political development; the art of compromise—never a highly prized skill in the North—was replaced with the art of the petrol bomb. It further undermined any attempt at peaceful mediation, providing evidence of the slide towards chaos charted with regularity that spring and early summer by the *Economist* and intensified after the unexpected Conservative win in the British general election.[3]

The flash-point of Hooker Street on the sectarian interface of north Belfast once again erupted. Running battles were fought into the night after a youth raised a Tricolour on a British army vehicle parked on the street to separate the crowds. With Bernadette Devlin in jail and no unified force linking the disparate ideological positions of the nationalist MPs in Stormont and Westminster, leadership in Belfast fell to Republican Labour, itself now hopelessly split on polit-ical strategy. Gerry Fitt placed the blame for the violence in Belfast on the intransigence of the Orange Order; his colleague Paddy Kennedy raised the stakes dramatically by complaining that if further Orange parades were not rerouted there was a danger of 'a holocaust that could envelop the whole of Ireland, north and south.'[4]

Dublin was not prepared to be pushed into precipitate action. In an interview with the *Sunday Independent,* Lynch chided Northern nationalism for its nihilistic propensity to engage in acts of self-fulfilling prophecy.

> The feelings of Miss Devlin's supporters at her imprisonment are under-standable, but it is sad that the expression of these feelings and the holding of Orange parades have led to further violence, suffering and even death. We hope that restraint will be exercised on both sides, even

in the face of provocation. I ask our own people in the Republic not to worsen the position in any way by word or by deed. I intend that the Government will keep in touch and deal with the situation as will best serve the interests of all the Irish people.[5]

The violence, and more importantly the arrest of Devlin, demonstrated the limitations of operating with the restraint that Lynch was now calling for. It was a measure of the Fianna Fáil Government's ideological retreat that the response offered by the leader of the opposition, Liam Cosgrave, revealed a much harder policy rationale. Cosgrave demanded an immediate ban on all parades.

> The violence associated with such outbreaks are consequences of the partition of the country. Until this national evil is ended such terrible events will recur.[6]

On the night of 27 June an incident occurred that was to have profound implications and to change irrevocably the strategic balance of forces within Northern nationalism. As rioting engulfed most of nationalist Belfast, the enclave of the Short Strand in the east of the city was exposed. The Short Strand, in the shadow of the Harland and Wolff shipyard, had long been vulnerable to attack when sectarian passions ignited; some of the worst violence associated with the 1920–22 pogroms was visited on the area. Once again it was to pay the price of sectarian demography. St Matthew's Church in Bryson Street, off the Newtownards Road, came under sustained attack after the death of three Protestants in Ardoyne prompted retaliation in east Belfast. The British army, though present, did not intervene. Apparently defenceless, the local community sent out an appeal to the Provisional IRA.[7] In the ensuing gun battle, which raged for more than five hours, three people were killed, including one IRA man.

In the aftermath of the violence the Catholic workers in the shipyard were expelled. As they trudged through the rubble of the Short Strand it was a scene, for the Catholic community, redolent of the nineteen-twenties. The fact that British soldiers were deployed on the streets and were unable to prevent the violence served only to heighten the sense of desperation—though little attention was given in republican accounts, then or since, to the fact that it was the attack on Ardoyne that provoked the attack on the church: if they were defenders, they had also helped create the atmosphere within which defence was needed.

The battle was critical for the credibility of the Provisional leadership: it not only demonstrated to sceptical nationalists the inability of the British army to provide adequate defence but outlined the possibility of an alternative to the politics of cowed oppression, an alternative that met fire with fire.[8] From the defence of St Matthew's onwards there was to be no turning back. The Provisional IRA had carved out a niche for itself; it had proved its capacity to defend Catholic areas from attack. Its authority was augmented by the introduction of a parallel policing service in nationalist ghettos as disenchantment with the RUC and British army intensified. The question was, could anybody intervene to damp down passions?

In Dublin the upsurge in Northern tension contributed to the steady erosion of Lynch's credibility. The Government was being buffeted from without and from within. The opposition parties demanded a full debate on the crisis in the North, a demand that Lynch rejected, saying that this could serve to exacerbate the situation. He was in effect curtailing the role of the Dáil in order to prevent the very real divisions within his own party from being exposed. As John Healy remarked in the *Irish Times,* 'he certainly acted more like a prisoner than a leader.'[9]

That essential difficulty was magnified when all charges against Neil Blaney were dropped the following day. District Justice Dónal Kearney determined that there was not enough evidence linking the former minister to the specific charge of conspiring to import weapons between 1 March and 24 April. Blaney, 'overcome with emotion' according to the *Irish Times,* was carried shoulder-high from the court; he then made a highly charged visit to Leinster House, accompanied by John Kelly, James Kelly, and Albert Luykx, with Séamus Brady meeting them at the entrance—the politician who had, more than any other, been responsible for the entire Arms Crisis, surrounded by the foot soldiers who would bear the responsibility.

Blaney brushed aside questions about his involvement in fomenting a crisis by saying that the importing of arms 'is something that is not relevant to me and certainly not one that I am prepared to discuss.'[10] He declared: 'I am Fianna Fáil, I always have been Fianna Fáil and will continue to be so.'

There is little doubt that the failure of the attempt to prosecute Blaney posed serious problems for the Government. One of the most powerful politicians in Fianna Fáil had been cleared in the courts of 'the slightest suspicion of wrong-doing,' which after all had been the reason behind the sacking in May. Any repeat of the St Matthew's incident, especially in the period leading up to the Twelfth of July demonstrations, had the potential to be used as a retrospective justification for the hard line adopted by Blaney before his dismissal. He immediately went on the offensive, stating that, while vindicated personally, he remained concerned about Northern developments.

> It is just as I predicted. I have the greatest fears for the people of the North from now until the twelfth of July.[11]

He repeated his long-standing view that the only solution lay in the British accepting responsibility for

> the whole sorry spectacle of fifty years of partitionist failure. They must sit down and negotiate a new deal for a united Ireland.[12]

Blaney's position was significantly strengthened by the heavy-handed reliance by the new British government on strategic imperatives set by the military. The new Home Secretary, Reginald Maudling, arrived in Belfast for his first visit, appearing to give the clearance for adopting such a purely military approach. The officer commanding British forces, General Freeland, had just announced that in the future, rioters faced the prospect of being shot on sight. On 1 July the Criminal Justice (Temporary Provisions) Bill was rushed through the Northern Ireland Parliament, bringing in a mandatory six-month minimum prison term for rioting.[13] Far from questioning the wisdom of such a strategy, Maudling declared that internment, the principal demand of the hard-liners in the Unionist Party, could yet be necessary. 'No government—and this does not reflect any change in policy—could rule out unconditionally and in advance the impartial use of this or similar powers in so far as they may be necessary for the protection of life and limb.'[14] In effect, London was acceding to the Unionist analysis that the only solution to the conflict was to be found in the stringent application of draconian law-and-order policies.

The imbalance in British strategy, designed, as Henry Patterson acidly notes, as an expedient 'to keep the British out of the bog of Irish politics, contributed powerfully to an upsurge in militant republicanism.'[15] It was to be the Provisional IRA that reaped the benefit of this polarisation of sectarian divisions, which served only to enhance their self-declared role as the only true defenders of the Catholic community. The political vacuum in nationalist politics on both sides of the border provided the Provisionals with an almost tailor-made capability to expand their influence far beyond the dreams of the Marxists in Dublin or the nightmares of those caught within the republican ghetto.[16] Nowhere was this more apparent than in west Belfast during the first weekend of July.

Acting on information about a cache of arms hidden in a house in the Lower Falls area, the British army began a crackdown on 3 July. A helicopter descended almost to rooftop level and a voice announced that the area was under curfew, and that anyone on the streets after the warning would be shot.[17] Serious rioting ensued as the military closed off the area for thirty-six hours. According to one account, Jim Sullivan, a leader of the Official IRA, ordered his men not to react and accepted the loss of whatever weapons the British army might discover. Official IRA sources, quoted by Bishop and Mallie, suggest that the Provisional IRA deliberately fuelled the violence by throwing grenades at the advancing British soldiers.[18] Either way, the Falls curfew was a significant turning-point.

The spectre of a nationalist community under siege brought the return of rallies outside the GPO in Dublin. Seán Keenan whipped up the crowd by calling for

> recruits to go where the fighting is. I come here tonight to call for unity, unity to drive the British Army out of the Six Counties for all time.[19]

That call was not restricted to the extremes of militant republicanism. In his memoirs, Paddy Devlin regards the Falls curfew as decisive in forcing a realignment of nationalist politics.

> Overnight the population turned from neutral or even sympathetic support for the military to outright hatred of everything related to the security forces. As the self-styled generals and godfathers took over in the face of this regime, Gerry Fitt and I witnessed voters in the Docks and Falls constituencies turn against us and join the Provisionals.[20]

What Devlin omits to mention, however, is that his own actions at the height of the curfew, in broadcasting an appeal for weapons, was indicative of the lack of political leadership that necessitated the creation of the SDLP in the first place. At the height of the curfew he was interviewed for the RTE programme 'This Week'. He was under no illusion about what was required:

> If the Catholic people are going to be treated in the way they have been treated at the present time, if this is going to continue, I think he [Jack Lynch] should be doing something more positive, and I'm not talking

about words … I don't want to spell that out any more. You can't be all that silly that you don't understand what I'm saying to you.[21]

At the end of the Falls curfew the British army allowed two Unionist ministers, William Long and John Brooke, to tour the area in an armoured car, a crass and unnecessary humiliation that served only to act as a recruiting focus for militant republicanism. The defence of St Matthew's and the alienation fashioned by what was seen as the heavy-handed pacification of the Falls allowed the Provisionals to move to Mac Stíofáin's second stage of 'combined defence and retaliation.'[22] The very tactical skill of the British response led to an escalation of provocation at a stroke, turning the civil rights grievances of the Catholics into a nationalist fight.[23] The keen tactics of the British thus encouraged the IRA to move from a defensive to an offensive campaign.[24] With Keenan's call to arms in Dublin, the absence of a unified opposition within Northern nationalism, and Blaney's open challenge as a vindicated patriot to the Fianna Fáil leadership from a substantially strengthened position—in narrowly defined legal terms—the situation was spiralling out of control.

Cathal Goulding was furious at the turn of events. A statement from his IRA Army Council condemned those responsible for introducing guns into the equation, whatever the provocation. The attack on St Matthew's was

> a vicious battle of Catholics against Protestants, which merits just as much condemnation as previous pogroms of Protestants against Catholics. The hatred and bitterness engendered by the killing of six Protestant civilians can only increase the likelihood of further pogroms in the future.

The statement concluded with a blunt rejection of the policies of the Provisionals. 'You cannot claim to love your country and its people and to lead a national independence movement if you are motivated by bigotry and have as your objective, or your means, the fomenting of civil war.'[25]

Dublin was under increasing pressure to act as a guarantor for the Northern minority.[26] When asked on RTE whether he would intervene, the Minister for External Affairs, Patrick Hillery, floated in a non-committal way the possibility of going northwards.[27] The following morning the minister, accompanied by a young diplomat, travelled to the Falls Road, where he met community leaders, including, incongruously, Aidan Corrigan, who had replaced Séamus Brady as editor of the

Voice of the North. In a press conference hastily arranged on his return to Dublin, Hillery declared that in his estimation people didn't want guns: they wanted 'intense diplomatic activity.'[28] There was recognition, however, of the slide towards anarchy with his comment that the community 'no longer regard the British army as their protectors.'[29]

The BBC programme 'Panorama' broadcast interviews with Hillery and Chichester-Clark; but the programme was considered so sensitive that

> the BBC feels that there is a danger that part of tonight's programme, if seen in Ulster, might serve not simply to inform but to inflame. The BBC has therefore decided that, in this particular case, 'Panorama' should not be transmitted in Northern Ireland.[30]

The programme made explicit the assessment that the fate of both parts of Ireland was linked. This was underlined by the contribution of Conor Cruise O'Brien, who argued that the Fianna Fáil Government itself had to bear some of the responsibility for the present turmoil, tracing its culpability to the failure to sack Blaney after his Letterkenny speech on 8 December 1969. 'We believe that the Lynch-Haughey-Blaney-Boland Government, which has now been dissolved, broken up and been succeeded by another Lynch Government—that that Government has a heavy responsibility for the tragic events which have followed.'[31]

The programme's importance rests not only on its graphic depiction of the polarisation of Northern attitudes but also on its demonstration that as a direct consequence of that polarisation, moderates had to adopt hard-line positions in order to retain potency in their own constituencies, which served only to deepen the polarisation. Hillery was careful in his interview to present a hard image. He talked of how the Falls Road area had been 'savagely attacked by the armed mobs the previous year, led by B Specials and police, burnt out, people killed.' He suggested that although weapons were found they were mainly antiquated.

> You can take it that these arms were there because of last year's savage attack on them. They were to protect themselves, so they are no longer protected.[32]

Hillery maintained that despite provocation, diplomatic pressure was the only viable means of achieving stability.

> No-one is entitled to take any action based on the assumption that our method has failed. We're doing it the way it can be effective and,

certainly, I think that the British government—the British people—will have to soon and adequately reassure the minority in the North that they're not being exposed to their enemies, that they're not being attacked by the forces of law and order.

The instability in the South, he declared, was a direct result

of the way in which the North has been handled. If it were being handled in a modern way by a modern government, then Mr Lynch would have no problems of leadership.[33]

He left little room for Northern compromise with his assertion that Chichester-Clark 'is totally wrong to think that in the modern world you can with force of arms, force of British money, keep a state there which is quite unusual and depends on tyranny at times.' Hillery was demanding not only an end to marching but also reunification.

You'll always find trouble in Ireland until we have our final re-unification. We're quite prepared to examine any kind of reunification: we don't want to impose any one culture on another.[34]

According to the presenter, Robin Day, it was an incredible intervention. Not only was Hillery giving the Irish Government's point of view but he was 'bluntly telling the British Government what to do in handling the internal situation in Northern Ireland, which is part of the United Kingdom.'[35] In essence, the message from Dublin was that if the British government and the Unionist government did not stand up to the Orange Order, it would do it for them before republicans forced their hand.[36]

Following the refusal of Orange leaders to accede to requests from Maudling to call off or curtail their parades, there was recognition and, indeed, sympathy for Lynch. Typical was the position of the *Economist,* with its argument that the Taoiseach had to be seen to be doing something 'mildly dramatic before Orange Day to stave off his own eclipse by the restless men of Fianna Fáil.'[37] Lynch, determined to show the advantage of the Hillery visit, declared in the Dáil that it was part of an initiative for peace. He apologised for the lack of 'diplomatic niceties' but felt that the circumstances on the Falls Road, with the people apprehensive and fearful, necessitated leadership from Dublin.

People in fear will turn almost anywhere for help. It is vitally important that this fear be not exploited by subversive elements for their own ends.

If a situation developed in which such people would turn to subversive elements there would be a very grave threat to peace and security not only in the Falls but in the Six Counties as a whole and possibly in the rest of the country.[38]

This was an overt change in strategy and represents the most important consequence of the Falls curfew in Southern elite politics. Lynch was in effect declaring war on the Provisional IRA, which, more than any other group, had now the potential to threaten the fragile peace, and his own Government. The most important contact in this repositioning was to be John Hume, who was increasingly alarmed about the drift towards the Provisionals in Belfast. A schoolteacher with a master's degree from Maynooth, he had cultivated contacts with the Department of External Affairs in Dublin. As early as 15 February 1970 he had had a secret meeting with Éamonn Gallagher, a senior official in the Department of External Affairs, at which plans for the creation of a new political party in the North were discussed. Gallagher reported to the Department of the Taoiseach:

> Mr Hume informed me in strict confidence yesterday that plans are going ahead for the creation of a new Opposition party in the Six Counties. The founding members are the three Independent MPs (Hume, Cooper and O'Hanlon), Mr Gerry Fitt (Republican Labour), Mr Austin Currie (Nationalist) and Mr Paddy Devlin (Northern Ireland Labour Party). If this succeeds it will be a most important political development as a coalition including Hume, Fitt and Currie will be very strong indeed and should eventually attract other Opposition MPs.[39]

The prime motivating factor for the new party, according to Hume, was the failure of NICRA to dissociate itself from the National Association for Irish Justice, Brian Heron's Marxist group in the United States. 'NICRA is now in the hands of extreme republicans and some extreme left wingers and the moderates are likely to get out of it.' It was evidence of the importance of the ideological debate in the United States, evidence too of how the initiative was passing into the hands of republicans, both 'green' and 'red' variants.

Hume's standing gradually rose as he sought to unify the divided opposition into a coherent force, which could provide a viable alternative to the military strategy envisaged by the Provisionals. When interviewed by the BBC he was presented as the most moderate man in the North. In setting up a political stall that was to become the hallmark of SDLP policy, Hume proclaimed that there was no alternative to the twin goals of fundamental reform and full representation within parliamentary structures inside the borders of Northern Ireland.

> On the one side, what use is one-man-one-vote if you are not there to exercise it? And on the other side, what's the use of maintaining a situation of privilege and power over a desert? The price of no solution is total destruction.[40]

What is interesting about Hume's intervention is that it offered a possible retreat from mutually assured destruction. It was a retreat that Lynch grasped as he began to fashion a new response to the Northern question, an approach that was to lead to Hume's eventual domination of Northern nationalist politics. The Hume approach, enunciated in the BBC programme 'Panorama', required the concerted co-operation of London, Dublin, and Northern nationalism. That was not achievable in July 1970, as most of the protagonists were locked into escalation positions—a fact recognised by Hume, who, despite his relatively hopeful long-term assessment, stressed the credibility gap associated with Maudling's handling of the brief. (In his visit, Maudling spent only forty-five minutes with opposition MPs.[41])

In Northern Ireland the very survival of the Protestant identity was pitted against a resurgent militant republicanism; in the Republic, logic dictated that only a retreat to fundamentalist concepts could retain potency. It was to be in America that that potency received material expression. Following the final failure of the arms shipments from the Continent, the leadership of the Provisional IRA decided to reactivate the contacts opened up by John Kelly and Seán Keenan in the winter of 1969. A network was quickly established that was to provide the Provisional IRA with the material for launching the most sustained guerrilla campaign since the end of the Second World War. Keenan and Ó Conaill were despatched to New York not only to organise arms shipments but also to establish a propaganda operation, the Northern Aid Committee. Under the trusteeship of Keenan and Jimmy Steele,[42] the day to-day-operations of Northern Aid were under the control of Mick Flannery, John McGowan, and Jack McCarthy. The founding principles were published in the July issue of *An Phoblacht,* an indication that the battle for Irish-American support had by then been won.

1. Provide financial assistance to the local defence committees who maintain the Defence Patrols that protect innocent people from the violence of British imperialism.

2. To alleviate the hardships of people who have lost their jobs and those who cannot take up employment or collect welfare benefits because of fear of arrest or being shot by sectarian extremists.

3. To assist persons who have lost their homes.

4. To provide assistance for persons imprisoned for defending their homes from attack.

5. To provide funds for defensive measures including first aid services.[43]

These principles give an insight into how the message was propagated in America. They present those prepared to take up arms as morally justified and are wide-ranging enough without explicitly condoning any act of armed violence from the IRA. Nor is there any mention of socialism. Northern Aid was specifically designed to act as an umbrella group, appealing to the broad range of Irish-American opinion. According to the civil rights lawyer Frank Durkan, such a development was necessary, as propaganda was almost impossible to overcome. Action in the North did not generate the kind of response that should have been expected.

> You are talking about a minuscule portion of the Irish-American community. There was a dearth of real information coming out, and as a result Irish-Americans, even those who would have been favourable towards the nationalist side of the North, were confused. There was such a wave of propaganda slanted against what was happening in the North, blaming everything on the IRA, as if there was no other cause for the violence.[44]

Throughout the spring and early summer of 1970 the Provisional leadership maintained to American audiences that its sole priority remained the defence of vulnerable Catholic areas. The possibilities of mass mobilisation offered by the realignment of the nineteen-sixties were ignored or played down to reassure sceptics, particularly in America, that no 'alien philosophy' would replace unity as the cardinal principle of the IRA. The first issue of *An Phoblacht* made it clear that the movement's goal was a unified Ireland first and foremost. The decision to use Cathal Brugha and Patrick Pearse, the most militarist of the revolutionary generation, as its chief iconic figureheads served to reinforce not only the Provisional IRA's primarily military emphasis but also to challenge the political cul-de-sac into which the preoccupation with socialism had led Sinn Féin. The Provisional Army Council issued a statement declaring in no uncertain terms that a military confrontation was both inevitable and necessary. 'We will erect the Irish Republic again in all its glory no matter what it costs and like Pearse, we know of no way which freedom can be obtained, maintained, except by armed men.'[45]

To this end the leadership of the Provisional IRA regarded it as of supreme importance to use political violence in the North to create the conditions for fundamental change. From the beginning this policy had a clear objective: the introduction of direct rule. As *An Phoblacht* explained,

> the abolition of Stormont would, as an interim measure be a step forward. It would make much easier the achievement of full rights and would bring us into direct confrontation with Westminster.[46]

Despite its elevation of the military instrument to the position of primary strategy, it would be a mistake to regard the Provisional IRA as an unthinking, anti-socialist movement. For Mac Stiofáin it was a question of changing the speech to suit the occasion, particularly when addressing conservative American audiences.[47] While it was true that many of the leading Northerners had little time for the socialist departure, others, including Ó Conaill and Ó Brádaigh, remained committed to using mass mobilisation to break out of the political isolation that a retreat to traditional methods by itself would necessarily entail. Indeed, early issues of *An Phoblacht* regularly proclaimed the value of the co-operative movement and of the importance of mass mobilisation. But there was a belief that unless there was recourse to a 'final confrontation with the forces of English imperialism and neo-colonialism,' the ultimate objective of national independence could not be achieved.[48]

It was to be this primary emphasis on Northern defence, coupled with a clearly defined short-term military strategy to create achievable political goals, that ultimately provided for the success of the Provisional IRA in Belfast in the summer of 1970. The commitment to the use of armed force to further the revolution gave the Provisionals added relevance to American activists, including those on the left.

The role played by George Harrison in organising arms shipments typifies the uneasy compromise at the heart of the Provisional movement. Harrison, once the most important link in the American connection, now lives in retirement in New York. The struggle against capitalism, neo-colonialism, McCarthyism and discrimination finds expression in the portraits and posters on the walls, in the book-cases filled with the works of Fidel Castro, published by the People's

Press in Moscow. Harrison's apartment is a monument to a lifetime of political activism, to the twin abiding passions in his life: Castro and Cuba, the IRA and the unfinished Irish revolution.

His decision to withhold support for the present peace process on the grounds that the Provisionals have betrayed the revolution gives an important clue to why Harrison supported them in 1970. While fervently left-wing in his personal politics, he was not prepared to countenance any sacrifice on essential principles. For the same reason his support for Castro against the 'inhumanity of the American trade embargo' remains constant.

Born in 1915, Harrison has not set foot in Ireland since 1938. His earliest memories are of the IRA prisoners released from internment camps after the Civil War. De Valera's Ireland was a betrayal.

> I viewed Dev as having betrayed everything he ever stood for, who had called the men out to fight and who had admitted the IRA were historically correct. He committed a blatant betrayal, and that is the way I still feel today.[49]

Harrison's involvement with the labour movement brought him into contact with Michael Quill and Paul O'Dwyer, prominent figures in the Irish-American community. Together with members of the Communist Party of the United States, their emphasis was as much on changing American domestic polity as on continuing the Irish revolution.

> It was not easy. There was a right-wing and racist element in the Irish community. I recall hoodlums called Christian Front, and their target at that time was Jewish people—to hang all Jewish people from lampposts—and I remember Paul O'Dwyer coming out and opposing them.

Harrison's career as a gun-runner began in 1953 through contacts arranged in the labour movement. Told in advance of the decision to relaunch the 'armed struggle' in December 1956, he viewed it as a

> resurrection of the spirit. We handled all communication in New York, we had left-wing contacts who ran off a few thousand copies, good mailing lists, and got the statement to all the United Nations delegations, which mortified the FBI.

Quill donated $6,000, ostensibly for the relief of prisoners but in reality for arms shipments. As the campaign petered out, Harrison saw once again the dead hand of de Valera.

He did everything he could to discredit the republic. Once he changed from being a republican to a Free Stater he was pretty consistent, a vicious hunter of his own comrades, just like Gerry Boland. Once people change they go galloping in the opposite direction. That is my experience in unions: if they change they leave you standing high and dry.

Harrison was unimpressed by the logic of the Goulding leadership's disavowal of armed struggle and received the cold shoulder when Goulding visited America. He kept in contact, however, with the Tyrone-born republican Eoin McNamee, a man Harrison refers to as the 'Emissary'. After the violence associated with the People's Democracy march at Burntollet he turned over any equipment he had to McNamee, and his first shipment was despatched to those who would make up the Provisional IRA.

Eoin said, 'Is there any tie-up?' I said, 'No, it is yours.' Sixty weapons, sixty to seventy thousand rounds of ammunition, as far as I can recall. The weapons were flown in and used for local defence. I knew it got there because a long time later Billy McKee said to me, 'You saved the day, because we had just about nothing.'

Though he did not meet Kelly and Keenan in November 1969, Harrison was friendly with Michael Flannery, who informed him of the split in the movement in December 1969. Despite his left-wing leanings, Harrison was in no doubt about who represented the true movement and immediately sided with the Provisionals, despite misgivings about the involvement of Blaney in arranging the financing of the visit.

I was aware of the visit [by Kelly and Keenan] through the Emissary. In later years Seán Keenan stayed with me. They were here to mobilise support, I guess. They got big crowds, and that was one reason that I stayed in the background. I believe that they met Paul [O'Dwyer]. I was very sceptical that Fianna Fáil would deliver; in a united Ireland they would not be top dog.

Along with others, Harrison was to provide the Provisionals with their most important supply of weapons. 'My reaction was to get as many weapons as possible—publicise it, but get as many weapons as possible.' But he remained on the periphery of Irish-American fund-raising activities.

For twenty-five years Harrison remained a loyal supporter of the Provisional IRA, until it too abandoned the principle of abstention.

They are revisionists within the Provisionals. They want to make this total. They are very concerned that there will be a nucleus left to pass on the message. They are very concerned that that will not happen. They want this to be the final campaign. We spent all our life trying to get out to break the connection with the empire of hell. People I worked with didn't die, didn't devote their lives to a reformed Stormont: they devoted their life to the establishment of a 32-county socialist republic, and that remains our goal. It seems we are the legion of the rearguard, but sooner or later we will be the vanguard again. If not us, then generations yet unborn.[50]

In 1970 Harrison believed in the promises put forward by Dáithí Ó Conaill that there would be no compromise on the destruction of the Northern state.

Dáithí told that he was setting up an organisation here to contribute to all the needs [of the Provisional IRA] and then asked where did we fit in. I told him if we were going to do what we wanted to do and be helpful then the thing to do was not to join Northern Aid, and he could see that point. Then he said we probably have other people working for us. I said I have no problem with that.[51]

Like McNamee, Harrison's commitment to Marxism sits uneasily with the decision to go with the Provisionals. It can be explained only by his personal commitment to the fundamentalist ideals of the unfinished revolution, ideals that the Provisional IRA was keen to stress from its inception.[52] Reflecting now, he argues that the problem rests on the fact that those who 'betrayed' the Provisional movement were interlopers from the beginning.

I guess you could date it back to some of the people who broke with the Officials in 1969 did not break for the right reasons. I don't think they broke on account of the drift towards Leinster House towards revisionism: I think some of them broke because it was the popular thing to do at that particular time.[53]

Viewed from such a purist ideological position, the policies of the Official IRA in July 1970 were as dangerous as fanciful and could not be tolerated. Goulding's support for a national liberation front emphasised the need to organise fraternal links across the barricades. Tomás Mac Giolla noted with some satisfaction that dialogue had begun between representatives from the Lower Falls and the Shankill; its impact was somewhat diminished when he revealed that so far it was only at the level of correspondence.[54]

The steps of the GPO were again used to warn of the danger of a return to the politics of the gun. The general secretary of Sinn Féin, Máirín de Búrca, counselled those present of the imminent return of the bomb and the bullet to 26-County politics. This would not occur through possible sectarian conflagration in the North but the passing through the Dáil of the Forcible Entry and Occupation Bill. Such a development, she said, once it came into law would mean 'no landlord's house, business, livelihood or life will be very safe.'[55] This was a reference to the Goulding wing's involvement in the squatting campaign of Dublin Housing Action Committee. The difficulty for the Officials was that this campaign and the use of military rhetoric to support it seemed an incongruous distraction when the North was exploding.

Two days later, as the massed ranks of the Orange Order marched through the streets of Northern Ireland in the midst of threats of civil war, the vanguard of the revolution was organising the occupation of Archbishop John Charles McQuaid's private garden in Merrion Square, Dublin, demanding its opening as a people's park. In such a febrile atmosphere, embarrassing the Catholic archbishop when his co-religionists faced real—if manufactured—danger served only to emphasise the irrelevance of the Officials to the realities of the situation in the only theatre that mattered for the IRA.

Dismissed by the Belfast Official leader, Jim Sullivan, as 'a collection of Glasgow Celtic supporters, backward nationalists, people on the make, and general ne'er-do-wells,'[56] the Provisionals were proving more relevant to a community that now found itself isolated and frightened. The ideological dispute was accompanied by an upsurge in violent confrontations between the two wings, originating in the sale of rival newspapers[57] and intensifying into accusations that the Provisionals set up the Officials over the Falls confrontation. The attack on St Matthew's Church and the very fact that the Provisionals took the credit for challenging the British action in the Falls reinforced their domination, not just in Belfast but, crucially, in America. That they had the tacit support of a significant section of Fianna Fáil made them even more dangerous and in the Northern arena more powerful, though that support was viewed as a liability by many of the Southern leadership.

An indication of this division was apparent in a special issue of *An Phoblacht* published in the immediate aftermath of the Falls curfew, which warned of the dangers of any association with Fianna Fáil.

We must beware of political adventurers like Blaney and Boland who would use the peoples struggle in the Six Counties to advance their own positions in Fianna Fáil. These are the political allies of Big Business, both foreign and native. A right-wing dictatorship like the Greek Colonels is not the end we see to Ireland's struggle.[58]

With tension running at dangerously high levels, Jack Lynch once again made the journey to the RTE studios to make a television address, drawing together the themes of the week. He outlined for the first time a new Northern policy, which was to begin the long process of changing the discourse of Irish nationalism.

The Irish poet John Montague from County Tyrone says: 'Old moulds are broken in the North.' We stand on the brink of a great achievement. There are those who would stop us—on both sides of the border. I speak to them first. I say to them that on this island there is no solution to be found to our disagreements by shooting each other. There is no real invader here. We are all Irish in all our different kinds of ways. We must not now or ever in the future show anything to each other except tolerance, forbearance—and neighbourly love.

I speak now to the Irish people, north and south, Protestant, Presbyterian, Catholic—and simply Irish. This whole unhappy situation is an Irish quarrel. I admit that others come into it, either because they misunderstand it or because they misuse it—but they are not an essential part of it. We must settle this quarrel among us.

I ask the Irish people of the majority tradition to recognise the truth of what I have just said. Let us not appeal to past gods as if past generations had said the last word about Ireland. We have our opportunity to say for our generation what is in our hearts and minds. I think that there is in us an instinct for good, for enjoyment, for beauty, and above all, for peace with our neighbours.

At the moment I speak to you I do not know whether the scheduled parades will take place in the North on Monday. But if they do, let me ask you to ignore those few who march to provoke you. For theirs is a mistake. If they must do this kind of thing, let you not yourselves prevent them—because one day they will know it is a wrong thing to do and stop themselves.

I now speak to the other great tradition in Ireland and in our history—that of the majority in the North. We have had invasions piled upon invasions. Danes, Normans, English, Scots, followed into Ireland our earlier migration and became part of our soil, of our blood and bone, of the green fields we cultivate.

Yours was our latest migration.

But some men, in their interests, which are not Irish interests, have kept us apart and have continued an unnecessary quarrel until today. Do you mistrust yourselves so much as to refuse to see that your home is here—not across any waters?

Since the Irish state was founded fifty years ago, my predecessors and I have said again and again that we have no wish to confront you or destroy you. Indeed, we think that a branch has been broken from the Irish tree.

If a few of you are so misled as to go on brandishing a domination over your nearest neighbours, no words of mine can stop you. But the world will not respect you. Do not be persuaded to sully your own great tradition. All Irish traditions are intertwined; let us cherish them all.

I now speak to the British government and people. Through the Minister for External Affairs my Government has done all humanely possible to prevent what your Home Secretary thinks might lead to bloodshed. Why should we, the Celts and the English, go on misunderstanding each other? There is no imperial role for you in Ireland. We have fought the good fight against each other. Neither of us should claim victory, because that is never the best result. Is it not better that we should both claim, as civilised peoples, the capacity to settle the last remaining disagreement between us by peaceful means?

In this affair I am committed to two things which I value deeply.

The first is my commitment to the idea that the most difficult problems can be solved peacefully if good will is first achieved—and ulterior motives are eliminated. Therefore, I will state my aim. It is that Ireland should be united. In this there is a motive, so I will state that too. It is that in this island there shall never again be fear, turning to hatred, turning to bloodshed.

My second commitment is to Anglo-Irish friendship. Our two governments have surmounted many difficulties to establish a unique relationship. Our peoples know and like each other. The Irish quarrel, in which your government has a responsibility, must not go on coming between us.

Dr Hillery has stated to the world press in the past few days the Irish Government's case. In their response—while I place no burden on them—I feel that they have become, in a sense, a protector of Northern Ireland from its own passions. Just grievances must be redressed. All the world is there to see where the failure lies.

There is no military means of preventing people determined on destruction from living out their disaster. This is not a job for soldiers.

And let me say on this that I much regret the injuries suffered by British soldiers during the course of the duties imposed on them in the North of Ireland; these young British boys find themselves in a position which must to them seem inexplicable.

It is for political leaders to govern wisely and justly. I accept the guarantees of the British government that they will do so. My Government is the second guarantor. Therefore, you who have suffered distress and indignity in the North are no longer unprotected victims. It is not in your interest to interfere, in any way, with any Orange parade. I ask you not to do so.[59]

The speech performed a number of crucial functions. It marked the beginning of the formal retraction of the nation to the state, and its implication that the problem was confined to Ireland abrogated British responsibility. It marked a staggering rejection of traditional formulations of Irish nationalism, more so because it was being made by the leader of Fianna Fáil.[60]

More telling was the fact that the speech was made on television rather than read into the record of Dáil Éireann, a further indication of the depth of division within the party, representing another downgrading of accountable government. For weeks before the speech, Lynch refused to offer his opponents in Fianna Fáil an opportunity to undermine his standing. Now he was speaking directly to the nation. As Conor Cruise O'Brien remarked with characteristic derision, it debased conceptions of a functioning democracy.

> What good is a parliament that the Taoiseach does not trust to discuss a matter of vital national importance, a parliament that has to be bypassed in the national interest? ... In effect, the Taoiseach is here asking for a personal popular vote of confidence at the expense of parliament, and his close associates are encouraged to proceed in the same way.[61]

The *Irish Times* believed that 'it was a great pity that the speech was not made many years ago; for if it had [been], the sounds now issuing from the unionists must have been different.' Nevertheless, it was now clear 'that the old game was up ... The problem of Ireland and of the relationship of the island to Britain can be looked at only in concert— that London, Dublin and Belfast must all be in on any major decision from now on.'[62] But first Lynch needed ideological support in the North. That was to be provided by recapturing the political initiative within Northern nationalism, nurturing those prepared to work within the system.

Reaction within constitutional nationalism was broadly in favour, an indication that there had been some consultation in advance. Gerry Fitt declared the speech 'a bloody good one,' in which Lynch 'has attempted to establish some dialogue with the Protestant majority, and it can no nothing but good, especially under present circumstances.'[63] Even Paddy Devlin, while he was critical of the failure to articulate the fear that Conservative policy was 'to draw on a Catholic backlash,' welcomed the broad thrust of the speech.[64]

The implication in Lynch's speech that the threat of violence came from nationalist extremists served to strengthen the resolve of those not prepared to reach a compromise either within Northern Ireland or in a broader Anglo-Irish arena. At the traditional Orange demonstrations throughout Northern Ireland the mood was much bleaker, with the order making a pointed decision not to include the traditional resolution of loyalty to the Stormont government or its ministers. Harry West, the hard-line MP, now positioning himself on the right of the party, told the demonstration that 'we must not—we dare not—allow any interference with this, the spinal cord of unionism.' For West, opposition to Orange parades was part of a calculated plot to destroy the Union.

> Today we have a softly-softly policy that has proved disastrous, no-go areas in two of our principal cities, and with self-appointed defence forces, no Specials and no-nothing policy in our government. All this, together with the threat of an armed insurrection from the Republic, presents a very great threat to our country.

Ulster required a 'strong-armed security force under the control of the Northern Ireland government and under the command of an Ulsterman.'[65]

Lynch continued with attempts to reduce the tension and to show that his diplomatic approach was gaining momentum. As Chichester-Clark travelled to London with his Minister of Home Affairs on 17 July, an interview given to the *Belfast Telegraph* was published alongside briefings to political correspondents. Lynch used the briefings to demand that the British government move further and faster in the implementation of reforms that would be of meaning to the ordinary Catholic. 'I do not doubt the guarantees of the British government, but could not the Northern Ireland government be induced to step up the pace of reform and reorganise the community in a manner proper to a modern society?' He argued that while decent

Orangemen believed they were members of a benevolent society, in reality the parades were demonstrations of arrogance and bigotry. If the Falls Road was to be raided, then east Belfast should as well. British soldiers should not be used to protect bigotry.[66]

The bitter irony for Lynch was that in shoring up his own position he was further weakening that of his opposite number in Stormont, thus setting in motion a chain reaction that destroyed the fragile equilibrium he so desperately wanted to uphold. The net effect was to further reduce Chichester-Clark's room for manoeuvre. He had already made this clear in the immediate aftermath of the Falls curfew when he plaintively exclaimed that he 'would not be prepared to hold any talks with Dublin, on any terms of any kind.'[67] The Irish Government's assertion of its self-proclaimed role as the second guarantor for the implementation of reform served to weaken still further the ability of the Northern Ireland government to compromise.

The Stormont government's decision on 23 July, under sustained pressure from London, to ban all public processions for six months was regarded in Dublin as having the potential to change the balance of forces in favour of the centre. Lynch commended the decision to the Dáil on 28 July, saying he considered it 'a most significant advance in community relations in the North.' The disarming of the RUC and the disbanding of the B Specials, to which Lynch obliquely referred as 'an armed militia virtually outside the control of higher authority,' were useful and important reforms; when they were considered in conjunction with the implementation of further reform, including the creation of a Department of Community Relations and the implementation of a Prevention of Incitement to Hatred Act, the stage was set for equal treatment. Lynch considered it imperative that 'we shall not have a repetition of the curious brand of consultation—with people opposed tooth and nail to any change in the North—and whose only purpose is to delay action or to make reform meaningless.'[68] He rather patronisingly advised the Stormont government to spend the summer proposing a response to the McRory Report on local government reform.

Lynch argued that such developments were necessary if there was to be any possibility of rescuing the Northern administration, on whose continued existence any attempt to wrest control from the extremes was predicated.

> They must understand that the basis of good community relations in the
> North is the recognition of the full rights of the northern minority to

express its political personality and to be respected in doing so by the organs of the state. Anything short of this would be incomplete, unsatisfactory and a confession of failure to govern wisely.[69]

He concluded with a warning that while reunification was an imperative, it could be achieved only

when the main Irish traditions are able to build together a new Irish society to their mutual good. Such a new Irish society must take into full account the various considerations put forward by the Irish minority as to how they see the form and shape of a society agreeable to them.[70]

To achieve this, Lynch suggested tinkering with the openly Catholic provisions of the Constitution of Ireland, so that

this society, in which other minority groups are involved, must be drawn together. In so far as there are constitutional difficulties which are legitimately seen by people to be infringements of their civil rights, then their views are worthy of intensive examination, and we should try to accommodate them in our Constitution and in our laws.[71]

The contributions of Boland and Blaney to the Dáil debate (following unsuccessful attempts to prevent them from speaking) seriously questioned Lynch's strategic vision and apparent willingness to uphold the Constitution. Without providing any evidence to support his claims, Blaney began by insinuating that, far from living in a society where democratic norms were upheld, the TDs were in effect living in a police state.

I am concerned about phone-tapping in this little statelet of ours. Phone-tapping was alleged months ago. As I understand it, it was apparently given to us to understand at that time that it had not taken place. My information since then is that very definitely it has been taking place. What I want to know is the circumstances in which phone-tapping is, in fact, legal.[72]

Next he alleged that 'the watching of people, keeping people under surveillance by the Special Branch, is on the increase.' Layer after layer of conspiracy was added. There had been rumours of two hundred extra Special Branch recruits. A secret police agency may have been established beyond accountability.

Is there a branch that is, in fact, based on ex-members of the Special Branch, and if so, who recruits these people? Who are they? To whom do they owe their allegiance? Who pays them? What is their job, and under what authority do they work? Is there such a special force? Is there, in fact, a B Special force in this country, and has there been such a force for a considerable time? Is it under the jurisdiction of the Minister for Justice, of our Government and our parliament, or is it not? … I wonder also how many of the deputies of this house are aware that Special Branch men are still roaming through the corridors of this house, and that you are likely to sit at the table next to them in our own restaurant here without knowing who they are.[73]

Warming to his theme, Blaney proceeded to question why the Fine Gael leader, Liam Cosgrave, had not been investigated for receiving sensitive state information from the very people he condemned for operating a police state.[74] The purpose of the attack was clear: Blaney was daring Lynch to censure him, to risk throwing him out of the party.

The Provisional IRA might be attempting to destroy the Northern state, but in Blaney's estimation it was a laudable patriotic objective when set against the nefarious activities of a police regime in the Republic. The minority, if under attack, were morally entitled to decide to defend themselves with arms. In particular, the violence associated with the defence of St Matthew's Church was justified, and the supply of weapons was considered implicitly acceptable, in this graphic description.

I wonder today if they had succeeded and got through that night and had there been no defenders, inadequate though their equipment may have been, to defend the church, the convent, the nuns, the girls, what would have been the outcome. If the church had been burned as the sacristy was burned, if the convent was razed, as it might have been, what might have happened to the nuns, to the girls, and to the priests? Had they been murdered, ravaged, abused, or whatever you like, what would be the attitude of any of us in this house tonight if we were recalling that particular episode? Would we feel that the minority that night had a right to protect themselves, their church and convent, their nuns and girls in that hostel? Unless we are blatantly and totally dishonest, we must admit that had that been the outcome we would feel very much aggrieved that nothing could have been done to save the situation.[75]

Blaney was rejecting any possibility that reform in the North could be acceptable to Irish nationalism as he understood it, a premise that was to underpin the ideology of the Provisionals until the ending of abstention in 1986. His central argument was that no-one had the right to betray the right of the revolutionary generation, least of all a Fianna Fáil Government.

> I believe in the republicans of past generations, in the republican traditions of past generations, both those who died for the cause and those who fought for the cause. I do not believe, and I do not accept, that in this generation we can invent a new form of Irish republicanism merely to placate the ascendancy of the Six Counties and their vested interests. I firmly believe we cannot do this. I do not accept that we can trim our republican sails to suit the needs of the carpetbaggers existing in our society.[76]

He rejected any suggestion that peace existed in Belfast, comparing the situation to that of Budapest in 1956 and Prague in 1968.[77]

> It is not peace: it is merely keeping the thing down at the moment. By all means try that in any way you can, but it is no answer. It is no final cure. It can erupt again, and possibly because of its being repressed in that way it may erupt with all the more force.[78]

Blaney set out the grounds for an alternative strategy for securing the unity of the country without recourse to violence. This, he argued, was based on the unparalleled situation where

> after fifty years of trial and error—mostly grave errors—the regime in Belfast is tottering on the brink of extinction, and we should recognise this to be the case. Instead of trying to bolster it up by gestures of co-operation we should be telling the world about how the sorry impasse has been reached.[79]

He argued that partition remained the root cause of the problem and that there would be no peace without it being resolved. What was required was the recognition by Britain that it was the root cause—an explicit rejection of Lynch's argument that the problem was confined to Ireland. Britain had to give a commitment to withdraw within five years, with the subvention phased out over fifteen years.[80] Public representatives had a responsibility not to damp down passions but to inject a new sense of civic responsibility, lost in the pursuit of wealth in the sixties, in which the primary loyalty to the national revolution had been jettisoned in favour of personal avarice.

> We in this parliament, the public representatives, must bring home to the people our responsibility to the ideal of nationhood, and I say 'nationhood' deliberately … It is only when Britain will have got out of this

land that we will get together and live together and become not only a united territory but a united people and, in a few words, a nation once again.[81]

Lynch's ideological difficulties were compounded by an economic crisis, and it is significant that in the adjournment debate he sought a continued mandate to rule primarily on his policies for ending that crisis. For Lynch the task was to change the definition of patriotism to include diligent work in ending economic and social problems. Inflationary pressures were destroying wage restraint and making Irish exports uncompetitive. Wage increases from 1968 to 1969 were 11 per cent—twice the level of Italy, Ireland's nearest rival. Strikes were widespread. The cement industry was paralysed by a 21-week stoppage, and as Lynch spoke the financial system was being undermined by a bank strike.[82] Real urgency was needed in dealing with economic problems, compounded by the difficulty in urging wage restraint and stopping trade unions from pressing home sectional advantages. He concluded that restraint, partnership and leadership must be combined to prevent those formidable difficulties from destroying the economy, and that 'everything is impossible except chaos.'[83]

That chaos in large part was the consequence of the working out of Fianna Fáil politics in the sixties. The loyalty of the working class was sorely tested by the increased standing of the business community. The inculcation of corrupt practices in the body politic through speculative land deals and shady business associations, including those associated with Haughey and Blaney, challenged the populist nature of Fianna Fáil. Repressive social legislation and the jailing of squatters served only to provide a vehicle for the increase in support for Marxists, whom the Department of Justice had earlier identified as the greatest threat. As Garret FitzGerald remarked, the very fabric of Southern society was being torn apart by speculative forces from above and revolutionary force from below.

> We see all around the growth of unrest among the oppressed. We can see a multiplication of the forces of those who want to encourage that unrest. We have created a situation in which it is becoming increasingly easy for those who want to destroy our society to secure the support of the ordinary people.[84]

It is important not to under-estimate the consequences these social and economic problems had in the articulation of policy and their importance in the power struggle within Fianna Fáil. The party perceived itself as having an almost divine right to rule, even if it showed itself a master of very worldly material politics.[85] Its ideological supremacy was based on its ability to transcend class-based concerns. Now, just as in 1948, an economic crisis threatened its credentials. The entrepreneurs of Dublin and other cities whose conspicuous consumption so appalled FitzGerald and infuriated the radical left were very much creatures of Fianna Fáil, their rise reflecting the destabilising relationship between politics and economics in 1970. Rising social discontent accentuated the political distance between the party and its base; all that was left was the ideological appeal for restraint for the 'national good'. If 1948 demonstrated that such a strategy could not work even when the party itself was unified and Northern nationalism was quiescent, in 1970, with Lynch virtually condemned as a traitor by Blaney and Boland, the ultimate party-machine men, Fianna Fáil was set to self-destruct.

It was a fact implicitly acknowledged by Lynch in his closing speech to the Dáil on 30 July, in which he explicitly rejected any suggestion of phone-tapping or the existence of a second Special Branch.[86] Neither was he guilty as charged of displaying an abject approach to Anglo-Irish relations: instead he felt it was the only sensible approach to dealing with the complexity of the situation. He suggested that the great achievement intimated in his speech of 11 July referred to an increased co-operation between London, Dublin and nationalist community leaders that had the potential to

> break the cycle of provocation followed by violence, followed by more provocation and more violence. I think I can say tonight that developments since the thirteenth of July continue to move in a favourable direction.[87]

Closing a debate that John Healy regarded as 'one of the sharpest in the history of the Dáil,' Lynch made it clear that he would tolerate no more dissent within Fianna Fáil.[88] 'So long as I have the support and strength and influence—and I have these in abundance—I shall let nothing, no organisation, no opposition, no clique, no person, no matter from where he comes—I shall let nobody assail or undermine the unity and strength of the Fianna Fáil Party.'[89]

It was fighting talk. It also went to the crux of the ideological chasm dividing Fianna Fáil. Lynch was saying in effect that the time had come to bury the dead, to allow new political circumstances to create new goals, even if that meant jettisoning core values. For

Blaney and Boland such a move questioned the very nature of Fianna Fáil's unique place in Irish society.

Despite the power struggle, Haughey, Blaney, Boland and Ó Móráin all voted for Lynch, who received his greatest ovation since becoming Taoiseach in 1969. As the Dáil rose for the summer, however, it was far from guaranteed that the Cork man would be its leader when it returned in October. Lynch was a hostage to fortune, a fact clearly recognised by Blaney and the Provisional IRA.

The collapse of Stormont had now become an imperative strategic goal. On 31 July, British soldiers, during a confrontation lasting five hours in which CS gas and water cannon were liberally used, killed Danny O'Hagan in the New Lodge, Belfast. The riot was dispersed only after a battalion of six hundred men saturated the area in the early hours of Sunday morning. According to an eyewitness,

> when they made their entry from North Queen Street at 2.30 a.m. yesterday, the residents of the high flats did not conceal their anger. Missiles that were hurled from balconies included chairs, paving stones, tables and even a child's rocking horse. They crashed sometimes on top of the big Army Saracens [armoured cars] and sometimes just inches from troops in riot gear.[90]

On 2 August the Stormont government increased to £50,000 the reward for information leading to the conviction of those responsible for a series of explosions, following the blowing up of the telephone exchange in Newcastle, County Down, and attacks on an electricity showroom in Lurgan and a customs house in Armagh. This was the second time that financial inducements were used to try to prise the nationalist community away from the grip of the paramilitaries. The aim, according to the Minister of Home Affairs, Robert Porter, was to

> bring the insane acts of violence to an end. They are being carried out by potential murderers who have a wanton disregard for the lives of men, women and children living in this country.[91]

Within unionism, internment was increasingly mooted as the only answer. The *Belfast Telegraph* complained that the government was forced into a corner: 'if there are continuing pointers to IRA involvement in the disturbances, or subversive activities from any quarter, it may yet have no other alternative.'[92]

The rioting following the Dáil debate marked a change in that open confrontations between the British army and Catholic youths were now becoming commonplace. The cycle of violence that Lynch had said was coming to an end was in fact intensifying in frequency and severity. Coming in advance of Anglo-Irish talks in London, it was interpreted as a deliberate escalation.[93]

Senior Provisionals, such as the Kelly brothers in Belfast and Ó Conaill in County Donegal, retained their belief that the Northern conflict could achieve a changed dynamic in Southern politics and that it was in the republican movement's interests to force a change in the elite in order to accommodate this. The aim was not necessarily to promote the candidacy of Blaney but to destabilise the Lynch Government, forcing a rejection of the policy of unity by consent. Viewed through a Northern republican prism, there was reason to believe that such a strategy could conceivably work. *An Phoblacht* complained: 'Mr Lynch cannot be allowed to continue with impunity to smear the aspirations of the Northern minority as subversive, nor can he smear the honour and integrity, the moral and physical courage of those who have stood between that same Northern minority and their would be exterminators.'[94]

The most glaring example of the intersection of these agendas occurred at two ceremonies in August 1970. The first, in County Antrim, marked a public change in the Provisional IRA's political and military strategy. The second, in County Cork, implicitly gave the Provisional IRA the imprimatur of veterans of the War of Independence. What was significant about both occasions was that the ceremonies were not only attended by the usual supporters but had high-level political involvement. Paddy Kennedy attended the Northern commemoration and used it to call for the resignation of Lynch; Blaney attended the Southern commemoration and used it as a vehicle to show continued support for those prepared to use force to advance their cause, a policy that brought him into a considered collision with the Taoiseach.

The divisions in Fianna Fáil were mirrored within Northern nationalism. Following the demise of the Nationalist Party, the political leadership fragmented. Gerry Fitt, because of his dual role as Westminster and Stormont MP, increasingly urged restraint and tried, along with John Hume, to adopt a conciliatory policy to both the Unionist government and, after June, the Conservative government in London. His party colleague Paddy Kennedy meanwhile was adopting an increasingly hard-line position. During the Arms Crisis, Kennedy had in effect thrown down a gauntlet to Dublin to act. This was also an implicit criticism of his party leader, who had moved away from the demand for weapons. Kennedy saw in the crisis an opportunity to advance the core demand of unity and found it 'incompatible with republicanism that anyone who calls himself a republican should run to Stormont or Westminster instead of Dublin.'[95] Any possibility that Republican Labour could retain both Kennedy and Fitt disappeared when Kennedy addressed the commemoration ceremony for Roger Casement on 2 August. He told the crowd: 'Let us tell our British masters that there is only one reform which we will accept, and that is the reunification of this country. It is only when we get that basic civil right that all other civil rights and reforms will follow.'

A declared socialist, Kennedy then proclaimed that no-one had the right 'to foist on the Irish people any alien form [of organisation] or any alien political philosophy.' Republicans had to unite to break the connection with England and bring about the reunification of the country. He accused Lynch of engaging in

> a dirty, filthy combination with the British government. The Taoiseach has sold and betrayed the Irish people and will be judged very harshly.

Kennedy left his audience in no doubt that a change in the Fianna Fáil leadership could change the situation, ushering in a new dynamic. 'There are men in high places or formerly in high places who would have done as one would have expected any Irishman to do and who stand charged with the same crime Roger Casement was executed for.'

Sharing the platform with Kennedy were Seán Keenan and Billy Kelly.[96] Keenan told the crowd that 'it is necessary to have an army to protect the people of this country, and if the [Irish] army is not being used for this purpose then I say let them disband that army now and hand the guns to the people who are prepared to use them to provide protection.' Billy Kelly, chairman of New Lodge Defence Committee, gave a eulogy to Danny O'Hagan and condemned the behaviour of the British soldiers in Belfast, accusing them of carrying out atrocities similar to those Casement reported in the Amazon and the Congo. Kelly also publicly acknowledged the basis of the IRA strategy.

> These boys in the New Lodge road and Northern Ireland generally are the cream of this nation. They are not fighting for civil rights as such; they are fighting for the Tricolour, and that is the flag they have in their houses and on the walls in the streets. It may be foolish and it may sound like hooliganism, but it is a feeling that is within the people of the North today, a feeling of resurgence and a feeling that at last we're on the brink

of a great achievement, as Jack Lynch said. But it is not the great achievement that Jack Lynch intended: it is the achievement of a 32-county Irish republic. Thank God we have young boys in this country today who will stand by that and die for it if necessary.[97]

It was to be the rhetorical linkage between the unfolding crisis and the War of Independence that informed two crucial interventions by Neil Blaney in August 1970. Firstly, he issued a statement calling for Irish soldiers to be stationed in minority areas of Belfast and Derry pending a withdrawal of British forces. It was a deliberate rejection of the Government's stated position of empathy with the plight of British soldiers. Far from receiving sympathy, for Blaney the British army stood charged with 'killing and terrorising ordinary people, abusing women and children, and raising once again before Irish eyes the spectacle of repression by foreign forces.'[98] This was also a deliberate challenge to the Taoiseach's authority following Lynch's warning in the Dáil that he would not tolerate any clique threatening the ideological stability of Fianna Fáil.

Blaney reinforced the challenge three days later by his presence, along with Boland, at the commemoration of the fiftieth anniversary of the Kilmichael ambush in County Cork, one of the most celebrated incidents in the IRA's campaign against the Black and Tans.[99] In his address Tom Barry accused the Government of adopting sloppy talk and sloppy actions in its prosecution of Northern policy; he rejected the principle of consent as enunciated by Lynch.

> There is now a heresy that the question of the unity of this country is a matter for the people of the Six Counties. This can never be accepted, because the unity of this country is a matter for every man, woman and child within it.

Unity would never be achieved by peaceful means, he declared in what amounted to a call for a renewed armed campaign.

> Are we going to continue to see our Six Counties under the repression, the terror of imperialism? Are we going to go on allowing this, or are we going to do our thinking for ourselves?[100]

Though Blaney neither spoke at nor played a prominent role in the official commemoration, veterans were photographed shaking his hand and congratulating him on his policy on the need to force the British from Irish shores. His mere presence suggested that he was prepared to countenance the use of force to solve the crisis once and for all. This challenge came just as the realisation was dawning on the establishment in London and Dublin that the IRA campaign was changing direction, clearly influenced by the ideological imperatives operating in the Republic itself. For Kennedy and the Provisional IRA leadership in Belfast it was a powerful, if irresponsible, endorsement that under a new leadership they could expect more than rhetorical support. A leading non-Provisional quoted in the *Irish Times* on 5 August said, 'Everything is falling into the Provisionals' hands at every turn.'

London was increasingly agitated by the turn of events. The *Economist* proclaimed that 'Mr Maudling and the rest of Britain may have to accept that Ulster cannot solve its own problems, and that the Stormont system must be wound up.'[101] The magazine noted two factors that were working to ensure that Britain would stay involved. Firstly, there was increased polarisation: those who could were leaving; those who remained had 'no option but to wait behind the communal defences which they were brought up to rely on in extremity.' Secondly, and more importantly, the Unionist Party was losing control. Banning parades was not a feasible option for stability, as it marked only the visible alienation of what had come to look like a liberal government from its visibly illiberal electorate.

The *Economist* was dismayed at what it saw as attempts to return to Protestant domination and the lack of government action in London. It accused the British government of complacency, warning that 'something may well turn up all right; it may be another round of communal rioting, or it may be that the sane Mr Lynch and his advisors will not be able to keep the lid on in Dublin.' The British government had no option but to introduce direct rule. 'What is the value beyond temporary convenience, or going on with the Stormont system?'[102] The article was widely publicised in Ireland, and there is little doubt that the Provisionals would have regarded it as evidence of the success of their strategy. In July and August 1970, for the Provisionals operating in Belfast the facts of life were that unity was not only achievable by force but also highly likely.

The British army went on the offensive as rioting continued throughout August; soldiers swamped the flashpoints in Ardoyne, New Lodge, Antrim Road, and the Falls. The constant drone of helicopters with searchlights playing across the rooftops became part of the background of life in large parts of Belfast for the next twenty-five years. The Provisionals correctly calculated that the bombings would lead to increased pressure on the Unionist government and the British state for a policy of repression. British government acquiescence in the more repressive measures that Stormont declared were necessary to prevent a drain of support to the Protestant extremists; and increasingly hostile relations between British soldiers and Catholic communities from which the Provisionals operated allowed the Provisionals to intensify their campaign. The *Economist* suggested in a hard-hitting editorial that 'a civil war is going on in the United Kingdom.' It unambiguously called for the introduction of direct rule; 'the only way to get Northern Ireland to simmer down and to isolate the wilder men from their own constituencies is to remove the partition question from everyone's mind.'[103]

The time had come for the counter-offensive, and the Social Democratic and Labour Party now emerged from the shadows. The first hint that something was stirring came on Monday 17 August, when the *Irish Times* speculated that a new formation was likely by the end of the week. Throughout the week other media strengthened the momentum, giving rise to the acerbic comment by Barry White in the first issue of the Belfast magazine *Fortnight* that the SDLP is 'probably the only political party in history to which the media acted as midwife.'[104]

Republican Labour denounced Gerry Fitt and Paddy Wilson and promptly threw them out of the party. Others, including Eddie McAteer, complained that they were not consulted; People's Democracy saw green Tories; and Sinn Féin denounced a neo-Redmondite party. The fact remained that for the first time, the opposition had provided an alternative based on 'the trappings of a six-county party'.[105] Hume, kept in the dark by Fianna Fáil in the past and dismissed by the hawks when they were running Northern policy, now appeared to be the one person able and willing to provide a new focus for Northern nationalism. His vision, nurtured by the political staff in the Department of External Affairs, including Éamonn Gallagher, now had the potential to change yet again the dynamics of Irish politics away from territorial unity.

As the battle for advantage raged throughout the summer, Haughey kept his counsel, despite repeated attempts by Blaney and Boland to link him to the strategy for unseating Lynch. To a certain extent this was because the prospect of a trial loomed large in his considerations; it also reflected a recognition that such an approach would lead to accusations that the pursuit of personal advantage overrode the primary loyalty to the party that informed his statement at the height of the crisis. If Lynch was to fall, Haughey was determined that he would not be blamed. It also meant that Haughey now represented an even greater threat, a threat that could be neutralised only if the SDLP prospered. The arms trial, now scheduled to begin in September, would not only determine the guilt or innocence of an individual Government minister but also had the potential to determine the leadership of Fianna Fáil.

CHAPTER SEVEN

Nobody Shouted Stop

The Dublin Arms Trials

T HE Four Courts complex on the Dublin quays occupies a central place in the history of the Irish revolution. It was here between 28 and 30 June 1922 that the young Seán Lemass stood shoulder to shoulder with Cathal Brugha and the anti-Treaty IRA in repudiating the right of the majority to compromise on the right of national self-determination.[1] In 1970 the ghosts of the past were called to mind as preparations were made for the first trial involving a minister of the Irish state, that of Charles Haughey, son-in-law of the great Fianna Fáil strategist.

It was a moment of unprecedented gravity and drama. The conflict in Northern Ireland had challenged core assumptions underlying the legitimacy of the Republic. The question posed to the jury was not so much whether the attempted importing of weapons was legal or not but rather what the country perceived to be the proper limits of nationalism. At stake was nothing less than the ownership of the Irish revolution.

The sense of unease about the implications of the trial was evident as early as 24 July, when the president of the High Court, Mr Justice Aindrias Ó Caoimh, noted that there was a profound reticence within the judiciary to even try the case. In the event Ó Caoimh himself—a former Attorney-General and associate of Haughey—opened the proceedings on 22 September 1970. There was a further indication of the feverish atmosphere created by the trial when a member of the jury panel was excused on the grounds that he had 'a nervous disposition'.[2] Only twenty-two journalists were allowed access to the court; a public address system relayed the proceedings to three adjoining courts, where more than a hundred reporters and leading figures from Fianna Fáil, including Neil Blaney and Kevin Boland, strained to catch each word of the most important trial in the history of the state.[3] Jack Lynch studiously stayed away.

The senior counsel for the state, Séamus McKenna, immediately focused on Charles Haughey, outlining the telephone conversation with Peter Berry on 18 April concerning the request for security clearance for the shipment coming into Dublin Airport. The state alleged that the phone call was 'of paramount importance,' the final act in a conspiracy in which the accused jointly and illegally agreed to import weapons and ammunition, in contravention of the Firearms Acts. Counsel for the state also made it abundantly clear that the main instigator of the conspiracy was not in court—a veiled reference to the central role played by Neil Blaney, against whom the District Court had denied informations on 2 July. That, however, was irrelevant, according to McKenna: all that was necessary for the prosecution was to prove that once a conspiracy came into existence, any person who by agreement joined in it was equally guilty of conspiracy with the originators.

The four defendants pleaded not guilty to the charges; but there was a significant divergence in defence strategies. While Captain James Kelly, John Kelly and Albert Luykx openly admitted their role in the planned importing, they claimed they were merely facilitating Government policy, as enunciated by Blaney, Haughey, and Gibbons. Haughey accepted that he tried to arrange the covert importing but only because he wanted to facilitate Military Intelligence and because he was under the clear impression that the shipment was required under the contingency plans agreed by the Government. At no time was he aware that the shipment included arms and ammunition.[4] This was an each-way bet, and it angered the other defendants. James Kelly regarded it as 'a clever but dishonest ploy ... mean and selfish.'[5] John Kelly thought it typical of the fact that the Belfast Defence Committees had, 'like lambs to the slaughter, entered a wolves' den of politicians.'[6]

The hoped-for outcome of the trial, in the eyes of Lynch and his supporters, was that a conviction would 'gut Haughey, and gut him fast.'[7] The prosecution sought to demolish any suggestion that Haughey was unaware of the arms importing. The evidence of his personal secretary, Anthony Fagan, was specifically designed to achieve this. Fagan's evidence implicated Haughey on three counts: the attempted importing at Dublin port, the attempted importing at the airport, and—crucially for Haughey—the involvement of Government money in the financing of the entire arms operation.[8]

Fagan had a long association with Haughey, serving under him in the Department of Agriculture before transferring to Finance following the defendant's promotion in 1966. He informed the court that he had followed up a request made by Captain Kelly on 19 March to grant customs clearance for a consignment to arrive by sea at Dublin, which would not be what the manifest described as mild steel plate. After ascertaining that the Department of Finance could, under ministerial direction, exercise such powers, Fagan briefed Haughey. 'The minister thought for a moment and said, "Yes, it's okay to do this."'[9]

Further evidence of Haughey's involvement came from the fact that Fagan admitted in court that the following day Captain Kelly and John Kelly held a meeting in the minister's office in Merrion Street, after which Captain Kelly had told him pointedly that 'customs were okay.' As a result of this conversation, Fagan made a second representation to the Revenue Commissioners, explaining the purpose of the subterfuge. He passed instructions to Captain Kelly by telephone that arrangements had been made with a Revenue official, Bartholomew Culligan, that when the cargo arrived in Dublin he was to present himself by name to the duty customs officer.[10] Fagan further testified that on 18 April he received a telephone call from Tomás Tóibín of the Revenue Commissioners to the effect that a cargo was arriving in Dublin Airport later that day. The customs official had said that it would be necessary to contact Chief Superintendent Fleming to confirm that the Government was prepared to allow the cargo in. According to Fagan, when he consulted Haughey

> I think I recall him saying, 'Blaney has told me.' Mr Haughey said I should contact Mr Fleming and say that if he had any difficulty in this he should contact Mr Haughey.[11]

Shortly afterwards Haughey rang him back to say that he had consulted Berry and that it was considered wise to call the entire thing off. Fagan confirmed that Captain Kelly had phoned from Vienna on the Sunday evening, 19 April, looking for instructions from the 'boss man'.[12] The following day Haughey told Fagan that, after discussions with the Minister for Defence, James Gibbons, both men had agreed that the operation be aborted.

The difficulty for Haughey was magnified by Fagan's interpretation of a further conversation on 8 May, before the issuing of Haughey's statement denying involvement in the illegal importing of weapons. According to Fagan, he was asked to read through the statement, and he reminded the minister of the attempts to secretly import a consignment in March.

> So I recalled to him my conversation with him about allowing an item through Dublin port without customs clearance and that I had got his authority to speak to the Commissioner of Revenue agreeing to this, and Mr Haughey said, 'I see: I will have another look at the statement.'[13]

In the long run, the most damaging evidence for Haughey was the oblique reference to the Baggot Street accounts used to finance the entire operation. Fagan confirmed that he had introduced Captain Kelly to the sub-manager of the Munster and Leinster Bank in Baggot Street. Curiously, the issue was not significantly addressed in the arms trials, but it was to provide the basis for the hearings of the Committee of Public Accounts established in December 1970.[14] The mention of the financing of the shipment was introduced by Captain Kelly's counsel, James Darcy, to buttress the assertion that Kelly was at all times authorised by Government ministers to conduct his business. This was considered necessary because the next principal witness to be called by the state was the former Minister for Defence, Jim Gibbons.

Gibbons's testimony was crucial to the entire prosecution case. Under the terms of the indictment, the prosecution had to prove that the importing was illegal because the minister was not involved. In his evidence Gibbons went further, stating that he had categorically refused a request by Haughey and Blaney to provide the written authorisation.

> I was asked on one occasion to do that. I said definitely that I would not do so. I did not do so.[15]

Gibbons provided a rare insight into the workings of Fianna Fáil and the raging battle taking place for ideological supremacy. It revealed a climate of fear and suspicion and raised more questions than it answered in relation to Gibbons's role in the entire affair. First there was the complex relationship between Haughey, Blaney and Gibbons over Northern policy and just who was running Captain Kelly. Gibbons testified that he knew that it was Blaney's design to get weapons into the North—itself in clear contravention of the

Government's stated position—yet he did not tell the Taoiseach. He suspected that a conspiracy was afoot and that the confusion over what exactly official policy was could be ironed out if the North was discussed more frequently in the Government, 'and I expressed this opinion to the Taoiseach.' Yet he did not tell Lynch specifically of his concerns; he asked Haughey to intervene on his behalf. This approach was adopted, he reasoned, because of Haughey's

> very senior position in the Government and my very, very junior one with the Taoiseach to get the Government's position in regard to the handling of the Northern affair on a regular basis. I asked Mr Haughey whether he was aware of any conspiracy to import weapons into the country, and he replied—and I don't purport to quote him verbatim, but he said something like this: 'No, Jim. My views about this are precisely the same as yours: the Government must act together in a matter of this kind.' I continued to say that this type of squalid hugger-mugger activity would have to be terminated and appealed to him to speak to the Taoiseach to have the general matter of our relations with the various aspects of the Northern problem especially discussed. Mr Haughey said he would do what he could.

Gibbons was aware of Captain Kelly's existence and his work as an intelligence officer in the North long before his first meeting in March, and had knowledge that Blaney was in fact controlling the operation. In Gibbons's presence, Blaney had referred to Kelly as 'his wee man'. Yet Gibbons further testified that despite his concerns he did nothing to get Kelly out. By his own admission Gibbons claimed that the importing was illegal, suspected that Captain Kelly had changed allegiance, had been told of the attempted importing at Dublin port, and still allowed Kelly to remain in place. Nothing was done even after the Minister for Justice told him that the Special Branch had Captain Kelly under surveillance.

Again Gibbons asked Haughey to intervene. 'On a couple of occasions—several occasions—I would say I raised the question of what I considered the urgency of the provision of the job outside the army for Captain Kelly, and Mr Haughey said he would co-operate.' He adopted this position because Haughey was going to help him sort out the problem by making the captain a smuggling prevention officer.

> My opinion was [that] the most discreet thing to do in the confident hope of his rapid removal from the army into another job in the public service was to do it the way I was doing it.

> *And I must further suggest to you, Mr Gibbons, that by your acquiescence*
> *in his continued duties in the army you led him to believe that you were*
> *authorising what he did. Do you understand me?*
>
> No ... I gave no such authorisation. My intention was that Captain
> Kelly would leave the army without any sense of being kicked out of the
> army or of being got rid of after the service he had rendered in the
> North. Because of his particular position as an intelligence officer he had
> access to a great deal of confidential information, which, if he left the
> army with any sense of grievance, of being got rid of, I felt could be
> improperly used to the detriment of the state.[16]

Mr Justice Ó Caoimh wanted to know why it had not been directly
put to the former Minister for Defence that he had assented to the
importing of some of these consignments of arms.[17] Defence counsel
argued that the case had been made that Gibbons was in fact aware of
Kelly's existence and had done nothing to stop him, a course of action
that implied consent.[18] The judge disagreed, arguing that Gibbons's
testimony that Kelly had changed allegiance had not been rebutted.

Gibbons then returned to the witness box. Again the questioning
centred on the legality of the importing. Gibbons was emphatic.

> He [*Captain Kelly*] *told you that the people who were on that delegation had the*
> *intention to import the weapons and that he proposed to assist or help them ... I*
> *suggest to you that, as an officer of army intelligence, he was engaged in assisting*
> *in the importation of arms into this country.*
>
> No. On the contrary, my understanding was that, because the
> importation of arms was illegal, he felt that it was necessary for him to
> resign from the army.[19]

Yawning gaps in the credibility of Gibbons's evidence began to
appear, particularly in relation to the Government directive of 6
February and the transfer of weapons to Dundalk. Gibbons conceded
that contingency plans had been established, but these were to deal
with 'what I would call a "doomsday" situation, where it might be
necessary to contemplate mercy missions of a very limited nature.'
Gibbons argued that there was never any possibility of weapons being
handed over to Northerners, or of doing anything outside collective
decision-making. This assertion was undermined when astute
questioning by Séamus Sorahan, counsel for John Kelly, elicited the
information regarding the transfer of weapons to Dundalk.[20] Sorahan
asked about 'late-night moves or decisions in high places or a decision
by the army to send five hundred rifles to Dundalk Barracks to be in

readiness for sending across the border if needed.' Tellingly, Gibbons replied, 'Do I have to answer that?'

It was at this stage that Gibbons started implicating Blaney, saying that the Minister for Agriculture had told him that the Taoiseach was in west Cork and could not be contacted immediately. Gibbons understood that a driver had been despatched to the holiday home with an urgent message. The judge intervened by suggesting that Sorahan had gone too far. Counsel for the prosecution, Séamus McKenna, complained that the line of questioning

> must have so exceeded the bounds of relevance that there is a grave risk that the jury may, through no fault of their own, be distracted from their primary duty of trying this case. This is without any disrespect to your lordship. If this line is pursued by him, I will have to apply for the discharge of the jury.

Sorahan retorted: 'It is obvious I have struck a very sensitive nerve on the state side.' This is something of an understatement. The significance of the Dundalk revelation was that it opened up two crucial lines of questioning, which further implicated Gibbons. Firstly, he was shown to be operating at the behest of Blaney, a man whom he had earlier testified was pursuing a policy not agreed by the Government. Secondly, it tied in the contingency plan to the Bailieborough meeting of October 1969, which discussed ways in which the Defence Forces could co-operate with the Northern Command of the IRA, a central part of the strategy developed by Captain Kelly and John Kelly.

The following day Gibbons returned to the witness box for more damaging revelations, which again brought Blaney back to the centre of the conspiracy allegations and in the process raised serious questions about why, if there was in fact a case to answer, he was not prosecuted. Defence counsel elicited from Gibbons the fact that he felt Blaney was attempting to implicate him in the conspiracy by handing him a letter from the German arms dealer Otto Schleuter. Gibbons said he did not authorise any arms importing, yet he went to a meeting on 23 April in Blaney's office that, according to Gibbons's own testimony, centred on

> the failure and breakdown of a scheme to import guns and ammunition through Dublin Airport. I think the object of the conversation was to determine by what means the situation could be dealt with.
>
> *Who did most of the talking?*

> Mr Blaney ... I cannot recall a great deal of the detail but it concerned the situation that had arisen, and my interest in it was the preservation of secrecy, if that was possible. Although I should say that on the previous Monday I had instructed the director of intelligence, Colonel Delany, to prepare a report on the whole affair for the Taoiseach.[21]

This evidence dovetailed neatly with Lynch's stated position that the first he knew of the attempted importing was on 20 April, when 'the security forces at his disposal' informed him. What remained unanswered was the question whether, if Gibbons had told Lynch in advance of the attempted importing, the fiasco would have been avoided. And if he did, would it have made a difference?

The performance was a disaster for the Government case. As Tom MacIntyre remarked,

> there are participants in this trial who the experience will mark for life, men whose breath—six months in the Alps, year on the Costa Brava—will never quite free itself from the rancid air of this courtroom. Place the witness now leaving us among those men.[22]

Mícheál Ó Móráin was then called to give evidence. The former Minister for Justice was necessary because, apart from the Department of Defence, only the Department of Justice had the authority to import weapons, and Ó Móráin had not authorised any such importing nor given a licence or authority to the named defendants. But the prosecution had made a major miscalculation in calling him after Gibbons. What should have been limited to the technical evidence was transformed into a destruction of key parts of the main prosecution witness's testimony.[23] The atmosphere soured almost immediately when Ó Móráin alleged that the Government, in the person of the new Minister for Justice, Des O'Malley, had refused permission for him to consult contemporaneous notes.

> I think I may save time if I say this here and now: these events with which the court is concerned took place six months ago or more. I tried last Friday to see the documents with which I was concerned, on some of which I made some notes, and I was refused permission to see them by the present Minister for Justice and the Attorney-General. So on the question of dates and, indeed, any of these matters, I am under quite great disability.[24]

Ó Móráin provided a number of telling observations, however, about the lack of clarity in Government thinking about the North. He confirmed that members of the Special Branch had been sent clandestinely to get an objective view of the situation there. 'At this stage there were very conflicting reports from the North, and we felt that it would be better to get an objective report on matters up there, and that was the main purpose.' Crucially, he revealed that Military Intelligence and the Special Branch were working at cross-purposes, a development that Ó Móráin claimed he raised with both the Taoiseach and Gibbons, but he was ignored. He further confirmed that the entire Government were aware not only of Captain Kelly and his activities but that John Kelly had been mentioned. Ó Móráin testified that the contingency plans were not only a matter of discussion at Government level but that they included the supply of weapons.

These revelations were serious setbacks for the prosecution case. When combined with the perception that the Department of Justice had deliberately withheld co-operation to a former minister in his preparation for giving evidence in a most important case, it allowed the defence to claim that this was a political prosecution. And in court no. 1 perception, not fact, was what mattered.

Similar problems for the prosecution surrounded the evidence of Colonel Michael Hefferon, the former director of Military Intelligence. He said he gave specific instructions to Captain Kelly not to enter Northern Ireland some time in September and certainly not later than early October 1969. This was in direct conflict with Gibbons's assertion that Hefferon had agreed there was a substantial risk that the British army could pick him up. At the same time Hefferon advised him to contact the ministers and advise them that in his opinion he could not carry on with this work as a serving army officer. Hefferon told the court that the matter was being dealt with between the ministers and Gibbons; this, he said, was necessary from a security point of view only.

Hefferon gave no indication, however, of a change of allegiance. He maintained that at all times the arms would be kept under effective military control, claiming privilege when Mr Justice Ó Caoimh demanded to know exactly where. Short-tempered exchanges followed, with the judge in effect taking over the cross-examination. Under duress, Hefferon conceded that they would have been stored in a monastery in County Cavan. The revelation shocked counsel for John Kelly. 'I am horrified, and I protest, even if I do it alone,' he said, to which the judge replied:

Does counsel want the truth or not the truth? ... I do not see how, consistent with public administration of justice, we are going to have evidence in open court by writing it down and handing it to the jury and allowing nobody else to see it. I am not ready to adopt that course.[25]

The prosecution sought to undermine Hefferon by progressively revealing the breakdown in the military command. Captain Kelly may have been acting under orders, but orders from whom? If the prosecution could establish that military discipline had been broken, a crucial part of the defence case could be undermined. Hefferon sidestepped the issue. He argued that the ultimate authority was the Minister for Defence, because Captain Kelly was at the time a serving officer undertaking a Government mission. But Gibbons had already testified that Kelly was not reporting directly to him. The prosecution then asked to whom Kelly reported. Hefferon replied that he was Kelly's superior, and then confirmed that he did not give him any orders to import weapons. It was a minor victory, but the general import of Hefferon's evidence broadly confirmed Captain Kelly's version of events, in particular the view that contingency plans included arming Northern nationalists. 'There was no question but that they would be used eventually in Northern Ireland if the contingency arose, in a somewhat similar situation to that of the previous August or perhaps worse.'[26]

Hefferon was turning into a hostile witness for the prosecution. He revealed that he had not informed his successor as head of Military Intelligence, Colonel Patrick Delany, of the scale of Kelly's operation. Hefferon, who retired from the army on 9 April 1970, felt that the operation was so sensitive that even the new head of Military Intelligence could not be informed. The importing issue was one sanctioned by the Government sub-committee, and it was up to them to inform Colonel Delany.

On 29 September 1970 the first arms trial unexpectedly collapsed, amid a welter of recrimination. The secretary of the Department of Justice, Peter Berry, had been giving evidence about his contacts with Albert Luykx. He proceeded to read out information contained in a certificate stating that Luykx had not been engaged in subversive activity since entering Ireland. Luykx's counsel, Ernest Wood, protested that he did not want his client's personal affairs bandied around the court, and alleged that the presiding judge had failed to prevent Berry from continuing because of bias. Wood declared that he strongly suspected that the reason his lordship wants the letter read is that it might hurt my client. It is only illustrative of the rather unfair tone in which his lordship, at times, has been conducting the trial.[27]

After a pause, Mr Justice Ó Caoimh adjourned proceedings until after lunch. When he returned, he caused a sensation by announcing his withdrawal from the case.

> In a case of this kind I do not recollect an accusation of that kind being made in the course of a trial to the judge trying the case, nor have I any recollection of this occurring during my practice at the bar ... You will recollect that in July I was reluctant to take on this trial for the very reason that, no doubt, was behind Mr Wood's observations. Whether I was right or not in being so reluctant, you can well understand that when an accusation of the kind now being made here has been made in open court in a trial of such importance, the judge cannot properly continue the trial and expect the public to believe that he is unbiased.[28]

As a consequence, Mr Justice Ó Caoimh said he had no alternative but to withdraw from the case and discharge the jury. Wood apologised and offered to withdraw from the case. Counsel for Haughey suggested it was an over-reaction, an injustice to his client, who had been made the principal figure in it; he added that such a development could stop any court case in the future. Ó Caoimh retorted:

> Then you would have to start all over again. There are six other judges, and it could happen to them, but then it would be some time before you would be back to me again.[29]

As he left the courtroom, Haughey reportedly hissed with rage,

> Get off the bench, Ó Caoimh. You're a disgrace.[30]

It was a remarkable move in a remarkable saga. As the *Irish Times* editorial remarked, 'the fact that such a trial was to be held at all has already proved a shock; the revelations made in court were in keeping; Mr Justice Ó Caoimh's discharging of the jury is an earthquake.'[31] It was indicative of the tension that the editorial made a direct comparison with concerns in 1932 about whether the institutions of the state would withstand the impact of the entry of Fianna Fáil into government. The *Irish Times* concluded that while the events in the North had sent shock waves throughout the country, by and large

> we have made a state worth living in. It can, and will be improved on. The national nerve need not be shaken.

In the pages of the same issue the paper reported that the Provisional IRA had regularised its position and was about to intensify its campaign.

The second arms trial began on 6 October 1970. The prosecution took care to eliminate the risk of Gibbons's testimony being rebutted by Ó Móráin by changing the order of appearance. It also refused to use Colonel Hefferon as a prosecution witness.

It was not until eight days later that the trial really ignited, in consequence of a speech from the dock by John Kelly. It was a remarkable performance from a 'stocky boyish figure, ghetto accusation in the black eyes, and you wonder for a moment. Is this man armed?'[32]

Kelly refused to give direct evidence, because of the danger that he would compromise the safety of others. He then proceeded to give a stinging indictment of Jack Lynch. Despite attempts by the judge to limit the content of Kelly's remarks to the compass of the charge, Kelly's speech cut through the rhetorical underpinnings of the state. He was being charged for defending his right as an Irishman to defend himself, a right Dr Hillery had announced to the United Nations in August 1969. Kelly quoted from that address the following passage:

> 'The claim of Ireland, the claim of the Irish nation to control the totality of the island had been asserted over the centuries by successive generations of Irishmen and Irishwomen and it is one which no spokesman for the Irish nation could ever renounce.'
>
> It is my conviction that I stand here and those who stand with me, that we are here as a matter of political expediency, and not from any desire that the course of justice be impartially administered. My lord, I find it a very sad occasion indeed that these institutions for which so much was sacrificed, which had been gained by such nobility, should be abused in this manner. There is no victory for anyone in these proceedings, my lord. There is only an echo of sadness from the graves of the dead generations.[33]

When he finished, at least one member of the jury applauded.[34] Even trenchant critics of the Provisional IRA, including the Labour Party spokesman, Conor Cruise O'Brien, regarded it as 'a highly effective piece of patriotic rhetoric' in the classic republican tradition.[35]

On 19 October, Charles Haughey swore an oath to tell the truth, the whole truth, and nothing but the truth. It was the moment everybody was waiting for. The opening questions by his senior counsel, Niall McCarthy, were designed to show not only long and loyal service to the state but also the willingness of his client to clamp down on subversives if necessary. Much was made of the fact that as Minister for Justice in 1960 Haughey authorised the re-establishment of military tribunals to rid the state of the risk that juries might be intimidated or might take irredentist rhetoric as spurious justification for armed struggle.

Haughey presented himself as a senior Government minister who at all times acted in the interests of the state, a firefighter who was on constant watch, given the fact that other ministers retreated to rural constituencies at the weekends. This was crucial, given the fact that the attempted arms importing took place on the weekend of 18–19 April. More importantly, he too gave a clear insight into the mechanics of Government decision-making in relation to the North and to his central role in relation both to the financing of the Northern Defence Committees and to the Government's contingency plans.

> I was given a very, very free hand ... There was no question of determining the amount. It was the view of the Government, and my personal view, that, considering the trials and tribulations those people were undergoing, that as far as we could help by making money available to them for the relief of distress there was no question of restricting the amount.[36]

He revealed that the Government sub-committee met only once, because it was not logistically possible to meet more often; and he accepted that in the directing of Northern policy he discussed the matter with Blaney more often than with the others. This, he protested, was because of the former Minister for Agriculture's contacts and experience in dealing with the North. Haughey specifically denied that he was aware of the extent to which Blaney was briefing Captain Kelly, though he acknowledged the role played by Kelly as the link between the Defence Committees and the Government. While outlining his own responsibility in determining who would in fact receive Government funds, he rejected any suggestion that he knew that money was being diverted towards the supply of arms. Yet he admitted providing funds for delegations, including representatives of the Defence Committees, who had continually asked for weapons. According to Haughey, it

> was an inveterate topic of conversation. We were all under pressure from people within the Six Counties to supply arms.[37]

The prosecution made a number of attempts to demonstrate that Haughey was both profligate and irresponsible in the handling of the relief fund. First there was the question of who was to receive funds. Haughey maintained that the money was to be distributed by 'a committee of respectable, reputable Six-County people.' He maintained that, given the fact that the Irish Red Cross Society could not operate within Northern Ireland, there was no alternative but to channel the money through bank accounts controlled by the Defence Committees.

You would agree that every citizen knows that the Red Cross Society does not traffic in guns?

I would think so, yes.

It does deal with blankets and foodstuffs and other commodities for the alleviation of physical distress?

Yes, and indeed would make relief payments of money in certain circumstances.

Did you use the Red Cross as a cloak and a blind to conceal the fact that this money was being paid to the Defence Committees?

No. I was very much aware of the role which the Defence Committees were playing inside Belfast city, where they were responsible for policing large areas, for feeding people, for the organisation of all sorts of humanitarian activities. The Irish Red Cross would normally assist these people.[38]

Haughey denied any knowledge of the fact that the money was transferred from the Clones bank accounts to Baggot Street or of how the money was dispensed thereafter. It was a tactic he was to use throughout his testimony. He was engaged in general policy, not the mechanics of the operation.

I take it that the disbursement of £100,000 of public moneys would be a matter of considerable concern to you as Minister for Finance?

It certainly would.

It would be important to check and be satisfied that this was being properly administered and applied?

Well, I have no doubt but that would be done by the Department of Finance. Once I have taken the decision that it was to be given and the sort of people who were to get the aid, then I presume this would be a matter of mechanics for the Department of Finance and the preparation of a supplementary estimate and the presenting of a supplementary estimate to the Dáil and the answering of any questions in relation to it.[39]

The evidence then turned to the circumstances in which weapons could be transferred directly into the hands of Northern nationalists. Here was the correlation between the relief of distress and the contingency plans. In a crucial section of his evidence, Haughey argued that arms would be transferred to the Defence Committees.

> It would be an integral part of the contingency plans as I saw it that the army would have to provide for itself a supply of arms which would be supplied to the people inside the Six Counties if that decision was ever taken.
> *By the Government?*
> By the Government ... I would have regarded it as a very normal part of army preparations in the pursuance of the contingency plans that they would have provided themselves with, and store here on this side of the border, arms which might, ultimately, if the Government said so, be distributed to other persons.[40]

Haughey maintained that

> my view all along was that the Government should take whatever action it was going to take through the army. Only in this way could we control it, make it official, that it would achieve the purpose we wished.

Throughout his evidence Haughey was careful to introduce details to support his version of events. It added significantly to the credibility of his statements, though not necessarily their accuracy, as evidenced by his conversation with the secretary of the Department of Justice on 18 April. Haughey told the court that, given the danger of unwelcome publicity if there was a seizure at Dublin Airport, he had an obligation to contact Berry. He was 'the man who down the years had a very special responsibility for the security of the state, the man who in effect ran the Special Branch, and therefore was in a position to know what exactly was going on and why.' The insertion of the fact that a child or a young person answered his phone was in flat contradiction of Berry, who, in giving evidence, had made use of what he claimed were contemporaneous notes. According to Haughey,

> it was exactly half past six, because when whoever answered the telephone first of all left it down to go and find Mr Berry or get him to the telephone, I could distinctly hear the half past six Radio Éireann news in Mr Berry's house. I could hear it over the telephone. I heard it come on.

In cross-examination Haughey remarked that the Special Branch might have had the airport under observation to seize illegal publications, a reference to pornography.[41] He specifically rejected any suggestion that he gave any guarantees about the shipments. He could not account for the divergence in testimony between himself and Berry; nor could he account for the discrepancies in the accounts of his meetings with Gibbons.[42]

Haughey introduced a quantity of factual evidence to support his assertion that he simply had not got time to discuss the Dublin Airport importing with Gibbons until late in the afternoon of the Monday. His secretary, Brendan O'Connell, who showed the minister into Haughey's office, confirmed Haughey's evidence. He said it could not have been Friday, because he was not at work that day. Again it was part of a strategy to undermine the truthfulness of Gibbons's evidence by demonstrating that Haughey had a clear recollection of events. On the substance of the discussion, Haughey maintained that he did not make the remark that the 'dogs in the street' knew about the plan nor that he asserted that he would call it off for a month.

> That did not happen … My understanding of the situation was that it was an army intelligence operation in pursuance of the contingency plans, that the Special Branch seemed to have blundered into the situation and it was going off the rails, and that Mr Gibbons came to me to get my advice and we both agreed that it should be called off, but as far as I was concerned it was Mr Gibbons's business, or at least army business.

The weakness of Gibbons's testimony was a constant factor in the final address to the jury by the defence team. Haughey's counsel suggested that it would be reasonable to conclude that this was a prosecution conceived in panic, nurtured in rumour, born in malice, and brought in spite, particularly in the calling of evidence. The case against his client revolved around several alleged conversations. McCarthy demolished Gibbons on the basis of the Fort Dunree training and the extent of his knowledge of the aborted operation in Dublin port the previous March. 'The prosecution was an ill-conceived monster, and I suggest that it is time it should be buried.'[43]

Tom Finlay, for Kelly, suggested to the jury that if they looked at this case in the broadest possible terms it was a situation in which 'nobody shouted stop.' Gibbons demonstrated a frailty and inaccuracy of recollection in relation to the crucial meeting at Bailieborough at which Captain Kelly noted the concerns and strategy of the IRA Northern Command. For Finlay, the credibility of Gibbons as a witness was seriously undermined because of the deceit over the training

at Fort Dunree. He had lied to the Dáil about the training, the implication being that he was just as capable of lying at the Four Courts.

Séamus Sorahan, paying tribute to the prosecution, made another
side-swipe at the Government. Barristers, he said, like jockeys, had to
get their instructions from the trainer or the owner. The decision not
to call Hefferon, 'horrible and disgraceful though it was,' should not
be laid at the door of the prosecutors but 'at the door or doors of
people in high places in the state.' He concluded with a flourish: 'For
God's sake, gentlemen, throw out this smelly, shameful, disgraceful
prosecution.'

Ernest Wood also launched into an attack on Gibbons, calling him
a liar—even though his testimony was not relevant to his client's case—
a development that prompted a scathing response from the prosecution.
Wood, it was alleged, had done his client no favours by conducting a
defence based on Gibbons, 'an intemperate diatribe … done in the
sort of way that one might associate with a blind rhinoceros charging
in the direction of every sound it heard.'[44]

As the trial was coming to a close, Jack Lynch was in New York,
using the General Assembly of the United Nations to outline his
vision of the future. London and Dublin were keenly aware that, just
as the events that led to the prosecutions had a profound impact on
the politics of the North, so too could a negative verdict. Lynch made
a deliberate attempt to move his discourse with the British government
onto a new plane. He spoke warmly of Britain as a 'freedom-loving
country' and outlined a policy based on London and Dublin acting as
equal guarantors of the rights of the minority in Northern Ireland. In
perhaps the most conciliatory section of the speech he maintained that
he did not doubt the sincerity and integrity of the Northern Ireland
Prime Minister, James Chichester-Clark, or his predecessor.

> We believe that one day that local community—long since Irish, as it
> knows itself to be—will see that the future lies with us, that we have a
> desire for the good of Ireland to see this and no desire to destroy their
> values. Long before the United Nations was conceived we renounced
> any intention of compelling their adhesion to us.

Lynch argued that domination led to a cycle of violence in which
revolt and tyranny went hand in hand. 'It is a terrible thing when
those who should be brothers are driven to hatred and destruction
because rulers lack the vision to govern justly.' For Chichester-Clark
and O'Neill before him there was above all sympathy.

I do not question their dedication in the face of petty intrigues and manoeuvres of lesser men. We have inherited a historic problem. We are determined to resolve it peacefully. We have asked those who have suffered to be patient.

Then Lynch proceeded to lay the basis for his optimism. He argued that Britain had in effect accepted Dublin's role as a guarantor of the rights of the minority.

We have said to those who suffered from deprivation of human rights in the north of Ireland that Britain will keep her word. My Government have guaranteed this. There is a fund of good will between Ireland and Britain, derived from a surer and deeper understanding of each other, reached through quiet diplomacy and personal conversation. I am satisfied that it is intended to restore peace with justice in Northern Ireland and to do this quickly and generously as the situation demands. I am confident that when this is accomplished the Irish people will them-selves put an end to ignoble relics of ancient disagreements and create the conditions which will fully restore the Irish nation, in all its diversity and cultural richness. In this regard we have put our trust in the good faith between our countries.[45]

Britain had a responsibility in this matter, and it was a responsi-bility that, Lynch argued, it had adhered to in its determination to proceed with a reform programme. In the circumstances of 1970 this was a remarkable olive branch.

Britain had a responsibility. We had a responsibility. We charged Britain with her responsibility when the Northern society had broken down. Britain responded with a firm declaration made at Downing Street on August 19th last year, and repeated in the Security Council, that human rights would be respected in the areas of Ireland over which she claims jurisdiction. We accepted that declaration as the true decision of a country which, despite many unhappy things in the past—and there comes a time to stop feeding on such things—we know to be herself a democratic and freedom-loving country with which Ireland has many ties of friendship and mutual interest.

Wrapping himself in a quotation from Terence MacSwiney, that 'it is not those who can inflict most but they who can suffer most will conquer,' Lynch subverted the ultimate goal. He was in effect ending the Irish revolution. The Irish nation had been truncated in the insti-tutionalisation of the 26-County state, with the promise that Dublin would try to persuade London and Belfast to improve the lot of Northern nationalists. It was an audacious move in the midst of the biggest political crisis facing the state since its formation. The speech was broadly welcomed by the British government, one source telling the *Irish Times* that it 'is a breaking out of the bog of misunderstanding onto firm ground.'[46]

The diplomatic offensive began as Northern Ireland was once again perched on the edge of the precipice. The demand for the introduction of direct rule, made with such clarity during the summer in the editorial pages of the *Economist,* was accompanied by the resurgence of right-wing forces within the unionist community. In the background the Provisional IRA had solidified its position, and in Dublin the danger of a reawakened commitment to turn the rhetoric of republicanism into strident policy remained real. In October 1970 the Irish question was very much to the top of the agenda in both Westminster and Leinster House. The danger was magnified because of the coalescence of interests in destabilising Chichester-Clark. The debate on the Central Housing Authority Bill and the McRory Report on local government proposals caused consternation in grassroots unionist circles, since, if implemented, they would in effect take away the main pillar of sectarian control in local government.

The paradox for the British and Irish governments was that in forcing the pace of institutional change they had brought the country to the edge of civil war. The bulwark of unionist hegemony, the Orange Order, the other loyal orders and the siege mentality, while useful in creating unionist dominance, had now become a force moderate unionism could not control. The re-emergence of the IRA, in large part fuelled by the adventurist policies adopted by Haughey and the other Government ministers, had created expectations that the Irish question could be solved once and for all. What neither government took into account in their considerations was that the terms of the debate had shifted dramatically. The campaign for civil rights was always, for the republican movement, a means to an end. With Stormont teetering on the edge of collapse, the terms of reference had changed dramatically. The governments' hope that reform would be enough to stem the violence was an illusion.

On 23 October 1970 Mr Justice Séamus Henchy addressed the jury for the last time. He stressed the importance of the case and specifically directed them to disregard the possible political consequences of their verdict. He told them they should exclude the fact that other people may have been involved who were not charged. There was, he said, no assurance that other people would not be prosecuted, and they should not allow that fact to influence them. He maintained that there was no question that the Attorney-General was right in bringing the case to trial, despite the epithets used by various defence counsel. This was so because the statements and material before him did suggest that the law had been broken.

> My opinion, for what it is worth, is that this was a proper prosecution to bring. This prosecution was instituted by the Attorney-General. The Attorney-General occupies one of the great constitutional offices of the state. To him is committed the decision in a case such as this which is to be tried by jury, whether the prosecution should be commenced or not, and in so deciding he must act in a quasi-judicial way, that is, he must act as if he were a judge. He must assess the statements and the material before him, and I think that in this case, having regard to the material before the Attorney-General, he was justified in bringing the prosecution. I even go so far as to express the opinion that he would be unjustified in not bringing it.[47]

According to Mr Justice Henchy, there were three key areas in which the law appeared to have been broken, all of which placed Haughey at the centre of the allegations. Firstly, Gibbons had alleged that Haughey had said he would stop arms importing for a month. Unless the Attorney-General considered that Gibbons was totally wrong, that alone would justify a prosecution.

> Either Mr Gibbons, it seems to me, has concocted—invented, as counsel put it to him—this conversation, or it happened in substance. Mr Haughey denies it and cannot see how his former colleague could say it is so. It is not like something said in the course of a conversation that could be misinterpreted. It seems to me, and you are free to dismiss my opinion, [that] either Mr Gibbons concocted this and has come to court and perjured himself, or it happened. There does not seem to me to be any way of avoiding a total conflict on this issue between Mr Haughey and Mr Gibbons.[48]

Secondly, there was the reference to the telephone conversation with Peter Berry in which Haughey was alleged to have offered guarantees on the shipments going directly to the North, then reluctantly saying he would call it off. According to Mr Justice Henchy, unless the Attorney-General was to reject such statement as unworthy of being tendered to a court, he was justified in bringing a prosecution.

It seems to me that you will have to come to a conclusion as to whether Mr Berry concocted this conversation, and has come to court to swear what was false … I would like to be able to suggest some way you can avoid holding [that] there is perjury in this case. You have a solemn and serious responsibility to decide in this case, firstly whether Mr Gibbons's conversation took place or not, and secondly, whether Mr Berry's conversation took place or not.[49]

The third count surrounded Anthony Fagan's evidence that Captain Kelly rang from Vienna looking for instructions from the Minister for Finance. Again this was, according to Mr Justice Henchy, clear *prima facie* evidence that the law had been broken. It was for the jury to decide on the quality of Gibbons's statements, to mediate on the discrepancies in his accounts of the training in Fort Dunree; it was up to them to decide whether they fell 'within the category of technically correct statements which are made in parliament by politicians, or whether they show Mr Gibbons to be a man given to half truths and lies and whether as a result you should treat him as being discredited as a witness.'[50]

The jury took less than two hours to deliver its damning assessment. As the foreman read out the 'not guilty' verdicts, the court erupted. John Kelly jumped with joy. Kevin Boland, in the public gallery, was heard shouting, 'Who's vindicated now!' John Kelly was carried shoulder-high out of the court into the entrance hall, where a crowd clamoured for Haughey. 'We want Charlie!' Haughey obliged with a short statement.

On behalf of myself and my fellow-patriots, I would just like to say that I am grateful to you all, each and every one of you, especially the people from my own constituency, every single one of you, for your loyalty, devotion and faithfulness you have shown me during these recent difficult times.[51]

Blaney, Boland and Ó Móráin, along with Paudge Brennan, the parliamentary secretary who resigned in protest at the sackings, were then carried shoulder-high out of the building and into the glare of the television cameras. At a press conference, Haughey demanded the resignation of Lynch. 'I think those who are responsible for this debacle have no alternative but to take the honourable course that is open to them.'[52] Significantly, Haughey added that he did not believe that Lynch's New York speech articulated the true meaning of republicanism, though he maintained that it would take some time to formulate a new definition.

Haughey was clearly furious. He regarded the verdict as a complete vindication of his position and remarked:

> The political implications will be far-reaching. There is some dissatisfaction with the Taoiseach at the moment. I will confine myself to that remark.

He said he was never in any doubt that this was a political trial. Significantly, he endorsed the position of John Kelly and the Provisional IRA by arguing that 'in all my time in politics I have never met a finer man than John Kelly.' It was a clear attempt to be associated with the whiff of cordite. Haughey had emerged from the arms trials ambivalent towards political violence, a position that was to become the hallmark of his political style in future years. He now became the standard-bearer for the implementation of a hard line on the North, as both Blaney and Boland in effect stood aside.

Blaney told reporters that he regarded the trial as 'an international joke, and a sick one at that.' He predicted that Fianna Fáil would change allegiance within the next week. Boland discounted the possibility of a special ardfheis but hinted that the meeting of the parliamentary party the following Wednesday could provide the opportunity for real change. Haughey was careful also not to call for an election, rather the displacement of the leader, provoking the leader of the Labour Party, Brendan Corish, to charge that Fianna Fáil had forsaken democracy.

The stage was set for a renewed leadership challenge as five hundred Haughey supporters gathered at the Four Courts Hotel to the constant refrain of 'A Nation Once Again'. It appeared that Lynch's hold over Fianna Fáil was comprehensively undermined; but as the arms trial diarist Tom McIntyre noted sarcastically, 'few governments would have survived the tumultuous aftermath of the trial—but in Dublin, the Party, long in power, kept power.'[53] The reason touches on the central purpose of Fianna Fáil politics: the pursuit and maintenance of power.

The Government was clearly placed under increased pressure by the 'not guilty' verdicts. On the one hand the moral arguments by Haughey and the others that they had been the victims of a political trial had greater credibility. Secondly, the position of Gibbons was seriously undermined. Not only was he the most obvious symbol of the division within the party but the acquittals, in the light of Mr Justice Henchy's argument that either Haughey or Gibbons had lied, provided the implication that a serving minister had been guilty of perjury in the courts, and left the Government open to ridicule. The opposition charged that the trial demonstrated the total collapse of collective responsibility, that Government ministers could lie with impunity.

Fine Gael issued a statement suggesting that parliamentary democracy was as much imperilled by Gibbons as by the troika of Haughey, Blaney, and Boland.

> If we now face a situation in which Ministers feel free to deceive Dáil Éireann about any matter where the truth might inconvenience them, then in effect Ministers have become no longer answerable to parliament, and we have moved over to a system of government by junta. In such circumstances parliamentary proceedings can be nothing but a hollow farce.[54]

Ministers had been shown to be meddling in other departments with dubious authority; money was used to buy arms but was not agreed by the Dáil or open to scrutiny. The reputation of the country had been trampled underfoot, and Lynch was seen as ineffective until it was too late. There was much truth in the Fine Gael charge that the 'picture which emerges is one of sordid intrigue combined with extreme incompetence and gross laxity in the handling of public business.'[55]

Lynch, who was still in New York when news of the acquittals reached him, issued a statement claiming continued justification for his actions.

> In taking the decisions I took last May in relation to the attempted importation of arms, I felt it was there my duty lay as Head of the Government. I am convinced now as I was then that I made the right decision.[56]

He repeated his assertion that only the acceptance of the principle of unity by consent could provide a lasting peace.

Lynch decided to raise the stakes while still in New York, a strategy in which honour played little part. He told reporters:

> No-one can deny that there was this attempt to import arms illegally. Blaney was involved too.

He also responded to the criticism of Gibbons, saying there was no question of him asking for the resignation of a loyal minister. He maintained that Gibbons had taken action to stop the importing as soon as he understood what was going on, glossing over the knowledge of the attempted importing in March. Lynch concluded that there was no room in his Government for Haughey, adding:

> Republicanism doesn't mean guns. It doesn't mean using guns. It is the state of a nation.[57]

John Kelly was furious at the apparent questioning of the judicial process. He called it 'a piece of arrogance and vindictiveness and an insult to the integrity of the judicial system.' As Lynch was laying down the law in New York, in Dublin the Provisional IRA formally launched Sinn Féin at Liberty Hall. A twelve-member executive was set up, and Ruairí Ó Brádaigh was elected its president. For Ó Brádaigh the leadership of Fianna Fáil was immaterial: the dispute about republicanism missed the point.

> Irish homes have been raided in good old British style by the same 26-County forces, and two groups locked in a power struggle within Fianna Fáil vie with each other as to which is the more republican. Our comment is that neither are. Both elements have persecuted republicans, have jailed and coerced them. Mr Boland and Mr Haughey do not apologise for their concentration camps [i.e. 1957–62], their military tribunals, their harassment of Republicans, all in collaboration with Britain and in response to British pressure. All of them support the Free Trade Agreement with Britain and the EEC sell-out.[58]

The task facing Fianna Fáil was to minimise the disruption caused by the unrealisable expectations. This was to be achieved by keeping the illusion of unity at the forefront of policy while ensuring the participation of nationalists in a reformed Northern Ireland. It was the natural consequence of the speech of 11 July in which Lynch had argued that Ireland could not allow itself to be imprisoned by the past. It also reflected the logical consequence of the assertion by Lemass that there would always be a Northern Ireland government but that that government might not always be a part of the United Kingdom.[59] The strategy was to achieve unity within Northern Ireland, opening the way for possible unity later on—the essential sub-text of the Belfast Agreement negotiated in 1998. Once Northern Ireland was unified, then all options opened. This was the essential legacy of Lynch's vision and the real reason for Ó Brádaigh's denigration of Fianna Fáil.

Blaney and Boland again called for the resignation of the Taoiseach.[60] But, just as during the summer, a discreet distance began to emerge between Haughey and the two main instigators of a political heave against Lynch. Any prospect that an offensive could succeed dissipated as soon as the plane carrying Jack Lynch from New York touched down at Dublin Airport on Monday 26 October. The entire Government, with the exception of Patrick Hillery, who was returning from New York by sea, and Seán Flanagan, Minister for Lands, who had a speaking engagement in London, gathered to welcome him. Also there were surviving members of the 1916–23 generation, including Frank Aiken and Seán MacEntee. President de Valera's representative also attended. Michael McInerney pointed out in the *Irish Times*:

> If anyone, after that display wishes to say that they are better Republicans than Mr Lynch in Fianna Fáil, then they have a formidable task. They would have to answer that airport argument of yesterday. It was the Republic par excellence.[61]

Lynch was successfully deploying the same formula used in May, when the crisis broke, and again in June, when Boland was calling for his resignation. He played the loyalty card, the most important currency in Fianna Fáil. He made it clear in interviews in New York before his departure that all elected representatives in the Fianna Fáil leadership had signed a pledge to support the party in the Dáil, and to resign if called on by the National Executive. The message was clear: Lynch was determined to enforce his will. The dissidents in the party would have to accept his mandate, a mandate that included Gibbons, or leave the party. A general election in view of the economic crisis was political suicide, a fact not lost on the more sophisticated political dissidents.

Haughey had clearly made up his mind that now was not the time. He had made a major miscalculation in wrapping the Green Flag around him. It had touched a raw nerve, exposing the Republic to ever closer involvement in a political crisis that in 1970 represented an even greater threat to its security than in the febrile month of August 1969.

The *New Statesman* was scathing.

> Suddenly at their much publicised celebrations, brilliantly arranged by their public relations advisors, they all looked again like the old gang that Mr Lynch had ousted, and quite unlike the sea-green uncorruptibles their promoters had promoted them [as] in recent months. Many Fianna Fáil Dáil members who had wavered in their loyalty to Mr Lynch took fright at the prospect of these men running the state. The danger of an aggressive and perhaps undemocratic government in Dublin, which seemed to be near last weekend is now much more remote.[62]

At the meeting of the Fianna Fáil parliamentary party on Tuesday night Lynch received an overwhelming majority of 70 to 3 in favour of the motion that they would support him if a vote of no confidence was proposed by the opposition. It is understood that Haughey reversed his position by the end of the meeting and said he would support the Government. Lynch played down any suggestion of a split in the party and made it clear that the coming Dáil debate on the party's economic proposals would in effect be a vote of confidence in the Government.

The Dáil resumed on Wednesday 29 October. The country was facing a record deficit of £21 million, an alienated labour force and trade union movement, and a recognition that the harsh measures needed to balance the budget would amount to electoral suicide if the party fell. The Minister for Finance spoke of unreasonable and un-sustainable pay agreements and the need for serious economies. Lynch then decided that he had enough of the activities of his detractors within the party and personally tabled a motion calling for a reaffirm-ation of confidence in 'both the Taoiseach and the other members of the Government.'[63] This was designed to head off the threat posed by the tabling of a Fine Gael motion that singled out Gibbons.

In the vote of confidence, much of the court cases was relived, with tenacious questioning by Garret FitzGerald in particular, evincing from Gibbons the further knowledge that he had been aware of the arms conspiracy for some months.

> I had a pretty good idea for some months that the Special Branch of the police was on to Captain Kelly and on to this arms conspiracy generally. I had confirmation of this from the then Minister for Justice [Mícheál Ó Móráin] about this time too; as I have already said, I felt that since this was the case, it relieved me of the distasteful task of acting as policeman.

Here Gibbons went even further than in his evidence at the trials that he had a vestigial knowledge of Captain Kelly and his operation. Lynch's claim that the first he knew of the crisis was on 20 April rang increasingly hollow.[64]

Boland refused to support the Government, accusing Lynch of duplicity. He concluded that all he himself had left was his honour, and he intended to retain it. For the party he left behind, the imperative was staying in power, and if that meant gliding over the truth, then so be it. Gibbons was not going to be sacrificed. As the *Irish Times* pointed out in the immediate aftermath of the arms trials, they are hanging together—Fianna Fáil is a great organisation. So is the Mafia.[65]

For the moment at least, the fire of ideology had been extinguished. Blaney retreated to the political wilderness of County Donegal, his dreams of power obliterated. Haughey, the consummate politician, retained the whip, in large measure by debasing himself by voting against a no-confidence motion proposed in the Dáil by the opposition over Lynch's handling of the issue.

There was to be one final attempt by Boland to rescue Fianna Fáil from itself. At the 1971 ardfheis, held from 19 to 21 February, he mounted a savage attack on the leadership. It was a very public coup attempt, replete with alternative podium. Hillery was called on to respond on behalf of the leadership. Fianna Fáil, he declared, would remain loyal to the policy of Jack Lynch. 'We will continue that policy in spite of the bully boys within or without the organisation.' As pandemonium broke out, he shouted:

> Fianna Fáil will survive, as it did before. You can have Boland, but you can't have Fianna Fáil.[66]

Patriot games had ended with Lynch indisputably in charge of the party. From presenting an opportunity for a heave against a caretaker leader, the crisis in the North eventually offered that leader an opportunity to rid himself of the nationalist wing of the party. For the first time, he held undisputed control over his own party.

CHAPTER EIGHT

Provisional Verdict

T WENTY-NINE years, to the day, after the acquittals at the Four Courts, Charles Haughey travelled to Cork to attend the state funeral of Jack Lynch, the architect of his downfall and the man he eventually succeeded as leader of Fianna Fáil in 1979. The crowds thronging the streets outside St Patrick's Cathedral were universally hostile. The insults directed at Haughey, the immaculately groomed nemesis of the dead Taoiseach, as he walked alone into the cathedral reflected the bitter questioning of the nature of modern Irish society and the very different legacies bestowed by each man on the nation. Ireland is now attempting to come to terms with a political culture whose defining characteristics of greed, self-promotion and ostentation represent the antithesis of what Lynch stood for.[1]

It was a measure of Lynch's own distaste for the politics of modern Fianna Fáil that the funeral eulogy was not to be given by the present leader of the party, Bertie Ahern, but by Des O'Malley, the former leader of the Progressive Democrats. He formed the Progressive Democrats in 1986 after being expelled from Fianna Fáil, accused by Haughey of unbecoming conduct. A lapse in protocol led to Haughey sitting next to O'Malley as the latter prepared for a final attack on his great adversary. Haughey, visibly shaken by the hostility before the service, decided not to attend the burial. It was a wise choice. At the graveside O'Malley launched into a coruscating attack on the legacy of Charles Haughey and the dangers of irredentism.

Thirty years ago as a nation we were confronted with a dark choice. We could have caved in to sinister elements and put our country at mortal risk. But Jack Lynch chose not to. Confronted with some of the most difficult decisions to face any Taoiseach of the modern era, he took determined and resolute action to defend democracy and uphold the law.[2]

The personal animosity between O'Malley and Haughey knows no bounds and stems in large part from the positions taken during the Arms Crisis. O'Malley was an important ally of Lynch's during the Arms Crisis and was appointed Minister for Justice following the sackings of May 1970. His decision to withhold access to files from Mícheál Ó Móráin and his subsequent actions in clamping down on the IRA from 1970 to 1973 demonstrated not only his loyalty to Lynch but also his aversion to the republican movement. The oration, coming as Haughey already faced personal ruin and a possible prison sentence for obstructing the tribunal of inquiry into his personal finances, was designed to bury him politically in a way that the arms trials and subsequent inquiry by the Committee of Public Accounts had signally failed to do. But the eulogy of Lynch was perhaps as unwarranted as it was lacking in fundamental truth.[3]

O'Malley has always insisted that Jim Gibbons and Peter Berry were telling the truth in the arms trials and, as a consequence, that Haughey was clearly not. In a television interview in 1998 O'Malley repeated the charge. 'The fact that some people might not altogether agree with some of the verdicts that the jury came to is part of the price we pay for a democracy,' he proclaimed.[4] For O'Malley, in 1970 as in 1998 and again at Lynch's funeral, the imperative was to reject any suggestion that Lynch knew what was going on. In his rush to defend Gibbons, however, uncomfortable realities are glossed over, not least the culpability of Lynch himself in abdicating responsibility at the beginning of the crisis.

By contrast, Haughey, who until the Arms Crisis broke had never been publicly associated with nationalism, has been depicted as a dangerous machiavellian politician bereft of principle or scruple. Considerable surprise was expressed at the time of the ministerial sackings that Haughey had been involved in what appeared to be such adventurist policy-making. He seemed to epitomise the mohair generation as he gleefully enjoyed the high life in the Dublin of the nineteen-sixties. His background was not conducive to political advancement within Fianna Fáil either, until his marriage into the revolutionary generation provided access to the higher echelons of the political establishment.

Haughey assiduously courted the image of a pragmatist, the political fixer who delivered results. He appeared uninterested in the passions concerning Irish or the limitations of the revolution. He would indeed become a patron of the arts, offering tax concessions, but the suspicion remained that he lacked depth, lacked principle, a stain that even a marriage into the family of the country's most influential political strategist could not erase. It was one reason why Haughey was forced to withdraw from the succession race in 1966 in favour of the compromise candidate, Jack Lynch.

Haughey also assiduously courted that machine while ensuring that he positioned himself to take control, control he believed was pre-ordained. The emerging conflict in the North changed the dynamics of Southern politics, offering him the potential to accede to the leadership. There can be little doubt that Haughey did in fact use the conflict and his position as Minister for Finance to further his own personal objectives; but there was more to it than that.

It is imperative that we guard against over-neat interpretations of history, using the present as a prism for viewing the past. In our rush to pass judgment on the undoubtedly corrosive nature of Haughey's tenure as Taoiseach, we would do well to reflect on the impulses triggered by the outbreak of violence in 1969. These are impulses whose manipulation many in Irish society would prefer to forget.

The Government papers for 1969 clearly reveal that Lynch knew more about what was going on than has previously been understood. There was an acceptance in the civil service that the conflict within Northern Ireland offered opportunities to end partition within ten to fifteen years.[5] Destabilisation was possible precisely because important figures in Fianna Fáil were prepared to use the ownership of the national question to assert their position inside the party, the state, and ultimately the nation. It was a defining moment in Irish political history, a moment when the rhetoric of the nation became viewed as the most dangerous threat to its stability.

The central role in forcing the hand of the Government was played by Blaney, whose power and influence in the Fianna Fáil machine in the sixties has been largely written out of history. It was Blaney who pushed Lynch into making a hard-line speech in August 1969 and whose motivation all along was to destroy the Northern state, whatever the consequences. He was ably supported by Kevin

Boland, who portrayed himself as the conscience of Fianna Fáil.

Haughey's role was more ambiguous and more complex. As Minister for Finance he provided the money for the arming of what became the Provisional IRA, but his motivation has remained oblique, as even his most trenchant critics, such as Garret FitzGerald, would concede.

> Haughey has a very strong streak of Anglophobia which is close to republicanism. Some of the things he did were clearly motivated by Anglophobia. He had locked them [the IRA] up; the last internment warrants were signed by him. I always felt in dealing with him that he was very hostile to the IRA because they were a threat to his power if nothing else. On the other hand, there was this Anglophobia. It is very hard to work out the balance of forces that motivated him, and nobody has quite managed it.[6]

Haughey's family connections and first-hand knowledge of the subservient position of the Catholic minority in the North gave him a natural empathy when the calls came for weapons. Two other factors complicated his response to the outbreak of the conflict, each with a significant potential impact on the dominant position of Fianna Fáil in Irish society. Fianna Fáil had begun the move away from economic nationalism associated with its traditional policy. As a result, its ability to handle the disparate demands of various interest groups began to fail as wage restraint weakened and the ostentatious display of wealth emphasised the gap between rich and poor. Rising resentment in the form of work stoppages and unofficial strikes sapped confidence in the foreign investment sector that was to provide an alternative.

Haughey was exceptionally vulnerable to left-wing criticism, both as an architect of economic dislocation and as a central figure in the new nexus of power emerging through the fund-raising organisation Taca, which linked Fianna Fáil to the property developers and speculators now coming to the fore. It was ground that the politicisation of the republican movement under Cathal Goulding and Roy Johnston sought to undercut, putting forward the idea that fundamental change would also mean a change in Fianna Fáil power. As Fianna Fáil director of elections in 1969 Haughey played an important role in elevating ideology over policy in the 'Cuban socialism' attack on the Labour Party. This strategy also had the effect of emphasising the yawning gap between rhetoric and reality when the violence in Northern Ireland punctured the 1920–22 settlement.

Haughey was determined not to leave the nationalist arena to Blaney alone; he also wanted to crush any possibility of an ideological challenge that threatened the capitalist ethos he represented. It was imperative that the destabilisation of the country be managed, and it was for this primary purpose that he sought to use the Defence Committees as a vehicle with which to destroy the Goulding leadership.

For the leadership of Provisional Sinn Féin there had always been a reticence about the promises of Haughey. The militants within the IRA Army Council, including Ruairí Ó Brádaigh and Seán Mac Stiofáin, were from the start sceptical about the promises of Fianna Fáil gold. But Belfast had become the only arena that mattered, and little attention was paid there to the implications of the apparent support offered by Haughey and the others until the split had occurred. Ó Brádaigh argues that the Belfast commanders made a serious miscalculation in not attending the 1969 IRA convention. The actions of Military Intelligence ensured that the conflict was hermetically sealed within the Northern state.

> My view was that it was all getting very murky, and I was very opposed to it because I felt that we would be all dropped when it suited them. Fianna Fáil's interest and in particular a certain section was purely selfish, that it was to advance their political power and the power of certain individuals.[7]

To a large extent Haughey was a victim of his own success. When the IRA split, the danger to the stability of the Southern state weakened demonstrably, fundamentally shifting the balance of power within the Fianna Fáil Government. Now irredentist rhetoric appeared to be no longer just a response but a dangerous one through which the Southern state could be sucked into the vortex. It was a game played for exceptionally high stakes. A senior Government source close to Haughey suggests that there was a real belief that continued pressure on the Northern state would force its disintegration and allow for a renegotiation of the Anglo-Irish Treaty. Throughout his political career Haughey maintained that the Irish question was one to be determined between London and Dublin, a formulation that minimised any possibility of two separate identities sharing the territorial space of Ireland, each deserving mutual respect. Political violence could not only be seen to serve the ultimate goal of Fianna Fáil but could also undermine the authority of Lynch, while elevating Haughey to the rarefied heights of Irish patriot, a sobriquet he self-consciously adopted in the immediate aftermath of the acquittals.

Just as the civil rights movement had shifted beyond the control and purpose of the republican movement in 1968–9, however, so too the Provisional IRA was now following an agenda no longer controlled by Military Intelligence. The political monster created and nurtured in the ghettos of Belfast had mutated, and control over the Irish question became much more unstable. Advocating or condoning political violence now appeared simply irresponsible.

For the Provisionals to grow they required the continued alienation of the Catholic community. The heavy-handed security response to Provisional aggression created a vicious circle that heightened tensions and increased the unrealisable ambition that unity was achievable without causing an all-out civil war. This, ultimately, was what the Provisional IRA was threatening from Easter 1970 onwards and demonstrating from that autumn, as Ruairí Ó Brádaigh explains.

> In fact when the struggle developed in the North, the powers that be in the South regarded it, rightly or wrongly, as a much graver threat to their whole situation, involving the whole people of Ireland with Britain. It headed into a new political arena, a new all-Ireland political arena and a new kind of politics based on the distribution of wealth in the community rather than the personal antagonisms of the Civil War. That is were the real threat came in the end.[8]

According to a highly placed source, Haughey continued to believe that such a risk was justifiable if it meant securing the aim of Fianna Fáil. He had little time for the SDLP and disparagingly referred to John Hume as 'the high priest of compromise'.[9] The careful nurturing of the SDLP was a bulwark against the rise of the Provisionals and a defence against any domestic challenge within Fianna Fáil. Northern Ireland had become a proxy for the feuding factions within Fianna Fáil.

Following the acquittals, a cross-party consensus emerged to prevent the situation ever again getting out of control. Lynch played a pivotal role alongside Fine Gael in this retraction of the needs of the nation by establishing the Committee of Public Accounts. The hearings opened on 11 December 1970. Ninety-two meetings were held as lurid tales were read into the record. The final report itself conceded that

> the evidence received contained much that was irrelevant, hearsay or personal opinion. The arms trial and its consequences seemed to have coloured and polarised the attitudes of some witnesses.[10]

Peter Berry was advised by his political superior not to give evidence. He did, however, give the committee a private briefing. Garret FitzGerald remembers it as a moment of high drama.

> Berry didn't give evidence. He did say, rather dramatically, that he had served under every Minister for Justice from Kevin O'Higgins until the present time, and of all the Ministers of Justice that he served under the most effective was Charles Haughey, and this man set me up to be murdered. He felt he had been left holding the baby vis-à-vis the IRA, he was at risk, and he was now guarded by sixteen guards in rotation. He produced the gun and slammed it on the table and made the member of the committee he was facing jump sideways. It was a very dramatic moment.[11]

The veracity of the evidence was not the task in hand. The hearings were specifically designed to destroy any credibility pertaining to Charles Haughey. To this day many people, among them Garret FitzGerald, remain convinced that the acquittals marked a miscarriage of justice.

> It was a totally perverse verdict. They were intimidated. The atmosphere in the court was such that the jury were afraid to convict and unwilling to convict, and they weren't going to convict. They totally disregarded the evidence.
>
> *Was that the sole purpose of holding the Public Accounts Committee hearings into the money?*
>
> Well, we were all pretty frustrated after the trial, certainly, yes. And Lynch must have been. He agreed to it. He was being challenged by the verdict. His comments were blunt. So, yes, he was very unhappy about the verdict.
>
> *So there was a consensus among the political parties in the Republic that the implications of the verdict would be minimised by speedily holding an inquiry?*
>
> Offset rather than minimised, yes.
>
> *So that was a conscious decision by the political parties?*
>
> People didn't sit down and plot it, but that was everybody's natural reaction. Certainly when someone who had set out to betray the state while in government and got away with it and was seeking to undermine the law and demanding that the Taoiseach resign—we couldn't take that. There was a great sense of solidarity against the undermining of the state. In a crisis like that party politics are not that significant.[12]

The Department of Justice stonewalled the committee and again withheld information requested by Ó Móráin. Berry was humiliated by O'Malley. Further difficulties emerged for the Government with the revelation by Gibbons that he had in fact been told by Captain Kelly in April that the arms shipments would be paid for out of the exchequer, laundered through the Baggot Street accounts. It stretched credibility that Gibbons would not have informed Lynch before he told the Dáil on 14 May that

> I made specific inquiries as to whether any moneys could have been voted or could have been paid out of Exchequer funds or out of any public funds in respect of a consignment of arms of the size we have been dealing with. And I am assured that there was not and could not have been.[13]

The committee reported that no blame should be attached to the Taoiseach, who had acted in good faith on the strength of assurances given to him by the Department of Finance.[14] Gibbons was criticised for not relaying the information directly to Lynch, putting him in the position of 'unintentionally giving wrong evidence on this matter to the Dáil.'[15]

Further difficulties in accepting this interpretation come from the evidence of one of the report's own authors. According to FitzGerald, when Berry gave his briefing he mentioned in passing that within the arcane world of the civil service there were frequently different levels of internal communication. This prompted the committee to recall Charles Murray, who read out a report from Berry to Murray dated 21 May 1970. 'The first paragraph was blanked out; the second stated, "If you check you will find that the money came from the Red Cross Fund."'[16] The report was never published nor its implication probed.

O'Malley claimed in a television interview that Haughey was responsible for dividing Fianna Fáil out of base political ambition. The doubts that many people had about the validity of the prosecution evaporated because of the revelations in the tribunals about the credibility of Haughey as a witness. For O'Malley, then, the question of Lynch's role in the crisis ceased to be of relevance.

> I think that many of the wounds, if you like to put it that way, were personified in Mr Haughey and the attitude he took at that time, and indeed took for a very long time afterwards. But I think that even he came to realise that the very ultra-green course that he sought to pursue was really an inappropriate one. I wish that he had realised that sooner. I think it would have improved the atmosphere greatly if that realisation had come sooner.[17]

Lynch was presented as a man who saved the nation from itself, whose essential honesty redefined the nature of constitutional republicanism. His acceptance of the principle of unity by consent marked the institutionalisation of the 26-County state as the nation, the consequences of which still reverberate throughout the country. It is a view that crosses party boundaries. Garret FitzGerald, who was the Fine Gael spokesman on Northern Ireland in 1970 and who subsequently became leader of the party and as Taoiseach signed the Anglo-Irish Agreement in 1985, offers this assessment:

> His handling of the Arms Crisis in 1970 was very difficult for him: he was dealing with people who had deeper roots in the party than he had. His success in overcoming that difficulty and stabilising the Government and in marginalising those who had adventurous ideas about the North was of crucial importance to the stability of the state and of the island as a whole.[18]

This truncated definition of nationhood was significantly buttressed by Lynch's handling of Ireland's entry into the EEC in 1973. The distancing of the Republic from the carnage in Northern Ireland as the IRA went on the offensive from late 1970 onwards, coupled with the enthusiastic embracing of pooled sovereignty in the European context, has significantly weakened territorial attachments to unity south of the border. By the time Haughey gained power in 1979, despite a retreat to rhetoric, the moment of opportunity he sensed in 1969 and 1970 had gone.

This new ideological position now informs policy not only in Fine Gael and the Labour Party but also crucially in Fianna Fáil itself, as evidenced by its enthusiastic endorsement of the Belfast Agreement.[19] It was only in death that Fianna Fáil found in Lynch the architect of the current process. According to Albert Reynolds, the nation owes him 'a deep debt of gratitude' for bringing it through a very difficult time when the whole country could have exploded into violence and civil war.

> I always remember his view at the time that no taint of suspicion should attach to any of these ministers, and he followed that through. It was a good standard to set. In fact I have followed it through myself subsequently.[20]

Reynolds argues that the 'Celtic tiger' economy, with the Republic showing substantial economic growth, offers the opportunity of closer co-operation between North and South. It is a retreat to the economic determinism of Lemass and Lynch; but there is an important corollary: economic co-operation represents the final goal. The Belfast Agreement institutionalises a distance between North and South.

> There is no reason why the other part of the island cannot indeed be part of the growth and prosperity that we have, but they have to do it for themselves. They have to work out their own future. They have to embrace the Good Friday Agreement, which I hope they will, and they have to create a new society where guns and arms and ammunition are simply not required. You need to have peace and stability at home, and that I think is in their hands and not in anyone else's.[21]

It was a message underlined by Bertie Ahern at the Fianna Fáil ardfheis on 4 March 2000. He made a point of emphasising Lynch's contribution to the party, recalling him as 'a leader whose integrity and innate decency will always be deeply treasured.'[22] Ahern maintained that the Belfast Agreement represented the future, an agreement based on inclusiveness within the confines of Northern Ireland. In an important passage, he maintained that demilitarisation and decommissioning went hand in hand.

> I understand only too well the difficulties that some people have with the very idea of decommissioning. But if democracy is to flourish, if inclusive partnership government is to be sustained, then all the armies must be stood down … A few small groups still suffer from the lingering delusion that it is possible to bring about a forced unity. More than forty years ago Éamon de Valera predicted absolutely accurately that it would not work and that even if it could it would ruin national life for generations. The only alternative policy, and it has long been Fianna Fáil policy, is to move forward on the basis of agreement and consent, while insisting on an equality of rights.[23]

Ahern concluded that while the future could not be pre-judged,

> we will only ever unite with people if we are prepared to treat them as equals and friends, and respect leaders or parties whose function is to protect the basic interests of their community as they, and not we, see it.[24]

The speech marked a formal debt of gratitude to Lynch for beginning a process that was formalised by the Belfast Agreement. It was a fitting tribute to his role in creating a new consensus in Irish politics in which there is no ideological incapacity for either Fine Gael or

Fianna Fáil in pursuing long-term policies in relation to the North, now clearly defined as a separate place with a legitimate separate identity.

Ahern proclaimed that Fianna Fáil remained a republican party. The definition is remarkably similar to that used by Lynch in 1970 when he proclaimed in the immediate aftermath of the acquittals that 'the Republic does not mean guns. It does not mean using guns. It is the state of a nation.'

Notes

Preface (pp ix–xvi)

1. It is ironic that Haughey, his fingers once burnt by involvement in the cauldron of Northern politics, was, as Taoiseach, to pass the opportunity to find a solution to Albert Reynolds, who succeeded him as leader of Fianna Fáil.

2. Here a distinction must be drawn between the IRA and the ability of the IRA's campaign to influence the leadership of Fianna Fáil. The threat posed to the stability of the state changed dramatically following the sackings as the IRA campaign intensified. The result was a serious clamp-down on IRA activity through the introduction of the Special Criminal Court and restrictions on interviews with members of Sinn Féin.

3. The most extended treatment so far can be found in Kelly's *Orders for the Captain* and a companion volume, *The Thimble-Riggers*. Vincent Browne provided much new evidence based on the diaries of Peter Berry, former Secretary of the Department of Justice, in a series of articles for *Magill* in 1980. For an academic view see Cruise O'Brien, *States of Ireland*, and Patterson, *The Politics of Illusion*, 121–35.

4. *Irish Times*, 31 July 1998.

5. Bishop and Mallie, *The Provisional IRA*, 132.

6. Coogan, *The Troubles*, 97.

7. Coogan, *The Troubles*, 97–102. Coogan is correct in drawing attention to the fact that general order no. 8, precluding attacks in the Republic, long predates the formation of the Provisionals, but he fails to take into account the threat the conflagration in the North posed to the Republic. That Coogan himself doubts the veracity of his own

account is seen by the caveat that 'it's as accurate a résumé as can be furnished at the time of writing' (p. 98).

8. Maurice Hayes, 'Documents give only part of the story,' *Irish Independent,* 3 January 2000.

9. Interview with Garret FitzGerald.

Chapter 1 (pp 1–32)

1. IRA statement quoted by Hennessey in *A History of Northern Ireland,* 107.

2. Clayton, *Enemies and Passing Friends,* xiii. Clayton's central point is the characterisation of Northern Ireland as the remnants of a settler society (p. 227). See also Wright, *Northern Ireland: A Comparative Analysis.*

3. The potential for the labour movement to reduce sectarian tensions was short-lived, but one example concerned a dock strike in 1907. See Brewer, *Anti-Catholicism in Northern Ireland,* 80–81. See also Michael Farrell, *Northern Ireland: The Orange State,* 16–17.

4. Alvin Jackson, 'Irish Unionism, 1905–21,' in Peter Collins (ed.), *Nationalism and Unionism: Conflict in Ireland, 1885–1921* (Belfast 1994), 35–46.

5. *Portadown News,* 25 May 1912, quoted by Clayton in *Enemies and Passing Friends,* 35–6.

6. A complete account of the atmosphere in Belfast on the day of the signing can be found in Stewart, *The Ulster Crisis,* 58–68.

7. Ian Lustik, *Unsettled States, Disputed Lands: Britain and Ireland, France and Algeria, Israel and the West Bank-Gaza* (1993).

8. Historians are divided over the provenance of the covenant. Donald Akenson, in *God's Peoples: Covenant and Land in South Africa, Israel, and Ulster* (Ithaca, NY, 1992), 186, claims it is redolent with Presbyterian imagery, a claim that is rejected by Brewer, *Anti-Catholicism in Northern Ireland,* 83. What is clear is that the document, signed by almost the entire adult Protestant population of Ulster, was designed not only to exert pressure on London but also to conflate Protestant identity with citizenship.

9. *Northern Whig,* quoted by Paul Bew in *Ideology and the Irish Question,* 70.

10. Bew, *Ideology and the Irish Question,* 53.

11. Bew, *Ideology and the Irish Question,* 45. See also Graham Walker's perceptive essay 'Thomas Sinclair: Presbyterian liberal unionist' in English and Walker, *Unionism in Modern Ireland,* 19–40.

12. Clayton, *Enemies and Passing Friends,* 87. See also her examination of newspaper editorials on the definition of Ulster (p. 86–9).

13. Books with titles such as *The Ulster Scot* (1914), *The Truth about Ulster* (1914), *The Soul of Ulster* (1917), *Unconquerable Ulster* (1919) and *Ulster*

in the X-Rays (1923) proliferated. See Ian McBride, 'Ulster and the British problem' in English and Walker, *Unionism in Modern Ireland*, 7.

14. Eamon Phoenix, *Northern Nationalism: Nationalist Politics, Partition, and the Catholic Minority in Northern Ireland, 1890–1940* (Belfast 1994), 76.

15. For a chilling account see Hart, *The Irish Republican Army and its Enemies*.

16. Kelly, *Bonfires on the Hillside*, 15.

17. Hennessey, *A History of Northern Ireland*, 13.

18. *News Letter*, 13 July 1920.

19. *New Letter*, 15 July 1920, quoted by Kenna in *The Belfast Pogroms*, 115.

20. Kenna, *The Belfast Pogroms*, 16.

21. Kenna, *The Belfast Pogroms*, 36–8.

22. This is a prime example of the kind of representational violence identified by Wright in *Northern Ireland: A Comparative Analysis*, 11–20.

23. Laffan, *The Partition of Ireland*, 77.

24. Michael Farrell, *Northern Ireland: The Orange State*, 39–50.

25. Kenna, *The Belfast Pogroms*, 44–5.

26. Wright, *Northern Ireland: A Comparative Analysis*, 53.

27. Feargal Cochrane, *Unionist Politics and the Politics of Unionism since the Anglo-Irish Agreement* (Cork 1997), 83.

28. Quoted by Dunphy in *The Making of Fianna Fáil Power in Ireland*, 68.

29. Garvin, *1922*, 155.

30. Lee, *Ireland, 1912–85*, 155.

31. English, *Ernie O'Malley*, 31.

32. Bew, Hazelkorn and Patterson, *The Dynamics of Irish Politics*, 78.

33. The range of opinion is shown by contrasting the positions taken by Bew, Hazelkorn and Patterson, *The Dynamics of Irish Politics*, 66, Cronin, *The Blueshirts and Irish Politics*, and Lee, *Ireland, 1912–85*, 181. Bew, Hazelkorn and Patterson assert that fascism was a real threat; Cronin suggests that the Blueshirts were proto-fascists; while Lee argues that fascism was 'far too intellectually demanding. Blueshirts were simply traditional conservatives decked out in fashionable but ideologically ill-fitting continental garb.'

34. See especially Dunphy, *The Making of Fianna Fáil Power in Ireland*, 206–27.

35. English, *Radicals and the Republic*, 265.

36. Dunphy, *The Making of Fianna Fáil Power in Ireland*, 304.

37. Patterson, *The Politics of Illusion*, 85.

38. Mac Stiofáin, *Memoirs of a Revolutionary*, 1–14.

39. Quoted by Hennessey in *A History of Northern Ireland*, 101.

40. O'Halpin, *Defending Ireland*, 298.

41. Patterson, *The Politics of Illusion*, 90.

42. Martin Mansergh, 'The republican ideal regained,' in Porter, *The Republican Ideal*, 54.

43. Martin Mansergh, 'The republican ideal regained,' in Porter, *The Republican Ideal*, 52–3.

44. Henry Patterson, 'Seán Lemass and the Ulster question, 1959–65,' *Journal of Contemporary History*, vol. 34 (1), 145–59. Patterson argues that 'we can see anti-partitionism in this period primarily as an ideology of consolation for a nationalist project whose central material dimension had just been unceremoniously jettisoned' (p. 159).

45. Horgan, *Seán Lemass*, 329.

46. Horgan, *Seán Lemass*, 337.

47. *Dáil Debates,* vol. 225, col. 898–918, 11 November 1968, quoted by Manning in *James Dillon,* 380.

48. See English, *Radicals and the Republic,* for a detailed discussion of the aims and limitations of the republican left.

49. Bishop and Mallie, *The Provisional IRA,* 51.

50. The last inmates were released from Crumlin Road prison in Belfast in December 1963. Seán Mac Stiofáin recalls a letter from the veteran Northern republican Jimmy Steele bitterly complaining that the prisoners were kept inside because of the Dublin leadership's failure to call off a pointless campaign (interview with Seán Mac Stiofáin).

51. For a trenchant analysis see Patterson, *The Politics of Illusion,* 99–104.

52. 'The IRA in the 1970s,' *United Irishman,* January 1970.

53. For a useful résumé of Taca and its activities see Gene Kerrigan and Pat Brennan, 'A scandalous country,' *Sunday Independent,* 31 October 1969.

54. Interview with Ruairí Ó Brádaigh. The theoretical basis of this position is outlined in a statement issued by Tom Maguire, the last surviving member of the second Dáil, in 1969, quoted by Ruairí Ó Brádaigh in *Dílseacht: The Story of Comdt-General Tom Maguire and the Second Dáil* (Dublin 1997), 64.

55. Mac Stiofáin, *Memoirs of a Revolutionary,* 92.

56. See 'Where Sinn Féin Stands' (Republican Lecture Series, 1A) (1974), 2. This timing differs from that given by Patterson, *The Politics of Illusion,* 105, who suggests that the measures were adopted at the 1965 ardfheis. While Patterson is correct to argue that the plans represented a major policy departure, the reality was that Goulding and Johnston were not in the unassailable position he suggests.

57. Bell, *The Irish Troubles,* 131.

58. Interview with Seán Mac Stiofáin.

59. Interview with Seán Mac Stiofáin.

60. Patterson, *The Politics of Illusion,* 99.

61. An agent was severely beaten up, however (interview with Ruairí Ó Brádaigh).

62. Interview with Seán Mac Stiofáin.

63. Interview with Seán Mac Stiofáin.

64. Taylor, *Provos,* 23.

65. Interview with John Kelly.

66. This view is accepted wholeheartedly by Robert White, *Provisional Irish Republicans,* 54. White quotes Joe Cahill—a leading IRA man who was imprisoned in the nineteen-forties and who admits he played no part in the discussions in the republican movement throughout the late nineteen-sixties—to support the assertion that 'abstentionism is important. Military defence of the people is essential.'

67. Bell, *The Irish Troubles,* 140.

68. Bishop and Mallie, *The Provisional IRA,* 69–74.

69. Patterson, *The Politics of Illusion,* 97.

70. Ignatieff, *Blood and Belonging,* 164. Ignatieff's central point is that the conflict in Northern Ireland mirrors that in Croatia, Serbia and Ukraine and that it is the fear of domination that propels the spiral towards violence.

71. For an enlightening view of the strategy of the republican movement see 'Copy of the IRA Political and Military Plan,' included as an appendix to the report of the Scarman Inquiry, vol. 2, 45–52.

72. See Ó Dochartaigh, *From Civil Rights to Armalites,* 19–61, for an even-handed account of the role Derry activists played in the descent into chaos.

73. Éamonn McCann, *War and an Irish Town,* 99.

74. Hennessey, *A History of Northern Ireland,* 142.

75. David Harkness, *Ireland in the Twentieth Century: Divided Island* (London 1996), 99.

76. See Sacks, *The Donegal Mafia,* for an assessment of the Blaney machine.

77. By October 1968 Blaney was the most skilful political strategist in Fianna Fáil. He was well suited to the task of organising the vote and was quite prepared to keep the Civil War issue and Fianna Fáil's commitment to the ideal of national unity to the fore. One example was the by-election for Limerick East in May 1968, during which signs painted on roads proclaimed 'Remember the 77'—a reference to the execution of republican prisoners during the Civil War. See Keogh, *Twentieth-Century Ireland,* 296.

78. Bew and Gillespie, *Northern Ireland: A Chronology of the Troubles,* 9.

79. Interview with Seán Mac Stiofáin.

80. Following the split, the Provisional IRA reverted to this formulation.

81. Interview with Ruairí Ó Brádaigh.

82. Interview with Ruairí Ó Brádaigh.

83. See Richard Rose, *Governing Without Consensus.* Rose found that 70 per cent of Protestants did not admit that any discrimination took place in Northern Ireland.

84. See Goulding interview with *Belfast Telegraph,* 16 February 1966.
85. Interview with Seán Mac Stiofáin.
86. Arthur, *The People's Democracy,* 36–44.
87. Michael Farrell, *Northern Ireland: The Orange State,* 249.
88. Arthur, *The People's Democracy,* 41–2.
89. Interview with Seán Mac Stiofáin. In a separate interview, Ruairí
    Ó Brádaigh recalled a PD leader telling him in late May 1969 that he
    hoped the IRA had an armed strategy, because things were getting
    worse and serious violence was inevitable.
90. Michael Gallagher, *The Irish Labour Party in Transition, 1957–82*
    1982), 91.
91. Lee, *Ireland, 1912–85,* 410.
92. Interview with Michael Mills for 'Spotlight,' BBC1 Northern Ireland,
    10 March 1998.
93. Interview with Seán Mac Stiofáin.
94. Taylor, *Provos,* 46.
95. Taylor, *Provos,* 45.
96. Interview with Seán Mac Stiofáin.
97. Interview with Seán Mac Stiofáin.

Chapter 2 (pp 33–63)

1. See Father John Hassan's account in Kenna, *The Belfast Pogroms.* For a
   contemporary account of the role of the Orange Order in asserting
   supremacy see 'Spotlight,' BBC1, 26 May 1998. The organiser of the
   North Belfast Orange parade, when asked why the march could not
   be confined to exclusively Protestant areas, declared somewhat baldly:
   'What would be the point of that?'
2. Cruise O'Brien, *States of Ireland,* 160–1. Cruise O'Brien maintains
   that 'when Orangemen marched into, or alongside, a Catholic area
   what they meant was that Catholics must accept the fact of *Protestant*
   domination. Now, if Catholics were going to march in Protestant
   areas, what they meant was that *Catholic* domination was coming.'
   (Emphasis in original.) Cruise O'Brien's central point is that street
   politics had little to do with civil rights but involved a clash of
   sectarian forces. 'The people of the ghetto were not committed to
   civil rights doctrine. They were interested in the relation between
   "us" and "them," and in what promised a change in that relation:
   new tones of voice, new movements of feet.'
3. This description of the Ulster Special Constabulary comes from
   the International Commission of Jurists, which launched a scathing
   attack on the Northern Ireland legal system in a report published
   in June 1969. The fact that the general secretary of the ICJ at the
   time was Seán MacBride, the former Minister for External Affairs
   and previously a leader of the IRA, was enough for the

Stormont establishment to reject the findings. See *Belfast Telegraph*, 19 June 1969.

4. Submission on behalf of the RUC by R. R. Chambers QC, *Violence and Civil Disturbances in Northern Ireland in 1969: Report of Tribunal of Inquiry* [Scarman Report], 67.

5. *Violence and Civil Disturbances in Northern Ireland in 1969: Report of Tribunal of Inquiry* [Scarman Report], 72–3.

6. *Violence and Civil Disturbances in Northern Ireland in 1969: Report of Tribunal of Inquiry* [Scarman Report], vol. 1, 11.

7. *Dáil Debates*, vol. 241, col. 1401.

8. Harold Black, Cabinet Secretary to Sir Philip Allen at Home Office, Stormont, 3 August 1969, quoted in *Irish Times*, 3 January 2000. Black concluded that the British authorities 'should be in no doubt whatsoever that in the NI view, the suspension of a democratically-elected government would lead to a major constitutional convulsion and the repercussions in terms of violence and civil strife would be very grave indeed.' See also James Downey, 'Troubles blighted a generation,' *Irish Independent*, 3 January 2000, and Eamon Phoenix, 'Stormont gears up for security solution to north's political problems,' *Irish News*, 3 January 2000.

9. Maurice Hayes, 'Documents give only part of the story,' *Irish Independent*, 3 January 2000.

10. McCann, *War and an Irish Town*, 113–14.

11. Quoted by Purdie in *Politics in the Streets*, 42–3. While Purdie's analysis of the civil rights movement is primarily concerned with the history of the movement up to 5 October 1968, it is interesting to note that Keenan and the IRA in Derry do not merit any mention with regard to the take-over in July 1969. This is a serious omission. Keenan was to play a central role in the descent into violence, and it is clear that this was his intention from the beginning.

12. Bishop and Mallie, *The Provisional IRA*, 94–9.

13. McCann, *War and an Irish Town*, 114.

14. Bishop and Mallie, *The Provisional IRA*, 98.

15. Interview with Seán Mac Stiofáin.

16. Keenan had ordered that the barricades to the Bogside be raised at 3:30 p.m.—two hours before the RUC baton charge. The barricades were not necessary at that point to stop a bloodbath. See Bishop and Mallie, *The Provisional IRA*, 99.

17. Ó Dochartaigh, *From Civil Rights to Armalites*, 121.

18. Maurice Hayes, 'Documents give only part of the story,' *Irish Independent*, 3 January 2000.

19. Quoted by Hennessey in *A History of Northern Ireland*, 164.

20. James Callaghan, *A House Divided* (London 1973), 15.

21. John Chilcott, quoted by Rose in *How the Troubles Came to Northern Ireland,* 167.

22. Department of Defence contingency plan quoted by Ronan Fanning in 'Living in those troubled times,' *Sunday Independent,* 2 January 2000.

23. Rose, *How the Troubles Came to Northern Ireland,* 150–70.

24. Rose, *How the Troubles Came to Northern Ireland,* 177–8.

25. Maurice Hayes, 'Documents only give part of the story,' *Irish Independent,* 3 January 2000.

26. Cruise O'Brien, *States of Ireland,* 196.

27. Government minutes, 13 August 1969, 2000/6/957, S9361.

28. 'Partition and Policy,' note presented to Government, 13 August 1969, Department of the Taoiseach, 2000/6/957.

29. 'Partition and Policy,' Department of the Taoiseach, 13 August 1969, 2000/6/957.

30. Dáil Debates, vol. 241, col. 137.

31. *Irish Independent,* 21 October 1999.

32. T. Ryle Dwyer, 'Dangerous journeys round the rocks in the boat that Jack built,' *Examiner,* 21 October 1999. See also Cruise O'Brien, *States of Ireland,* 198–9.

33. Desmond Fisher, 'Irishman's Diary,' *Irish Times,* 25 October 1999.

34. This approach was typical of Lynch's handling of the North. Placing the blame for civil disturbances on partition alone was the bedrock of his Northern policy; partition was also blamed for the riots in Derry on 5 October 1968.

35. Text of Lynch's address, RTE (television), 13 August 1969. See also *Violence and Civil Disturbances in Northern Ireland in 1969: Report of Tribunal of Inquiry* [Scarman Report], vol. 2, 42–3. For a critical reading of Lynch's speech see Cruise O'Brien, *States of Ireland,* 198–9.

36. For an account of the background to the speech see Vincent Browne, 'The arms trial,' *Magill,* May 1980, the first of three influential articles published in successive issues. Browne's account contains fascinating information collated from the diaries of Peter Berry, Secretary of the Department of Justice. He captures the chaotic nature of events, but his approach shows the limitations of not viewing the Arms Crisis as a power play within Fianna Fáil; hence his interpretation that the Lynch speech amounted to 'a declaration of war against Northern Ireland.' *Magill,* May 1980, 36.

37. Bishop and Mallie, *The Provisional IRA,* 105. It is interesting to note that when the Catholic residents of the area gave their submission to the Scarman Tribunal, they claimed the incident was brought about by the 'ill-considered actions on the part of the police in an area where they knew there were a number of Republicans with hostile feelings to the police.' See submission on behalf of the Roman

Catholic residents of Lower Falls and Divis Street by H. G. McGrath QC, *Violence and Civil Disturbances in Northern Ireland in 1969: Report of Tribunal of Inquiry* [Scarman Report], 10.

38. Interview with Paddy Kennedy.

39. Submission on behalf of the RUC by R. R. Chambers QC, *Violence and Civil Disturbances in Northern Ireland in 1969: Report of Tribunal of Inquiry* [Scarman Report], 75.

40. Sharrock and Devenport, *Man of War, Man of Peace?*, 58.

41. *Violence and Civil Disturbances in Northern Ireland in 1969: Report of Tribunal of Inquiry* [Scarman Report], 74.

42. See *Violence and Civil Disturbances in Northern Ireland in 1969: Report of Tribunal of Inquiry* [Scarman Report], and the exceptionally useful McKittrick et al., *Lost Lives*, 33–40.

43. Interview with Paddy Kennedy.

44. The sermon was recorded, and excerpts were broadcast on 'Spotlight,' BBC1 Northern Ireland, 10 March 1998. For the full text of Father Egan's sermon see Coogan, *The Troubles*, 85–8.

45. *Violence and Civil Disturbances in Northern Ireland in 1969: Report of Tribunal of Inquiry* [Scarman Report], quoted by McKittrick et al., *Lost Lives*, 35.

46. *Evening Press*, 14 August 1969.

47. Submission on behalf of the RUC by R. R. Chambers QC, *Violence and Civil Disturbances in Northern Ireland in 1969: Report of Tribunal of Inquiry* [Scarman Report], 81–2.

48. *Irish News*, 16 August 1999.

49. Devlin, *Straight Left*, 106.

50. Devlin, *Straight Left*, 86.

51. See also McKittrick et al., *Lost Lives*, 38–9, for useful information on the role of the Fianna.

52. See Cruise O'Brien, *States of Ireland*, 186. The radical orators had nothing further to offer to the Catholic population; they needed defence in a situation partly produced by the radical orators themselves.

53. Coogan, *The Troubles*, 88. For audio version see 'Spotlight,' BBC1 Northern Ireland, 10 March 1997.

54. Press statement by Cardinal Conway, 14 August 1969, *Violence and Civil Disturbances in Northern Ireland in 1969: Report of Tribunal of Inquiry* [Scarman Report], vol. 2, 41–2.

55. Press statement by Cardinal Conway, 17 August 1969, *Violence and Civil Disturbances in Northern Ireland in 1969: Report of Tribunal of Inquiry* [Scarman Report], vol. 2, 43.

56. Press statement by Catholic Church, 23 August 1969, *Violence and Civil Disturbances in Northern Ireland in 1969: Report of Tribunal of Inquiry* [Scarman Report], vol. 2, 43.

57. Press statement by Catholic Church, 23 August 1969, *Violence and Civil Disturbances in Northern Ireland in 1969: Report of Tribunal of Inquiry* [Scarman Report], vol. 2, 43.

58. Submission on behalf of the Roman Catholic residents of Lower Falls and Divis Street by H. G. McGrath QC, *Violence and Civil Disturbances in Northern Ireland in 1969: Report of Tribunal of Inquiry* [Scarman Report], 120.

59. Submission on behalf of the RUC by R. R. Chambers QC, *Violence and Civil Disturbances in Northern Ireland in 1969: Report of Tribunal of Inquiry* [Scarman Report], 80.

60. James Chichester-Clark, speech to Stormont House of Commons, 14 August 1969, *Violence and Civil Disturbances in Northern Ireland in 1969: Report of Tribunal of Inquiry* [Scarman Report], vol. 2, 38.

61. Speech by James Chichester-Clark at press conference in Stormont Castle, 17 August 1969, *Violence and Civil Disturbances in Northern Ireland in 1969: Report of Tribunal of Inquiry* [Scarman Report], vol. 2 39–40.

62. Sir Andrew Gilchrist to Foreign Office, 14 August 1969, quoted in *Irish Times,* 3 January 2000. It turned out to be a prescient prediction. Demonstrators burnt the British embassy in Dublin on 2 February 1972 following a demonstration against the killing of thirteen civilians by the British army in Derry on Bloody Sunday. For a somewhat contrite account of how, along with other trade unionists, he was manipulated by the IRA in the burning of the embassy see Keogh, *Twentieth-Century Ireland,* 310, n. 75. While not doubting Keogh's own probity, it is beyond question that the nationalist passions ignited in the Republic were well captured by Gilchrist in August 1969 and retained their potency as late as February 1972. It took little effort to manipulate a peaceful protest into a riot.

63. For a searing indictment of the Lynch Government's response see Boland, *Indivisible Faith,* 206. Boland refers to the Government as a 'group of lazy smug, self-interested men starting a new secure five year tenure of office.'

64. Brady, *Arms and the Men,* 37. Brady was a significant participant in Fianna Fáil circles in the late nineteen-sixties. He was Blaney's chief speech-writer and was later to play a pivotal role in the propaganda war waged in the North and within Fianna Fáil, as described in chapter 3.

65. Sacks, *The Donegal Mafia,* 196. Sacks maintains that the Donegal Mafia wielded immense influence in Irish society and that its power was 'analogous to the [Mayor] Daley machine's power [in Boston] in America.'

66. Quoted in *Hibernia,* 29 August 1969.

67. See searing profiles of Ó Móráin in *Hibernia,* 11 April 1969, 5 December 1969, and 3 April 1970.

68. *Hibernia,* 27 June 1969.

69. Sacks, *The Donegal Mafia,* 75.

70. *Hibernia,* 29 August 1969. For a more sympathetic reading see Brady, *Arms and the Men,* 26–7, 33–4.

71. Important files relating to Government policy in 1969 were not released in January 2000. Files that would throw light on the extent of divisions in the Government were reported to be missing (*Sunday Tribune,* 2 January 2000); the chairwoman of the National Archives Advisory Council, Margaret MacCurtain, said that an investigation would be carried out. The files were later discovered and released. But important minutes appear still to be missing, or were not committed to paper. Lynch himself is reported to have taken a number of files with him when he resigned as Taoiseach in 1979 (interview with Garret FitzGerald).

72. Government minutes, 14 August 1969, 'Partition and Policy,' Department of the Taoiseach, 2000/6/957.

73. Interview with Tim Pat Coogan.

74. Coogan, *The Troubles,* 97–102.

75. Department of External Affairs briefing note, 16 August 1969, 'Partition and Policy,' Department of the Taoiseach, 2000/6/958. The civil service immediately requested the Gardaí to strengthen the security around Lynch's home in Dublin. A copy of the briefing was forwarded to Peter Berry at the Department of Justice.

76. Interview with John Kelly.

77. Anonymous, *Fianna Fáil and the IRA,* 23.

78. Transcript of interview with South Derry IRA member, provided to the author by Chris Moore.

79. Purdie, *Politics in the Streets,* 47. For an assessment of the impact the civil rights movement had on unionism see also Sarah Nelson, *Ulster's Uncertain Defenders* (Belfast 1984), 72.

80. Quoted by Brian Dooley in *Black and Green: The Fight for Civil Rights in Northern Ireland and Black America* (London 1998), 44.

81. Transcript of interview with South Derry IRA member, provided to the author by Chris Moore.

82. Military Intelligence documents in the author's possession.

83. Military Intelligence documents in the author's possession.

84. Military Intelligence documents in the author's possession.

85. Séamus Brady, situation report for Government Information Bureau, presented to the Government on 22 August.

86. 'Partition and Policy,' Department of the Taoiseach, 2000/6/958.

87. The meeting was organised by Paddy Kennedy. Kennedy had attended Maynooth seminary with Captain Kelly's brother; Kennedy confirmed this to the author.

88. Interview with John Kelly.

89. Fitt was later to feature prominently in the first attempt by John Kelly and Captain James Kelly to buy arms in London. See below.
90. Military Intelligence documents in the author's possession.
91. *Dáil Debates,* vol. 241, col. 1406, 22 October 1969.
92. *Dáil Debates,* vol. 241, col. 1413–14.
93. *Dáil Debates,* vol. 241, col. 1418.
94. *Dáil Debates,* vol. 241, col. 1460.
95. *Dáil Debates,* vol. 241, col. 1438.
96. *Dáil Debates,* vol. 241, col. 1439.
97. *Dáil Debates,* vol. 241, col. 1496.
98. *Dáil Debates,* vol. 241, col. 1535–6.
99. See Vincent Browne, 'The Arms Crisis,' *Magill,* May 1980, 38. Browne suggests that 'an inescapable conclusion … is that a great deal of the blame for what happened lies with Jack Lynch, not because of any deviousness or duplicity on his part, as some of his enemies would like to allege, rather because of an indecisiveness and weakness which was responsible for a great deal of the chaos that ensued.'
100. Interview with James Kelly.

Chapter 3 (pp 64–95)

1. Bew, Hazelkorn and Patterson, *The Dynamics of Irish Politics,* 99. The authors describe Lynch's decision as the most startling abdication of responsibility in the history of the state.
2. Taylor, *Provos,* 60.
3. Military Intelligence documents in the author's possession.
4. Interview with James Kelly.
5. Evidence of Charles Haughey to second arms trial, *Irish Times,* 20 October 1970.
6. *Dáil Debates,* vol. 249, col. 443, 3 November 1970.
7. Billy McKee, quoted by Taylor in *Provos,* 61.
8. Devlin, *Straight Left,* 116.
9. Interview with John Kelly.
10. The Department of Justice was horrified at the frequency with which IRA spokesmen, such as Goulding, appeared without adverse comment in the media, particularly the *Irish Times* and RTE. The department believed it was dealing with an unlawful, treasonable organisation, contemptuous of parliamentary democracy and committed to the establishment of a socialist republic; see Justice, 20/69, quoted in *Irish Times,* 3 January 2000.
11. Dennis Kennedy, 'Propaganda drive produced little,' *Irish Times,* 16 October 1969. Kennedy, the paper's diplomatic correspondent, was severely critical of the early period, with its heavy use of photographs, 'with rather emotive captions. This was too blatantly propaganda for many people.'

12. For circumstance of employment see *Committee of Public Accounts, 1968/69–70*, 219. Haughey had the power to recruit Brady because of the imperative of obtaining as much information as possible; see Haughey's evidence to the second arms trial quoted above.

13. Submission by Séamus Brady by way of a statement to the Dáil Committee of Public Accounts, *Committee of Public Accounts, 1968/69–70*, 189. For a flavour of his writing style see *Arms and the Men*, Brady's self-published account of the Arms Crisis and his involvement in it.

14. *Committee of Public Accounts, 1968/69–70*, 190.

15. *Committee of Public Accounts, 1968/69–70*, 191. That the pamphlets played an important role for the propaganda unit is clear from the fact that *Eyewitness in Northern Ireland* is included in the list of core texts sent out by the Government Information Bureau; see *Irish Times*, 16 October 1969.

16. See submission by Eoin Neeson, *Committee of Public Accounts, 1968/69–70*, 218–20. Neeson suggests that all he did was to listen to Brady, a man he described as a 'propagandist'. He continued: 'Since my views on propaganda, especially inciting and inflammatory material, were well known to and frequently conveyed to Mr Brady, and since he was clearly committed to this scheme which he claimed to have discussed in detail with the Minister for Finance I listened to what he had to say but did not comment upon it or argue about it.'

17. Hugh Kennedy had a direct line to Blaney in his capacity as an employee of An Bord Bainne, a state-sponsored body under the direct control of the Department of Agriculture.

18. 'C.R. members vote on discipline, policy,' *Irish Times*, 6 October 1969. It is interesting to note that this press conference was designed to promote what amounted to an official publication.

19. *Fianna Fáil and the IRA*, 40, suggests that Captain Kelly was following a predetermined brief to influence the rejection of Cathal Goulding, Roy Johnston, Séamus Costello, and Mick Ryan, the most prominent ideologists in the IRA.

20. See Patterson, *The Politics of Illusion*, 125–7, for a discussion of the ideological differences within the Belfast IRA. As Patterson makes clear, 'the Officials exaggerated the role of Fianna Fáil, but they did not imagine it.'

21. Interview with James Kelly.

22. Military Intelligence documents in the author's possession. Kelly prints a facsimile in *The Thimble-Riggers*, 19.

23. When the crisis broke in May 1970, Gibbons denied that training had been provided to Derry civilians. This was technically correct, in that the civilians had been inducted into the FCA to provide a cover for the operation; see *Dáil Debates*, vol. 249, col. 792. For a full

discussion of Gibbons's role in the crisis see below.

24. Seán Mac Stiofáin maintains that the intelligence picture he was receiving from Northern republicans indicated that in their dealings with Captain Kelly and Fianna Fáil ministers they were given certain guarantees; these included 'arms, facilities for training, and no anti-republican activities in the state in the summer of 1969' (interview with Seán Mac Stiofáin).

25. Interview with James Kelly.

26. *Committee of Public Accounts, 1968/69–70*, 29. Despite the exceptional terms of reference, the directive was never fully investigated by the Committee of Public Accounts or, subsequently, by academia. It is ironic that when the Government papers for 1969 were released in January 2000, Professor Ronan Fanning suggested that this minute 'was the most interesting discovery I unearthed in the Irish records … In trying to explain the significance of that minute, I cannot do better than to convey my immediate reaction: They gave Charlie Haughey a blank cheque.' In fact the terms of the Government decision formed the basis of the hearings of the Committee of Public Accounts and were published with the final report in 1972. This assessment is indicative of the failure of academia to investigate what Fanning himself refers to as 'one of the most injudicious cabinet minutes in the history of the government of independent Ireland' (*Sunday Independent*, 2 January 2000).

27. See statement by Mary Murphy, general secretary of the Irish Red Cross Society, *Committee of Public Accounts, 1968/69–70*, 217, and the support she received from Leslie de Barra, chairwoman of the society, p. 206.

28. *Voice of the North*, 12 October 1969.

29. *Committee of Public Accounts, 1968/69–70*, 192.

30. Berry himself had provided Ó Móráin with a memorandum as early as July 1969 suggesting that the time had come to 'drive a wedge between the rural members—the old faithful—and the doctrinaire republicans, mainly based in Dublin, who were sedulously propagating the gospel of a "workers Socialist Republic"'; see *Magill*, June 1980. It would appear that while such a course was the logical outcome of the Bailieborough conclave, Berry's subsequent actions may be predicated on the fact that either Military Intelligence was not communicating with the Special Branch or the department secretary felt slighted at being kept out of the picture.

31. *Magill*, June 1980.

32. Department of Justice, 18 March 1969, 20/69, quoted in *Sunday Tribune*, 2 January 2000. See also *Irish Times*, 3 January 2000.

33. *Magill*, May 1980. Berry alleges that he first became aware of Captain Kelly's involvement as early as September. In a diary entry dated 15

September 1969 he noted: 'I received numerous verbal reports of the border activities of military intelligence officers and the name of Captain James Kelly cropped up again and again as consorting with known members of the IRA.' See Vincent Browne, 'The Peter Berry diaries,' *Magill*, June 1980, 52.

34. Sir Andrew Gilchrist to Foreign Office, 10 November 1969, quoted in *Irish Times*, 3 January 2000.

35. Military Intelligence documents in the author's possession.

36. Vincent Browne, 'The Peter Berry diaries,' *Magill*, June 1980.

37. Boland, *Indivisible Faith*, 217–18. See also note 83 below.

38. 'Partition and Policy,' Department of the Taoiseach, 14 August 1969, 2000/6/957.

39. 'Partition and Policy,' Department of the Taoiseach, 2000/6/461.

40. Minute from Peter Berry, 5 September 1969, Government papers, 2000/6/659.

41. Confidential memorandum from Department of External Affairs to Department of the Taoiseach, 6 August 1969; 'Partition and Policy,' Department of the Taoiseach, 2000/6/958. The minute was copied to Berry.

42. *Fianna Fáil and the IRA*, 45.

43. 'Fianna Fáil plots take over of Civil Rights,' *United Irishman*, November 1969.

44. See statement by Colonel Michael Hefferon, Director of Intelligence, *Committee of Public Accounts, 1968/69–70*, 208–9. The statement makes it clear that the financial transaction was 'done clandestinely lest the connection of the office with any Government agency should be embarrassing or damaging to either party.' Hefferon somewhat disingenuously suggests that the office closed because of 'disagreements among the personnel running the office'; it is more likely that it closed because the disclosures in the *United Irishman* blew its cover. It was also a fact that precious little intelligence was garnered from talking to refugees; see also 'Refugee statements were little use to state,' *Examiner*, 10 January 2000.

45. Brady denied he was a Fianna Fáil plant. He told the Committee of Public Accounts that he would have sued the *United Irishman* but was informed by his solicitors that it was pointless, because the paper was not registered (*Committee of Public Accounts, 1968/69–70*, 194).

46. *United Irishman*, November 1969.

47. *Fianna Fáil and the IRA*, 47. John Kelly has confirmed to the author that he played a major role in the distribution of *Voice of the North* in the New Lodge area of Belfast (interview with John Kelly).

48. The finding of *Committee on Public Accounts, 1968/69–70*, 35.

49. For a full breakdown of the operation of the accounts see *Committee on Public Accounts, 1968/69–70*, 35.

50. A somewhat gleeful account of this is to be found in *Fianna Fáil and the IRA*, 33, which describes how Kennedy was 'more or less persuaded to write out a cheque for £2,000 and detained while an IRA volunteer went to Clones and collected the cash.' Understandably enough, Kennedy in his interview, while confirming the authenticity of his kidnapping, was not so glib. For an account sympathetic to the Official position see Paddy Devlin, *Straight Left*, 67–113.

51. Interview with James Kelly.

52. Military Intelligence documents in the author's possession.

53. *Voice of the North*, 8 November 1969.

54. In Captain Kelly's published account he omits any mention of his role in the financing of *Voice of the North* or the operating of an account held in the name of Ann O'Brien in the Baggot Street branch of the Munster and Leinster Bank, through which the money was channelled; see *The Thimble-Riggers*, 32, 268.

55. Eoin Neeson, *Committee of Public Accounts, 1968/69–70*, 220. This account differs substantially from the total denial quoted in the *Sunday Independent*, 10 May 1970. 'The Government Information Bureau had no knowledge of the publication beforehand. Therefore the question of giving consent and giving or withdrawing support had never arisen.'

56. Eunan O'Halpin, *Defending Ireland*, 307. O'Halpin is undoubtedly correct in describing the *Voice of the North* as a 'rabidly nationalist publication'. However, his contention that 'the Taoiseach cut off the funding when he learnt of it' cannot be substantiated from the sources quoted. It sits uncomfortably with the evidence of the Director of Information.

57. Brady, *Arms and the Men*, 96–7.

58. *Irish Times*, 24 September 1969.

59. *Irish Times*, 9 December 1969.

60. *Irish Times*, 10 December 1969.

61. Kevin Boland was a long-standing ally of Blaney, now in the Department of Local Government, succeeding Mícheál Ó Móráin, now the Minister for Justice. Blaney was seen as the voice of the rural Fianna Fáil machine, commanding enormous political power and patronage within the party. He pushed a number of buttons in his speech, including a call to move Government departments to provincial centres, a proposal put forward by Ó Móráin in 1968; see *Hibernia*, 19 December 1969.

62. *Hibernia*, 19 December 1969.

63. See Arnold, *What Kind of Country?*, 49–50. Arnold argues that as early as 1969 the 'sombre truth' was that republicanism was dead in the Republic—a fact that Lynch clearly recognised and articulated in his

Tralee speech. Blaney, suggests Arnold, was 'attempting to resurrect a form of republicanism which had laid for itself no foundations in reality, save in the reality of violence.' This, however, was the essential point. The Blaney speech in effect gave the Northern republicans a green light. It is easy to have perfect vision in retrospect, but in the context of December 1969 the fragility of Jack Lynch's tenure was never more apparent. For an interesting discussion of the power of rhetoric and its purpose in supplanting a stronger argument see the introduction to Hugh Lawson Tancred's translation of Aristotle, *The Art of Rhetoric* (1991). Lawson-Tancred argues that the central tasks facing the orator 'are to find aspects of the subject that can be employed in arguments designed to establish the features that need to be stressed and that can be used to induce the appropriate emotional state in the listener and to create the appropriate impression of character' (p. 17). Blaney's speech in Letterkenny, whatever its basis in contemporary reality, was a virtuoso Aristotelian performance.

64. Paddy Kennedy, quoted in *Irish Times,* 10 December 1969.

65. John Hume, interview on 'Seven Days,' RTE, quoted in *Irish Times,* 10 December 1969.

66. *Irish Times,* 11 December, 1969.

67. Neil Blaney, interview with 'This Week,' RTE (radio), 15 December 1969, quoted in *Irish Times,* 16 December 1969.

68. For an interesting examination of Northern nationalism's views of the Republic see McKeown, *The Greening of a Nationalist.* McKeown lived in Belfast throughout this period and was Northern correspondent of *Hibernia.* A contemporary perspective is offered by Fionnuala O'Connor, *In Search of a State: Catholics in Northern Ireland* (Belfast 1993), 223–71.

69. For an assessment of the sheer scale of the emotional outpouring see 'Relief groups see long-term need for their services,' *Irish Times,* 7 October 1969. The article details the various attempts to raise funds at local level. For Blaney it represented a possible rich vein to be tapped for electoral support.

70. Cruise O'Brien, *States of Ireland,* 201.

71. John Healy, 'In the Dáil,' *Irish Times,* 17 December 1969.

72. *Voice of the North,* 20 December 1969.

73. *Voice of the North,* 20 December 1969. To ram home the point, Paddy Kennedy, the Republican Labour MP, is quoted in the same issue as saying that Blaney's speech was 'honest and realistic. It is consoling to know that at least some Southern politicians are still concerned with our problem. I hope they all show the same concern as Neil Blaney.'

74. The news of the September coup attempt in Belfast leaked out six days after the Blaney speech; see *Irish Times,* 15 December 1969.

75. Interview with Ruairí Ó Brádaigh.

76. A third letter, dated 27 November, stated that the customer no longer required facilities. In evidence to the committee, the manager of the Baggot Street branch, when asked whether a cheque was cashed at the Piccadilly bank, replied: 'No, I don't think so. I think the final letter says "no longer requires facilities," so apparently there was no cheque cashed there.' The committee then requested that the originals of the letters be obtained; these were received on 15 March. On the back of the first letter (dated 17 November 1969), signed by the manager of the Baggot Street bank, the following initialled entries appeared:

    19.11.69 1500.

    21 Nov. 69 100.

    On 14 April 1971 a letter dated 6 April 1971 from the Piccadilly bank to the Baggot Street bank was transmitted to the committee, confirming that the two dates and accounts related to payments effected. The committee considered that the initial request to the manager of the bank to produce all relevant documents should have resulted in a thorough examination by the bank of all its papers and the consequent presentation of all the facts at the commencement of its examination of the bank officials; see *Committee of Public Accounts, 1968/69–70.*

77. Interview with John Kelly. Kelly further alleges that he discussed the encounter with Markham Randall with the nationalist MP Gerry Fitt at the Irish Club in Eaton Square. 'Gerry knew what Jim Kelly was about and knew that I had been seconded to go with Jim Kelly to organise a shipment from whatever source, so it was a matter really of bringing Gerry up to date as to what was happening. He wasn't surprised to see us there. He wasn't surprised to know what we were there for, what our business was.'

78. Interview with John Kelly.

79. Seán Mac Stiofáin, *Memoirs of a Revolutionary*, 119. Mac Stiofáin now argues that the leadership in Dublin exposed the funding of the *Voice of the North* to provide cover for a split that was already happening (interview with Seán Mac Stiofáin).

80. Interview with Seán Mac Stiofáin.

81. Interview with Ruairí Ó Brádaigh.

82. Interview with John Kelly.

83. The role of Irish America in the IRA split is an under-researched element of the roots of the conflict. The most considered account so far is to be found in Wilson, *Irish America and the Ulster Conflict*, 19–48. See also Holland, *The American Connection*, 27–62. For an account of the importance of Keenan's presence in the United States see Ó Dochartaigh, *From Civil Rights to Armalites*, 189–92.

84. For the reaction of the British and Irish diplomatic delegations to the United States see John Bowman and Rachel Donnelly, 'Bernadette Devlin fails to impress diplomats despite media attention,' *Irish Times,* 3 January 2000. Her meeting with the Secretary-General of the United Nations, U Thant, was regarded with derision by both Dublin and London; diplomats used similar language to criticise her verbosity and arrogance. As the tour continued, British communiqués became more sanguine: after all, she was doing a great self-destructive job. The embassy noted that, despite her considerable impact, the 'press on the whole has been fairly objective about Bernadette and the Irish question.' A further message from San Francisco noted how 'distinctly rattled' she was by rumours that some of the money raised would be used for buying arms for the IRA.

85. *Chicago Tribune,* 4 September 1969, quoted by Wilson, *Irish America and the Ulster Conflict,* 35.

86. Interview with Frank Durkan. Durkan is a nephew of the late Paul O'Dwyer, one of the most influential civil rights lawyers in the United States. Their firm, O'Dwyer and Bernstein, was later instrumental in constructing defence strategies for republicans caught attempting to smuggle arms. The two men also played a significant role in securing Bill Clinton's support for intervention in Ireland while he was campaigning for the Democratic presidential nomination in 1992; see Conor O'Clery, *The Greening of the White House: The Inside Story of How America Tried to Bring Peace to Ireland* (Dublin 1996), 11.

87. Proinsias Mac Aonghusa, 'The split among Irish-Americans,' *Irish Times,* 10 December 1969. Mac Aonghusa concluded that while Heron and those who supported him represented a minority voice, opposed by the Irish-American community, they were destined 'to play a more direct and decisive part in Ireland's affairs than any or all of the other Irish American groups. For they know where they are going, and why and how they are going to get there: they are in the mainstream of world youth revolt against the mismanagement and worse of their elders.'

88. Hennessey, *A History of Northern Ireland,* 101.

89. Interview with John Kelly. The antipathy towards Fianna Fáil was understandable. Flannery despised the 'party of reality'; see Dylan Foley, 'Rebel without a pause,' *Irish Echo,* 13 May 1992. Liam Kelly had been interned by the Fianna Fáil Government in 1957 and spent most of the years of the border campaign in the Curragh military internment camp.

90. For an example of the former see Bishop and Mallie, *The Provisional IRA,* 294–5. Taylor, *Provos,* 62, takes the latter view.

91. Interview with Seán Mac Stiofáin. For a full discussion of the formation of Northern Aid see chapter 7.

92. Ó Dochartaigh, *From Civil Rights to Armalites*, 189.

93. *An Phoblacht*, February 1970.

94. *Magill*, May 1980, 47. Again, there is no trace in the Government papers of such a memorandum.

95. Interview with Ruairí Ó Brádaigh.

96. Interview with Ruairí Ó Brádaigh.

97. Interview with Ruairí Ó Brádaigh.

98. Interview with Ruairí Ó Brádaigh.

99. Provisional IRA statement, *Irish Times*, 29 December 1969.

100. Interview with Tomás Mac Giolla.

101. Anonymous, *Fianna Fáil and the IRA*, 41.

102. McKeown, *The Greening of a Nationalist*. 84.

103. Interview with John Kelly.

104. Interview with Seán Mac Stiofáin.

105. It is not clear why Blaney should have stopped such a route. Certainly the use of Irish-Americans provided less risk of exposure than the vagaries of the international arms market. When the IRA split was formalised in January 1970 the American connection was to provide a ready-made market for the Provisionals and was to remain important until the establishment of links with Libya in the nineteen-eighties; see Holland, *The American Connection*, 116–17.

106. Interview with John Kelly. This is an important admission and reveals clearly Blaney's central involvement. Vincent Browne in *Magill* suggests that Captain Kelly cancelled the shipment.

107. 'Arms and the Ulsterman,' *Irish Times*, 2 December 1969.

Chapter 4 (pp 96–125)

1. Walsh, *The Party*, 102.

2. Sacks, *The Donegal Mafia*, 197.

3. *Hibernia*, 23 January 1970.

4. Boland, *Indivisible Faith*, 171–2. Boland has argued that the speech was misinterpreted as an attempt to defuse the tension in the party after the pro-Blaney speeches earlier in the ardfheis. 'What I had done was to state as party policy the ideas, which he was rejecting by his inaction. When I said there could be no concession "whether directly or by implication of any legitimate British interest in any part of our country" I was criticising in public and to the Taoiseach's face his slavish acceptance, by his silence of Callaghan's and Wilson's jingoism' (p. 172).

5. *Irish Times*, 19 January 1970.

6. Erskine Childers to Lynch, 28 August 1969; 'Partition and Policy,' Department of the Taoiseach, 2000/6/659. The second memo is dated 2 September 1969 and can be found in the same file. In a covering letter, Childers appeals to Lynch that 'unless we examine previously unacceptable ideas we will only have the old policy. I am

also convinced that, however impossible the task, we have to get beneath the skins of Protestants.'

7. For a scathing assessment of the speech see Brady, *Arms and the Men*, 101–3. Brady argues that the speech was 'masterly and deserves close reading ... Lynch had begun to shake the Republican party of the legion of the Rearguard away from its traditions and into a new era of open acceptance of partition.'

8. Arnold, *What Kind of Country?*, 51.

9. *Hibernia*, 23 January 1970.

10. The most vociferous advocate of the parallel government thesis is Dermot Keogh. He is extremely sympathetic to Lynch and argues that in effect there appeared to be a parallel administration whose agenda was surreptitiously endorsed by the Lynch Government. He further argues that the failure to sack Blaney stemmed from a recognition that it could have divided the party and forced his own dismissal as leader of Fianna Fáil in favour of a politician not committed to the anti-force pledge. See Keogh, *Twentieth-Century Ireland*, 307.

11. Confidential source.

12. Confidential source.

13. Charles Haughey interview, 'Seven Ages: The Story of the Irish State,' RTE1, 27 March 2000.

14. See Peter Barry, 'The consociational model and its dangers,' *European Journal of Political Research*, 1975. 'While it may be possible to maintain a system of party alignments cutting across a line of communal cleavage, it is usually possible to shift from this to a system where parties articulate the communal cleavage. But it is extremely difficult if not impossible to move in the reverse direction, because of the primitive psychological strength of communal identification and the effects of social reinforcement on maintaining the political salience of communal identification.'

15. See McKeown, *The Greening of a Nationalist*, 40–41.

16. The mystique surrounding Haughey's republicanism had a profound influence on young TDs, particularly in the nineteen-seventies, as he began to rebuild his career. Haughey's decision not to give any interviews, even when he became Taoiseach, added to his charisma. See 'The man who grew out of his mohair suit,' *Sunday Independent*, 30 January 2000. The article is a profile of Seán Doherty, Minister for Justice in Haughey's second Government, who was forced to resign from the Fianna Fáil front bench when the coalition of Fine Gael and the Labour Party exposed his role in the bugging of political correspondents' telephones. The most detailed exposition of the bugging scandal is to be found in Joe Joyce and Peter Murtagh, *The Boss: Charles J. Haughey in Government* (Dublin 1983). Doherty's admission in a television programme ten years later that Haughey had

authorised the bugging precipitated his final downfall. See Dwyer, *Short Fellow,* 425–32. Dwyer suggests that the admission was carefully designed to destroy Haughey, an act of revenge. After he had sacrificed so many colleagues in the pursuit of power, 'his past had finally caught up with him' (p. 431).

17. Charles Haughey interview, 'Seven Ages: The Story of the Irish State,' RTE1, 27 March 2000.

18. Cabinet minutes, 11 September 1969, confidential annex CC (69), 43rd conclusions, minute 3, Public Record Office, CAB 128/46. The minute records dissatisfaction with Lynch, noting that his attitude 'has not been helpful or easy to assess. Though he had specifically renounced the use of force, he had sent troops to the border and he had embarked on a world-wide propaganda campaign against the United Kingdom and Northern Ireland Governments. If he really wanted a united Ireland, he must conciliate Protestant opinion; but so far his tactics had done nothing but alarm it.'

19. The importance of this ideological distinction has long been ignored, largely to buttress the legitimacy of the truncated Irish nation as represented by the independent state. See, for example, Eunan O'Halpin, *Defending Ireland,* 310. O'Halpin argues that there was no justification for arming nationalists in the North because of the phased introduction of reform of the RUC and the disbanding of the B Specials. He also argues that the British government was 'clearly committed' to the introduction of measures to address specific nationalist grievances; 'in such circumstances, it was monumental folly to seek to put guns in the hands of Northern republicans, whose aim was the destruction of the Northern state rather than the acquisition of equal rights and security within it.' This was precisely the point. Blaney clearly despised the Northern state. According to a highly placed confidential source, this was a view shared by Haughey; the presence of British soldiers on the streets shoring up what he viewed as a corrupt state served only to deepen his anger. Haughey had a visceral sense of nationhood denied. While he believed that the ultimate solution lay in forcing Britain to change, he saw in the circumstances of 1969 and 1970 the possibility of a British withdrawal. The fact that such an approach proved useful in the leadership battle within Fianna Fáil does not necessarily mean that it was not a deeply held view. Likewise, O'Halpin's clearly felt view that the Provisional IRA was 'a cancer in the body politics of independent Ireland' (p. 314) clouds his analytical judgment. For Haughey, Blaney and Boland the Southern state alone was not enough; see Boland, *Indivisible Faith,* 172–3.

20. 'Loyalism' (Republican Lecture Series, 9), quoted by Brendan O'Brien in *The Long War,* 88–9. O'Brien, one of the best-informed

journalistic observers of the Provisional IRA, argues that 'there is much in this that found echoes in traditional Irish republicanism, particularly in Fianna Fáil. It was a philosophy embodied in Articles 2 and 3 of the Irish Constitution' (p. 89). Writing in the context of the nineteen-eighties, O'Brien goes on to make the point that the IRA was on its own because the nature of the conflict was foreign to most people's experiences south of the border.' This is undoubtedly true. The point is that in 1969–70 the perception that loyalism could not be compromised with was central to Haughey's political make-up, and he was prepared to finance those determined to confront it— regardless of the consequences.

21. Charles Haughey, presidential address to Fianna Fáil ardfheis, 16 February 1980, quoted in *Irish Times,* 17 February 1980. For detailed analysis of the evolution of Haughey's ideological position see chapter 8.

22. Charles Haughey interview, 'Seven Ages: The History of the Irish State,' RTE1, 27 March 2000.

23. Peter Berry had drawn up a strategy paper in 1969 advocating channelling resources to split the republican movement in the Republic. A Government source suggests that this was seriously discussed at the very highest levels.

24. Confidential source.

25. For even-handed discussion of the dilemma facing Goulding see Smith, *Fighting for Ireland,* 87–90.

26. Bew, Patterson and Hazelkorn, *The Dynamics of Irish Politics,* 100; also 136, n. 41.

27. 'Where Sinn Féin Stands' (Republican Lecture Series, 1), undated.

28. Adams, *Before the Dawn: An Autobiography,* 130.

29. 'Where Sinn Féin Stands' (Republican Lecture Series, 1).

30. See 'Building barricades,' *Hibernia,* 26 September 1969. The paper noted the 'real fear of the church authorities at the inroads of the left,' and also that the 'hastily erected heap [of barricades] at the end of the street was political dynamite.'

31. Sweetman, *On Our Knees,* 151. Sweetman is an Official acolyte, modifying Mao Zedong's maxim on power to buttress her support for Goulding. 'If political power comes out of the barrel of a gun, it's necessary to gather the political ammunition of the people before firing the gun' (p. 138).

32. See chapter 4 above and *United Irishman,* October, November and December 1970.

33. *United Irishman,* December 1969.

34. *United Irishman,* December 1969.

35. Michael Farrell, *The Orange State,* 270.

36. 'Where Sinn Féin Stands' (Republican Lecture Series, 1).

37. *An Phoblacht,* March 1970.

38. *An Phoblacht,* March 1970.

39. *An Phoblacht,* March 1970.

40. *An Phoblacht,* May 1970.

41. *An Phoblacht,* May 1970.

42. Neil Blaney interview, *Irish Independent,* 3 April 1970.

43. Des O'Malley was Parliamentary Secretary to the Taoiseach and Chief Whip of Fianna Fáil. He viewed it as quite reasonable that Haughey 'should be on any committee that might have to take decisions at short notice, decisions that might have financial implications' (quoted by Walsh in *Des O'Malley,* 29–30).

44. Quoted by Seán Carberry, 'A gallant brief defence,' *Irish Times,* 3 December 1969.

45. Boland, *Indivisible Faith,* 183.

46. See *An Phoblacht,* February 1970. For a full discussion of the rise of the Provisional IRA see chapter 6 below.

47. Neil Blaney interview, 'Timewatch,' BBC1, 27 January 1993.

48. Interview with James Kelly.

49. Captain Kelly maintains in his written account that the contact originated with the Northern Defence Committees; see Kelly, *Orders for the Captain,* 19.

50. In his written accounts Kelly states that the only reason he went to Germany was because there were difficulties in getting the Defence Committee representative to go. He also states that the Defence Committee gave the money to him (Kelly, *Orders for the Captain,* 18–19).

51. See, for example, Mícheál Ó Móráin's evidence to the first arms trial, 28 September 1970, quoted in *Irish Times,* 29 September 1970. 'There was a grave lack of co-operation between the two bodies [Military Intelligence and Special Branch], that one crowd didn't seem to know what the others were doing.'

52. The directive was not committed to paper and became one of the most contentious pieces of evidence in the arms trials.

53. Mícheál Ó Móráin, testimony to first arms trial, 28 September 1970, quoted in *Irish Times,* 29 September 1970. Ó Móráin was neutral within the Government on activities in the North but was obsessed with subversives in the Republic—an indication of the influence of Peter Berry (interview with Kevin Boland).

54. See Kelly, *The Thimble-Riggers,* 165–6.

55. Vincent Browne, *Magill,* May 1980.

56. See below.

57. Confidential source.

58. Colonel Michael Hefferon, testimony to first arms trial, 28 September 1970, quoted in *Irish Times,* 19 September 1970.

59. Interview with James Kelly.

60. Interview with John Kelly.

61. Kelly, *The Thimble-Riggers*, 34.

62. Jim Gibbons, testimony to first arms trial, 24 September 1970, quoted in *Irish Times*, 25 September 1970.

63. *Irish Times*, 24 September 1970.

64. Submission by Niall McCarthy, counsel for Charles Haughey, second arms trial, 16 October 1970.

65. Charles Haughey, testimony to second arms trial, 19 October 1970. This was to be a standard feature of the Haughey defence as the plan disintegrated, done purely for secrecy purposes. 'There was no suggestion at any time that the consignments would not have authorisations or licences. This was not involved—what was involved was the opening of the consignment by Customs.'

66. Colonel Michael Hefferon, testimony to first arms trial, 28 September 1970, quoted in *Irish Times*, 29 September 1970.

67. Interview with Seán Mac Stiofáin. Mac Stiofáin says he did not realise that the rendezvous was going to be Captain Kelly's house, and he was angered at the lack of security adopted by the Northern unit.

68. Interview with Seán Mac Stiofáin.

69. Jim Gibbons, testimony to first arms trial, 24 September 1970, quoted in *Irish Times*, 25 September 1970.

70. Bew and Gillespie, *Northern Ireland: A Chronology of the Troubles*, 26. See also Sharrock and Devenport, *Man of War, Man of Peace?*, 72–5.

71. Adams, *Before the Dawn*, 136–7.

72. Brady, *Arms and the Men*, 108–10.

73. Jim Gibbons, testimony to first arms trial, 24 September 1970.

74. Colonel Michael Hefferon, testimony to first arms trial, 28 September 1970.

75. Interview with James Kelly.

76. Neil Blaney interview, 'Timewatch,' BBC1, 27 January 1993.

77. There were sound reasons for believing that the violence could change the Government. See 'Lynch under threat by sabre-rattling' (editorial), *Observer*, 5 April 1970. The paper argued that Dublin could help Lynch dramatically by putting the question of the unification of Ireland on the agenda. 'There is widespread agreement here that a divided Ireland is a nonsense. Unfortunately the time never seems right for saying so.'

78. Colonel Michael Hefferon, testimony to first arms trial, 29 September 1970.

79. Prosecution opening statement, first arms trial, 23 September 1970, quoted in *Irish Times*, 24 September 1970.

80. See Vincent Browne, *Magill*, May 1980.

81. *Magill*, May 1980.

82. Charles Haughey, testimony to second arms trial, 19 October 1970, quoted in *Irish Times,* 20 October 1970.

83. Peter Berry, evidence to first arms trial, 29 September 1970, quoted by Tom MacIntyre in *Through the Bridewell Gate.* For a full transcript of the Berry evidence see *Irish Times,* 30 September 1970. Berry gave the same evidence to the second trial, 12 October 1970; see *Irish Times,* 13 October 1970.

84. See Niall McCarthy, opening address to the jury, second arms trial, 16 October 1970, quoted by Tom MacIntyre in *Through the Bridewell Gate,* 156.

85. Charles Haughey, testimony to second arms trial, 19 October 1970, quoted in *Irish Times,* 20 October 1970. This was to be a crucial exchange in the arms trial. Haughey suggested in evidence that he had passed word to his permanent secretary on the Saturday night that the operation was to be cancelled.

86. Jim Gibbons, statement of evidence, first arms trial, 25 September 1970. For an annotated version of the transcript see MacIntyre, *Through the Bridewell Gate,* 44.

87. For competing interpretations of Lynch's motivations see Vincent Browne, *Magill,* May–July 1980, Coogan, *The Troubles,* 101–3, and Arnold, *What Kind of Country?,* 60–63. Browne's account, based largely on Peter Berry's diaries, suggests that even after a meeting of security officials on 30 April the Taoiseach had decided not to take any action, telling Berry he would protect him from the wrath of Charles Haughey (Browne, *Magill,* July 1980). Coogan largely accepts Lynch's stated position that he knew nothing until Berry's intervention, arguing that the Taoiseach 'managed to remain oblivious.' Lynch's action is attributed to a secret meeting with the British ambassador on 1 May (Coogan, *The Troubles,* 101). Arnold takes a more sympathetic view, based on a reading of Lynch as imprisoned by the myths of nationalism. He argues that Lynch was understandably far more devious than was previously understood. He needed the impetus of outside intervention to combat within Fianna Fáil 'the republican ideals and shibboleths, the tribal loyalties and emotions, and the curious political rules and standards which can emerge from this background' (Arnold, *What Kind of Country?,* 63).

88. Vincent Browne, *Magill,* May 1980.

89. Vincent Browne, *Magill,* May 1980.

90. Hefferon's evidence at the first arms trial suggested that Kelly was acting under orders up to the attempts to import arms and that he had passed on this intelligence to Gibbons. He also stated that Kelly was 'acting as a go-between for the Defence Committees and the Government'; see 'Court report,' *Irish Times,* 29 September 1970.

91. Boland may be confusing this more explicit directive with that of 14
    August for the Department of Justice to 'expand the intelligence
    service maintained by the Garda Síochána in the Six Counties'; see
    'Partition and Policy,' Department of the Taoiseach, 2000/6/957.
92. Interview with Kevin Boland.
93. See Walsh, *The Party,* 120. Walsh suggests that the argument that
    Lynch had no intention of taking further action is seriously flawed.
    'He delayed taking action so that he could be sure of his ground, as a
    lawyer and as a politician, before he tackled them.'
94. For full details of the Blaney move see *Hibernia,* 3 April 1970.
95. See *This Week,* 8 May 1970. See also T. F. O'Higgins, *A Double Life*
    (Dublin 1994), 223–4. O'Higgins, a former Fine Gael TD and
    prominent lawyer, suggests in his memoir that Ó Móráin was not
    drunk but suffering from the stress of knowing that members of the
    Government were engaged in attempts to import weapons contrary
    to officially stated policy.
96. *Dáil Debates,* vol. 246, col. 279–80, 29 April 1970.
97. Interview with James Kelly.
98. Interview with James Kelly; see also Colonel Hefferon's evidence,
    Irish Times, 29 September 1970.
99. Jim Gibbons, testimony to first arms trial, 25 September 1970, quoted
    in *Irish Times,* 26 September 1970. At the second trial Gibbons
    suggested that he wanted the letter destroyed, because 'it would
    associate me—to some degree at any rate—with a conspiracy to
    import arms with which I had nothing to do' (*Irish Times,* 10
    October 1970).
100. Interview with Seán Mac Stiofáin.
101. It remains unclear who had initial ownership of the document.
    Coogan, *The Troubles,* 102, suggests that the document emanated
    from British intelligence and that the newspaper gave it to Cosgrave.
    Arnold, *What Kind of Country?,* 66–7, suggests that Cosgrave had
    attempted to pass it to the political correspondent of the *Sunday
    Independent,* E. B. Murphy. Certainly the implication of the *Sunday
    Independent* editorial the week after the story broke suggests that there
    was some degree of collusion between Independent Newspapers and
    Fine Gael. The paper wrote, somewhat melodramatically: 'The Editor
    … knew it was exclusive. If he published it he had a scoop. It was a
    story which might bring down the Government, which would
    certainly bring the Government into international disrepute and
    further endanger the tense situation in the North. The question
    confronting him was: where did his duty lie as a newspaperman, to
    his country or to his profession? The Editor decided not to print the
    story, holding that the proper place to have the matter raised was in
    the Dáil' (*Sunday Independent,* 10 May 1970, 3).

102. *Dáil Debates,* vol. 246, col. 518–19, 5 May 1970.
103. *Irish Times,* 6 May 1970.

Chapter 5 (pp 126–51)

1. 'How loyal is the army?', *This Week,* 15 May 1970. The magazine clearly had significant access to high-level sources. When the article was published it fed into a cycle of innuendo and rumour; in those heady days any story could become plausible. 'One story that grew so fast into an ominous monster had it that 100 Army officers had evolved into a close-knit association with a unified mind on the need for a stronger Northern policy. This speculation quickly extended into a hint that if Jack Lynch won a supporting vote from the Parliamentary Party a move might emanate from a section of the Army to take control.' *This Week* suggested that 'even a tenuous mention of his name in connection with the whole affair threw tremors of doubt into many concerning the credibility of Army loyalty at this critical juncture.'
2. Kelly, *The Thimble-Riggers,* 68.
3. *Irish Times,* 7 May 1970.
4. John Healy, 'In the Dáil,' *Irish Times,* 7 May, 1970.
5. *Dáil Debates,* vol. 246, col. 632, 6 May 1970.
6. *Dáil Debates,* vol. 246, col. 634, 6 May 1970.
7. 'The breaking point' (editorial), *Irish Times,* 6 May 1970.
8. John Healy, 'Review of events in politics longest day,' *Irish Times,* 7 May 1970.
9. There were obvious tactical and strategic reasons for supporting such a motion. If either was to assume the leadership of the party in the future—and both clearly believed they had every reason to expect such an event in the short to medium term—then such control was a necessary component of political power.
10. *Hibernia,* 13 May 1970, 4.
11. *Dáil Debates,* vol. 246, col. 641, 6 May 1970.
12. *Dáil Debates,* vol. 246, col. 642–3, 6 May 1970.
13. John Healy, 'In the Dáil,' *Irish Times,* 7 May 1970.
14. *Dáil Debates,* vol. 246, col. 643, 6 May 1970.
15. *Dáil Debates,* vol. 246, col. 645, 6 May 1970.
16. *Dáil Debates,* vol. 246, col. 645, 6 May 1970.
17. Garret FitzGerald, in an interview with the author.
18. *Dáil Debates,* vol. 246, col. 646, 647, 6 May 1970.
19. *Dáil Debates,* vol. 246, col. 648, 6 May 1970.
20. *Dáil Debates,* vol. 246, col. 654, 6 May 1970.
21. *Dáil Debates,* vol. 246, col. 655, 6 May 1970.
22. *Dáil Debates,* vol. 246, col. 658–9, 6 May 1970.
23. *Dáil Debates,* vol. 246, col. 694, 6 May 1970.

24. 'Loyalty' (editorial), *Irish Times*, 7 May 1970.

25. *Dáil Debates*, vol. 246, col. 714–15, 6 May 1970.

26. *Hibernia*, 13 May 1970 p 4.

27. Kevin Boland interview, *Irish Independent*, 8 May 1970.

28. *Dáil Debates*, vol. 246, col. 746, 8 May 1970.

29. *Dáil Debates*, vol. 246, col. 749, 8 May 1970.

30. *Dáil Debates*, vol. 246, col. 750, 8 May 1970.

31. *Dáil Debates*, vol. 246, col. 750–51, 8 May 1970.

32. *Dáil Debates*, vol. 246, col. 752, 8 May 1970.

33. John Healy, 'In the Dáil,' *Irish Times*, 9 May 1970.

34. *Dáil Debates*, vol. 246, col. 752. The Dáil debate took place as the conflict in south-east Asia was deepening; the United States had just begun bombing Cambodia. The deputy was referring to the self-immolation of Buddhist monks in Viet Nam, which began in 1962, and a similar protest by Jan Palach in Czechoslovakia in 1968.

35. Gibbons's evidence was to be crucial. If it could be proved that Gibbons had authorised the shipment, the charge of conspiracy to import weapons illegally could not be upheld. Indeed this was a central plank of Haughey's defence. He alleged that the operation had the approval of the Department of Defence and was carried out by Military Intelligence. He further testified that he did not know—or need to know—what it was the consignment actually contained.

36. Press conference by Paddy Kennedy, broadcast on RTE television and quoted in *Sunday Independent*, 10 May 1970.

37. *Dáil Debates*, vol. 246, col. 839, 8 May 1970. In evidence at the arms trials Gibbons referred to what he termed 'vestigial knowledge' of the planned importing. The inconsistency between his Dáil account and his court evidence did much to destroy his credibility as a witness.

38. *Dáil Debates*, vol. 246, col. 841, 8 May 1970. This interpretation also caused Gibbons serious problems in the witness box.

39. John Bruton read the statement into the Dáil record just after midnight; *Dáil Debates*, vol. 246, col. 971, 9 May 1970.

40. *Dáil Debates*, vol. 246, col. 861, 8 May 1970.

41. *Dáil Debates*, vol. 246, col. 863, 8 May 1970.

42. *Dáil Debates*, vol. 246, col. 864, 8 May 1970. The implication here is quite clear: Blaney saw no distinction between the Special Branch in the nineteen-twenties and Berry's handling of covert intelligence in 1970.

43. *Dáil Debates*, vol. 246 col. 864–6, 8 May 1970.

44. *Dáil Debates*, vol. 246, col. 866, 8 May 1970.

45. *Dáil Debates*, vol. 246, col. 868, 8 May 1970.

46. John Healy, 'In the Dáil,' *Irish Times*, 9 May 1970.

47. *Dáil Debates*, vol. 246, col. 885, 8 May 1970.

48. *Dáil Debates,* vol. 246, col. 887, 8 May 1970. Cruise O'Brien's colleague Justin Keating went even further, suggesting that Blaney exhibited 'a psychological disturbance [that,] even though we may understand it, totally unfits a person, in my view, for holding high offices in any country' (*Dáil Debates,* vol. 246, col. 917, 8 May 1970).

49. 'Come clean' (editorial), *Irish Times,* 9 May 1970.

50. *Irish Times,* 9 May 1970.

51. *Irish Times,* 9 May 1970.

52. *Dáil Debates,* vol. 246, col. 1302, 9 May 1970.

53. *Dáil Debates,* vol. 246, col. 1322, 9 May 1970.

54. *This Week,* 15 May 1970. The *Irish Press* later reported that Gibbons was the source of the story in *This Week;* see Tom O'Higgins, summing up for the vote of confidence in the Government, 'Dáil report,' *Irish Times,* 15 May 1970.

55. *Dáil Debates,* vol. 246, col. 971–2, 8 May 1970.

56. Statement by Charles Haughey, *Irish Times,* 9 May 1970.

57. *Dáil Debates,* vol. 246, col. 1317, 9 May 1970. For a scathing assessment of the attributes of the Fianna Fáil fallen see Owen Sheehy-Skeffington, 'They'll none of them be missed,' *Irish Times,* 11 May 1970.

58. 'The great cover-up,' *This Week,* 15 May 1970.

59. *Irish Times,* 11 May, 1970.

60. *Irish News,* 11 May 1970.

61. The Official IRA issued a statement the following week maintaining that none of its members had been involved. Violence at this time, it said, would be counter-productive: 'rather than bringing nearer the establishment of the Irish Republic desired by all sincere Republicans, uncoordinated acts of this nature play into the hands of sinister men who seek a federal arrangement and entry into the Common Market as the final solution to the Irish problem' (*Irish News,* 19 May 1970). This is indicative of the depths of fantasy to which the Official IRA had descended in the city. The politics of the Common Market were not even on the agenda in the febrile atmosphere permeating the city. The fear was palpable: defence and getting weapons was the only priority.

62. Statement by Sinn Féin, *Irish Times,* 12 May 1970.

63. Seán Mac Stiofáin has confirmed to the author that Captain Drohan approached him in Monaghan in November.

64. Statement from Northern Defence Committee, quoted in full in *Irish News,* 13 May 1970.

65. *Irish News,* 13 May 1970.

66. Blaney was tapping into a very real sense of unease within Fianna Fáil. The return to the politics of traditional nationalism offered an opportunity for those opposed to the ideological shift towards economic pragmatism becoming the party's sole determinant of legitimacy; see Mair, *The Changing Irish Party System,* 141, 182–4. Mair

regards the Lemass and Lynch administrations as following a corporatist agenda, 'eschewing the politicisation of social conflict and measuring nationalist success by wealth and economic growth rather than in cultural or territorial integrity.' Just as the Official IRA appeal imploded in the context of the unleashing of sectarian forces in Northern Ireland, the same forces led to a profound questioning within Fianna Fáil about what the fundamental purpose of power actually was. For a critical analysis see Cruise O'Brien, *States of Ireland,* 187–216.

67. 'Dáil report,' *Irish Times,* 15 May 1970.
68. Erskine Childers, quoted in 'Dáil report,' *Irish Times,* 15 May 1970.
69. Patrick Hillery, quoted in 'Dáil report,' *Irish Times,* 15 May 1970.
70. *Irish Times,* 15 May 1970.
71. *Irish Times,* 15 May 1970.
72. *Irish Times,* 15 May 1970.
73. Lynch was very badly advised by the Department of Finance in making this statement. The Committee of Public Accounts was exceptionally critical on this matter but placed the blame on the advice rather than on the Taoiseach himself. 'The Committee is satisfied that ... the Taoiseach acted in good faith in giving the assurance to the Dáil, but it does not feel that the terms of the assurance suggested to the Taoiseach were justified' (*Committee of Public Accounts, 1968/69–70,* 57).
74. *Irish Times,* 16 May 1970.
75. *Irish Times,* 12 May 1970.
76. *Sunday Independent,* 17 May 1970.
77. *Hibernia,* 12 June 1970.
78. *Irish News,* 28 May 1970.
79. Statement by Christopher Gore-Grimes, solicitor for Captain Kelly, *Irish Times,* 28 May 1970.
80. Statement by Christopher Gore-Grimes, solicitor for Captain Kelly, *Irish Times,* 28 May 1970.
81. Kevin Boland, quoted in *Irish Times,* 29 May 1970.
82. John Healy, 'No-one surprised at Boland's showdown,' *Irish Times,* 29 May 1970.
83. Neil Blaney, speech to Milford party organisation, 30 May 1970, quoted in *Irish Times,* 30 May 1970. Blaney was more discreet than Boland in soliciting support. It was reported that he held meetings with at least twenty-five to thirty TDs in an attempt to oust Lynch; see *Sunday Independent,* 31 May 1970.
84. *Voice of the North,* 7 June 1970. Boland somewhat mischievously told the Dáil during Taoiseach's question time on 14 May that he believed that the *Voice of the North* expressed Fianna Fáil policy with regard to the national question. Not surprisingly, Lynch demurred; see *Dáil Debates,* vol. 246, 14 May 1970. By 14 June the rhetoric had soared

into the realms of vague nationalist populism of the vintage type: 'The patriot felon stands alongside the afflicted poor. Ireland's history never changes' (*Voice of the North*, 14 June 1970).

85. *Voice of the North*, 29 November 1969.
86. *Voice of the North*, 17 May 1970.
87. *Voice of the North*, 24 May 1970.
88. Dáithí Ó Conaill, quoted in *Irish News*, 15 June 1970.
89. Interview with Ruairí Ó Brádaigh. The three-pronged strategy was enunciated by Seán Mac Stiofáin. For his own interpretation see Mac Stiofáin, *Memoirs of a Revolutionary*, 146; for an analysis of that strategy see Smith, *Fighting for Ireland*, 91–5. Smith emphasises the crucial but often-overlooked fact that although the Provisionals were a 'one-town organisation', the fact that this town was Belfast, where sectarian passions were most inflamed, placed it in the cockpit.
90. Dáithí Ó Conaill, quoted by Cruise O'Brien in *States of Ireland*, 221. It is interesting to note that while the *Irish News* carried the bulk of Ó Conaill's address, the final sentence, with its overt threat, is omitted.
91. Arnold suggests that the Arms Crisis 'had done less damage than had been anticipated by the more alarmist members of the opposition parties' (*What Kind of Country?*, 71–2). This approach is symptomatic of a wider failure to provide a holistic account of the impact on Northern politics of the Fianna Fáil power struggle, its fall-out, and the wider implications for the country as a whole. In Arnold's world view the conflicts, north and south, were not linked. Clearly such an approach has to be seriously questioned.

Chapter 6 (pp 152–86)

1. See two articles by the *New York Times* columnist C. L. Sulzberger reprinted in the *Irish Times*, 13 July 1970. Sulzberger was among a number of foreign journalists briefed by Dr Hillery in July. 'One cannot but suspect', he concludes, 'that Hillery himself reckons that he himself can gain control of the governing party.'
2. Gerry Boland, quoted in *Irish News*, 24 June 1970.
3. The *Economist* paid significant attention to events in Ireland throughout the crisis. It was broadly sympathetic to the positions adopted by Chichester-Clark and Lynch, decrying what it termed the wild men in both jurisdictions. Nevertheless it noted as early as May that each was a prisoner of more atavistic forces; see 'The gunman's shadow,' *Economist*, 16 May 1969, 18. 'There is a mood astir in Ireland now, on both sides of the border, which is more ominous, more threatening than anything that has happened since the nineteen-twenties ... The belief that reason will prevail in the republic is now in question. The slide has now begun, and there are too many who welcome it.'
4. *Irish News*, 27 June 1970.

5. Jack Lynch interview, *Sunday Independent*, 28 June 1970. This fear that hysteria could provoke a crisis is a common feature of editorials in the days leading up to the Twelfth of July celebrations. For an overt example see the *Irish Times*, 9 July 1970. The paper notes that 'it is easy to give in to mass hysteria. If enough people warn each other that trouble is bound to break out, it may indeed come about through a sharpening of suspicions and a tautening of nerves.'

6. Statement by Liam Cosgrave, quoted in *Sunday Independent*, 28 June 1970.

7. For a detailed account of the St Matthew's attack and its place in Provisional IRA folklore see Taylor, *Provos*, 75–8.

8. The *Times* reported that the rioting was part of an orchestrated campaign to prevent Orange marches from taking place. It quoted forensic scientists as saying that the IRA now had access to 'a simple highly-effective timing device' that could outstretch the security forces. It also suggested that the IRA was marching around in green battledress with berets (*Times*, 2 July 1970). This, of course, fed into unionist fears and strengthened the hands of those who declared that a military solution was required to restore order. The *Irish Times* echoed this by suggesting that 'information from sound sources of the arms held in certain Catholic districts is alarming to say the least' (*Irish Times*, 2 July 1970).

9. John Healy, 'In the Dáil,' *Irish Times*, 1 July 1970.

10. John Healy, 'In the Dáil,' *Irish Times*, 1 July 1970.

11. *Irish Times*, 3 July 1970.

12. *Irish Times*, 3 July 1970.

13. Michael Farrell, *Northern Ireland: The Orange State*, 273.

14. *Irish Times*, 2 July 1970.

15. Patterson, *The Politics of Illusion*, 150.

16. For a scathing and overtly ideological account that contends that the Provisionals were willing dupes of capitalist interests see Sweetman, *On Our Knees,* in particular her essays on Seán Mac Stiofáin, 149–61, and John Kelly, 201–13.

17. For a particularly graphic account of the Falls curfew see Devlin, *Straight Left*, 128–31.

18. Bishop and Mallie, *The Provisional IRA*, 160–61. Bell, who states bluntly that 'the Official IRA decided to take on the Brits,' disputes this account; see *The Secret Army*, 377.

19. *Irish Times*, 6 July 1970.

20. Devlin, *Straight Left*, 134. For Devlin the threat this posed was one of the main reasons that led to the establishment of the SDLP later in the month. The reality is that the plans to create the SDLP had a much longer progeny (see below).

21. Paddy Devlin interview, 'This Week,' RTE, 5 July 1970, quoted in *Irish Times*, 6 July 1970.

22. Mac Stiofáin, *Memoirs of a Revolutionary*, 138.

23. The Provisional leadership in Belfast saw in this an opportunity to harden that alienation. Moral appeals to shun the British military were accompanied by direct threats in *Republican News*, the periodical launched by the Provisionals in Belfast in June 1970; see *Republican News*, June 1970, July 1970.

24. Bell, *The Secret Army*, 377–8.

25. Statement by Official IRA, quoted in *Irish Times*, 7 July 1970.

26. For an honest assessment of the atavistic tribal feelings the developments provoked in even the liberal Southern intelligentsia see Cruise O'Brien, *States of Ireland*.

27. Dr Patrick Hillery interview, 'This Week', RTE, 5 July 1970.

28. *Irish Times*, 7 July 1970.

29. *Irish Times*, 7 July 1970.

30. The most openly controversial element in the programme contained an interview with Frank Morris, a former member of the IRA, who commented that guns might be required in the coming summer. The analysis, while overtly supportive of the British soldiers who had to undertake an 'unpleasant task', was unremittingly bleak.

31. 'Panorama,' BBC television, 6 July 1970.

32. 'Panorama,' BBC television, 6 July 1970.

33. 'Panorama,' BBC television, 6 July 1970.

34. 'Panorama,' BBC television, 6 July 1970.

35. 'Panorama,' BBC television, 6 July 1970.

36. See analysis by Dennis Kennedy, 'Fear of subversives motive for NI trip,' *Irish Times*, 10 July 1970.

37. *Economist*, 11 July 1970. See also the *Times*, 8 July 1970, which commented that the refusal of Orange leaders to call off parades was 'the most flagrant refusal to co-operate with the British government by substantial citizens in Ulster.'

38. *Dáil Debates*, vol. 248, col. 522–3, 7 July 1970.

39. 'Partition and Policy,' Department of the Taoiseach, 2000/6/101.

40. 'Panorama,' BBC television, 6 July 1970.

41. The editor of the *Voice of the North*, Aidan Corrigan, was more forthright, comparing in a speech in Dungannon the British army's handling of the Falls curfew with the behaviour of the Black and Tans during the War of Independence. Corrigan claimed that the purpose of the Maudling visit was to ensure Unionist support for the Heath government (*Irish Times*, 13 July 1970).

42. The most extended treatments of Northern Aid are to be found in Holland, *The American Connection*, and Wilson, *Irish America and the Ulster Conflict*. Holland is good on the early years and in particular on

the role played by George Harrison. Wilson takes a more academic approach, which, while thorough, tends to rely heavily on the printed record. His assessment of Northern Aid as being successful merely because 'the presentation of the Ulster conflict as one between Irish patriots and British invaders appealed more strongly to the traditional nationalism of Irish-American activists' (p. 42) lacks depth. It seems more likely that the relationship between the activists and the middle-class civil rights lawyers grouped around Paul O'Dwyer lay in the fact that the Provisionals had a strategy that was perceived as not only achievable but also capable of being sold to wider America.

43. *An Phoblacht,* July 1970. The first address used for donations was that of the Irish Institute in West 48th Street, New York. The same organisation provided $12,000 to Charles Haughey in November 1969; see letter of acknowledgment in Committee of Public Accounts records.

44. Interview with Frank Durkan.

45. *An Phoblacht,* February 1970.

46. Provisional Army Council, Easter statement, *An Phoblacht,* April 1970. The statement concluded with an indication that the next phase in the conflict was imminent. 'The Provisional Army Council assures the Irish people that no opportunity of furthering the cause of Irish freedom will be lost and that at the opportune time appropriate action will be taken to achieve full national independence.'

47. See Maria McGuire, *To Take Arms: A Year in the Provisional IRA* (London 1973), 108. She notes that when on speaking tours of the United States, IRA members were specifically warned that 'by no means should anything be said against the Catholic Church and all references to socialism should be avoided' (p. 108). McGuire was not attracted to the Provisionals because of 'the usual crude rhetoric about the heroes of 1916 and how the Irish should kick the British out' but rather because they had a 'constructive programme to break British economic and military control, to abolish both Stormont in the Six counties and Leinster house in the Twenty-six, and replace them with a new system of government embracing all thirty-two counties' (p. 15).

48. *An Phoblacht,* March 1970.

49. Interview with George Harrison.

50. Interview with George Harrison.

51. Interview with George Harrison.

52. That commitment to 'bombs and Bolshevism' has been a feature of the republican left and finds contemporary expression in the politics of Brian Keenan, the IRA's interlocutor with the International Commission on Decommissioning. On 11 May 1996 Keenan gave the oration at a republican commemoration in Milltown cemetery, Belfast, for an IRA hunger-striker, Seán McCaughey. He assured the crowd: 'Don't be confused about the politics of the situation, don't

be confused about things like decommissioning. The only thing which the republican movement will accept is the decommissioning of the British state in this country ... I'll tell you now, this struggle will go on ... for the old comrades here, for the young people coming up. It will not be defeated, and those who don't want peace will get war. If the conditions of conflict arise, and stay, they will be fought for, and in every generation there will be a Seán McCaughey' (excerpts broadcast on 'Spotlight,' BBC television, 6 June 1996, and again on 'Spotlight,' BBC television, 25 January 2000). Keenan, who makes no secret of his Marxist leanings, has consistently been named as a member of the IRA Army Council, as recently as *Belfast Telegraph,* 3 February 2000; see also Seán O'Callaghan, 'The decider' (a profile of Keenan), *Irish Independent,* 12 February 2000.

53. When the Provisionals themselves split over abstention in 1986, Dáithí Ó Conaill and Ruairí Ó Brádaigh were the most prominent dissidents. They left to set up Republican Sinn Féin, receiving the blessing of Tom Maguire, the last surviving member of the first Dáil. In the United States, Michael Flannery and George Harrison also opposed the change in direction and pledged support to Republican Sinn Féin and to the Continuity Army Council. Flannery became the first patron and on his death was succeeded by Harrison, who holds the position today; see *Saoirse,* January 2000.

54. *Irish Times,* 13 July 1970.

55. *Irish Times,* 13 July 1970.

56. Jim Sullivan, quoted by Patterson, *The Politics of Illusion,* 145.

57. The Provisionals prevented the selling of the *United Irishman* in Ballymacarrett in the Short Strand. The IRA issued a statement saying that 'while it is our policy to promote freedom of political expression we will not accept strong-arm tactics by sellers of any political organ aimed at sales promoted by coercion' (*An Phoblacht,* June 1970).

58. *An Phoblacht Bulletin,* 6 July 1970.

59. Jack Lynch, television address, RTE, 11 July 1970, reprinted in *Irish Times,* 13 July 1970.

60. For a scathing and caustic rejection of the Lynch approach see Kevin Boland's response in a speech to the Dáil on 30 July 1970 (*Dáil Debates,* vol. 248, col. 2678–85, 30 July 1970). See also Boland, *The Decline of Fianna Fáil.*

61. *Dáil Debates,* vol. 248, col. 2331–2, 29 July 1970. This final comment refers to the policies announced by the Minister for External Affairs to 'Panorama,' BBC television, on 6 July. See above for a full discussion.

62. 'In the other's weal' (editorial), *Irish Times,* 13 July 1970. The speech was widely welcomed in Britain. The *Economist* (18 July 1970, 13) regarded it as 'one of the most formative utterances on Irish affairs for half a century,' in which the Taoiseach 'skilfully expressed both his

government's concern with the north and its equal concern to avoid violence.'

63. *Irish Times*, 13 July 1970.
64. *Irish Times*, 13 July 1970.
65. *Irish Times*, 14 July 1970.
66. *Irish Times*, 17 July 1970; see also *Belfast Telegraph*, 16 and 17 July 1970.
67. 'Panorama,' BBC television, 6 July 1970.
68. *Dáil Debates*, vol. 248, col. 2170, 28 July 1970.
69. *Dáil Debates*, vol. 248, col. 2171, 28 July 1970.
70. *Dáil Debates*, vol. 248, col. 2172, 28 July 1970.
71. *Dáil Debates*, vol. 248, col. 2173, 28 July 1970.
72. *Dáil Debates*, vol. 248, col. 2569, 29 July 1970.
73. *Dáil Debates*, vol. 248, col. 2570–1, 29 July 1970.
74. *Dáil Debates*, vol. 248, col. 2572, 29 July 1970.
75. *Dáil Debates*, vol. 248, col. 2586, 29 July 1970.
76. *Dáil Debates*, vol. 248, col. 2595–6, 29 July 1970.
77. Interestingly, the August 1970 issue of *An Phoblacht* used a similar analogy on the front page, but also included Saigon.
78. *Dáil Debates*, vol. 2348, col. 2576–7, 29 July 1970.
79. *Dáil Debates*, vol. 248, col. 2574, 29 July 1970.
80. *Dáil Debates*, vol. 248, col. 2576, 29 July 1970.
81. *Dáil Debates*, vol. 248, col. 2596–8, 29 July 1970.
82. See Central Bank report, 1969–70, quoted by Jack Lynch in *Dáil Debates*, vol. 248, col. 2160–62, 28 July 1970.
83. *Dáil Debates*, vol. 248, col. 2162, 28 July 1970.
84. *Dáil Debates*, vol. 248, col. 2363, 29 July 1970.
85. This reached its apogee in the nineteen-eighties and early nineties under the baneful influence of the monetary politics associated with Charles Haughey's tenure as leader of Fianna Fáil.
86. *Dáil Debates*, vol. 248, col. 2847–8, 30 July 1970.
87. *Dáil Debates*, vol. 248, col. 2851, 30 July 1970.
88. John Healy, 'In the Dáil,' *Irish Times*, 31 July 1970.
89. *Dáil Debates*, vol. 248, col. 2858–60, 30 July 1970.
90. Andrew Hamilton, 'Troops' searches anger residents,' *Irish Times*, 3 August 1970.
91. *Irish Times*, 3 August 1970.
92. *Belfast Telegraph*, 4 August 1970.
93. Michael McInerney, 'Sense of urgency over NI talks,' *Irish Times*, 3 August 1970.
94. *An Phoblacht*, August 1970.
95. Paddy Kennedy, quoted in *Irish Times*, 16 May 1970.
96. As the political crisis in the North intensified, Paddy Kennedy increasingly aligned himself with the republican movement. When the veteran republican Joe Cahill was denied a visa for entry to the

United States, Kennedy deputised for him. Those who attended the
meetings say that at no point did Kennedy present himself as a
member of the republican movement; 'if he did he would have been
sent packing, just like Joe Cahill' (interview with Frank Durkan).

97. All quotations from *Irish Times*, 3 August 1970.
98. *Irish Times*, 7 August 1970.
99. For full details of the Kilmichael ambush and a deconstruction of the
nostalgia see Hart, *The IRA and Its Enemies*, 21–38.
100. *Irish Times*, 10 August 1970.
101. 'The losing battle in Ulster' (editorial), *Economist*, 1 August 1970,
14–15.
102. 'The losing battle in Ulster' (editorial), *Economist*, 1 August 1970,
14–15.
103. 'In this United Kingdom' (editorial), *Economist*, 8 August 1970, 9.
104. Barry White, 'The new parties: the SDLP,' *Fortnight*, 25 September
1970.
105. Barry White, 'The new parties: the SDLP,' *Fortnight*, 25 September
1970. For a more extended treatment see Barry White, *John Hume*,
94–108.

Chapter 7 (pp 187–213)

1. Lee, *Ireland, 1912–85*, 62–3; Coogan, *De Valera*, 313–26. The
Provisionals self-consciously claimed their ideological inheritance
from the fundamentalist position adopted by Brugha, who died from
wounds received in action in O'Connell Street following the Four
Courts siege. See *An Phoblacht*, February 1970.
2. *Irish Times*, 23 September 1970.
3. *Irish Times*, 18 and 23 September 1970. Mr Justice Ó Caoimh rejected
any suggestion that the public were barred from the court: the public
gallery remained open. See *Irish Times*, 24 September 1970.
4. In his testimony to the second arms trial, Haughey somewhat
moderated this stark defence. 'I did not know that Customs clearance
was directed to a specific consignment. It was directed to a general
arrangement whereby army intelligence would be absolved from
customs examination for any consignment they wanted to bring in. I
want to say that if I had known it was arms and ammunition imported
by army intelligence in pursuance of the contingency plans, it would
not have made any difference to my decision' (testimony to second
arms trial, 19 October 1970, quoted in *Irish Times*, 20 October 1970).
5. Kelly, *The Thimble-Riggers*, 92–3.
6. Interview with John Kelly. Kelly was no innocent: by the time of the
trial he had become a senior figure in the Provisionals and had been
given special dispensation by the Provisional Army Council to
recognise the court.

7. MacIntyre, *Through the Bridewell Gate,* 17.
8. The financing issue was curiously skated over in the Four Courts but became the sole focus of the hearings of the Committee of Public Accounts, further evidence of a concerted campaign to destroy Haughey. See below.
9. Tony Fagan, evidence to first arms trial, 23 September 1970, quoted in *Irish Times,* 24 September 1970.
10. According to Culligan, Fagan had told him explicitly that the importing was in relation to Government policy relating to the North and that the minister wanted the cargo imported without attracting any attention whatsoever (Bartholomew Culligan, evidence to first arms trial, 23 September 1970, quoted in *Irish Times,* 24 September 1970).
11. Tony Fagan, evidence to first arms trial, 23 September 1970, quoted in *Irish Times,* 24 September 1970.
12. In his evidence to the second arms trial, Haughey strenuously disputed this. He denied he even knew Kelly was in Vienna; see *Irish Times,* 20 and 21 October 1970.
13. Tony Fagan, evidence to first arms trial, 23 September 1970, quoted in *Irish Times,* 24 September 1970.
14. See summing up of Mr Justice Henchy, second arms trial, 23 October 1970, in which he specifically directed the jury to disregard the financing of the operation, out of fairness to the defendants and to Haughey in particular (quoted in *Irish Times,* 24 October 1970).
15. Jim Gibbons, evidence to first arms trial, 24 September 1970, quoted in *Irish Times,* 25 September 1970.
16. Jim Gibbons, testimony to first arms trial, 28 September 1970, quoted in *Irish Times,* 29 September 1970.
17. *Irish Times,* 29 September 1970.
18. See the argument presented by James Darcy SC, counsel for Captain Kelly, first arms trial, 28 September 1970, quoted in *Irish Times,* 29 September 1970.
19. Jim Gibbons, testimony to first arms trial, 28 September 1970, quoted in *Irish Times,* 29 September 1970.
20. It was one of the ironies of the case that Sorahan too had a close association with Haughey, going back to their student days. On 6 May 1945 students at Trinity College, Dublin, flew the flags of Allied countries, including the Union Jack, from the main building to celebrate Victory in Europe Day. The incident prompted a counter-demonstration by students from University College, who marched to Trinity; Haughey, along with Sorahan, set fire to a Union Jack (Dwyer, *Short Fellow,* 15–16).
21. Jim Gibbons, testimony to first arms trial, 28 September 1970, quoted in *Irish Times,* 29 September 1970.

22. MacIntyre, *Through the Bridewell Gate,* '53.

23. This mistake was rectified in the second arms trial. The proceedings were delayed because Ó Móráin was not ready to testify and the prosecution would not proffer Gibbons until Ó Móráin had testified, prompting an angry response from the defence barristers.

24. Mícheál Ó Móráin, testimony to first arms trial, 28 September 1970, quoted in *Irish Times,* 29 September 1970.

25. Mr Justice Aindrias Ó Caoimh, first arms trial, 28 September 1970, quoted in *Irish Times,* 29 September 1970.

26. Kelly, *Orders for the Captain,* 126–30.

27. Court report, *Irish Times,* 30 September 1970.

28. Mr Justice Aindrias Ó Caoimh, first arms trial, 29 September 1970, quoted in *Irish Times,* 30 September 1970.

29. Kelly, *The Thimble-Riggers,* 142.

30. MacIntyre, *Through the Bridewell Gate,* 75.

31. 'The national nerve' (editorial), *Irish Times,* 30 September 1970.

32. MacIntyre, *Through the Bridewell Gate,* 123.

33. John Kelly, address to second arms trial, 14 October 1970, quoted in *Irish Times,* 15 October 1970. See also full text in MacIntyre, *Through the Bridewell Gate,* 123–31.

34. Kelly, *The Thimble-Riggers,* 191.

35. Cruise O'Brien, *States of Ireland,* 255. Cruise O'Brien refers to Kelly as 'the real hero of the arms trials,' who 'brought to clear and deadly light the fact that the principles on which he had *acted* were the identical principles *professed* by the government which had put him on trial.' He concludes that 'our democracy, shabbily as it was working, was still better than anything the noble gunman was likely actually to deliver. But this truth was hard to defend against the mystic force invoked by John Kelly' (p. 258).

36. Charles Haughey, testimony to second arms trial, 19 October 1970, quoted *Irish Times,* 20 October 1970.

37. Charles Haughey, testimony to second arms trial, 19 October 1970, quoted in *Irish Times,* 20 October 1970. In cross-examination Haughey admitted that 'there are certain sections of the community in the Six Counties who are very determined people, and if they thought they needed guns for their own defence they would make determined efforts to get them' (quoted in *Irish Times,* 20 October 1970).

38. Charles Haughey, testimony to second arms trial, 19 October 1970, quoted in *Irish Times,* 20 October, 1970.

39. Charles Haughey, testimony to second arms trial, 19 October 1970, quoted in *Irish Times,* 20 October, 1970.

40. Charles Haughey, testimony to second arms trial, 19 October 1970, quoted in *Irish Times,* 20 October, 1970.

41. Court report, *Irish Times*, 21 October 1970.
42. See Michael Mills, 'The Arms Crisis,' *Irish Times*, 29 April 1998.
43. Niall McCarthy SC, counsel for Charles Haughey, second arms trial, 21 October 1970, quoted in *Irish Times*, 22 October 1970.
44. Éamonn Walsh SC, closing submission, second arms trial, 22 October 1970, quoted in *Irish Times*, 23 October 1970.
45. Jack Lynch, address to General Assembly of United Nations, 22 October 1970, reprinted in *Irish Times*, 23 October 1970.
46. *Irish Times*, 23 October 1970.
47. Summation by Mr Justice Henchy, second arms trial, 23 October 1970, quoted in *Irish Times*, 24 October 1970.
48. Summation by Mr Justice Henchy, second arms trial, 23 October 1970, quoted in *Irish Times*, 24 October 1970.
49. Summation by Mr Justice Henchy, second arms trial, 23 October 1970, quoted in *Irish Times*, 24 October 1970.
50. Summation by Mr Justice Henchy, second arms trial, 23 October 1970, quoted in *Irish Times*, 24 October 1970.
51. *Irish Times*, 24 October 1970.
52. *Irish Times*, 24 October 1970.
53. MacIntyre, *Through the Bridewell Gate*, 209.
54. The full text of the Fine Gael statement is printed in the *Irish Times*, 24 October 1970.
55. *Irish Times*, 24 October 1970.
56. *Irish Times*, 24 October 1970. The following day Lynch went further, telling reporters that 'no-one can deny that there was this attempt to import arms illegally.' He also accused Blaney. His comments prompted threats by John Kelly and Neil Blaney to sue for defamation (*Irish Times*, 26 October 1970).
57. *Irish Times*, 26 October 1970.
58. Ruairí Ó Brádaigh, address to Sinn Féin ardfheis, quoted in *Irish Times*, 26 October 1970.
59. See in particular two perceptive analytical pieces by Michael McInerney: 'A short walk from the Falls to the Shankill,' *Irish Times*, 27 October 1970, and 'From Whitehall to Stormont via Kildare Street,' *Irish Times*, 28 October 1970.
60. See in particular *Irish Times*, 26 October 1970, quoting RTE interview in which Blaney accused Gibbons of dishonesty; in effect he proposed Haughey as a leadership candidate. Fianna Fáil needed a traditional republican leader; if Haughey did not allow his name to go forward, Blaney himself would be prepared to stand.
61. See Michael McInerney, 'Cheers for Lynch mark line ahead,' *Irish Times*, 27 October 1970. Lynch received a further vote of confidence from Seán Lemass, who argued on the television programme 'Seven Days' that the Taoiseach's speech to the United Nations did

accurately reflect Fianna Fáil policy (quoted in *Irish Times*, 28 October 1970).

62. *New Statesman*, 30 October 1970. The *Economist* (31 October 1970) took a much more sceptical line, arguing that 'while Mr Lynch and the moderates are still just about on top in Dublin they know they are in for a fight.'

63. *Irish Times*, 29 October 1970.

64. The difficulties with Gibbons's evidence became apparent with the investigation into the misappropriation of Government funds conducted by the Committee of Public Accounts. Gibbons told the committee that he was aware that the weapons would be paid for out of the grant in aid (see Kelly, *The Thimble-Riggers*, 248–54). Kelly's counsel argued that the divergence in evidence amounted to the conclusion that Gibbons had conducted wholesale perjury either in the arms trials or to the committee (p. 252).

65. *Irish Times*, 30 October 1970.

66. *Irish Times*, 22 February 1971.

Chapter 8 (pp 214–24)

1. For a scathing comparison see Fintan O'Toole, 'Death of leader reminds us of end of innocence,' *Irish Times*, 23 October 1999.

2. *Sunday Independent*, 24 October 1999.

3. The only commentator to question the fawning approach was Vincent Browne, *Irish Times*, 25 October 1999.

4. Des O'Malley interview, 'Spotlight,' BBC Northern Ireland, 10 March 1998.

5. See in particular the briefing notes presented by Éamonn Gallagher, Department of External Affairs, based largely on conversations with John Hume, forwarded to the Taoiseach's office. As early as 12 September 1969 Gallagher argues that the civil rights movement offered the opportunity of ending partition, 'not as a historical necessity but as a social necessity' ('Partition and Policy,' Department of the Taoiseach, 2000/6/660).

6. Interview with Garret FitzGerald.

7. Interview with Ruairí Ó Brádaigh.

8. Interview with Ruairí Ó Brádaigh.

9. Confidential source.

10. *Committee of Public Accounts, 1968/69–70*, 25.

11. Interview with Garret FitzGerald.

12. Interview with Garret FitzGerald.

13. *Dáil Debates*, vol. 246, col. 1757, 14 May 1970.

14. *Committee of Public Accounts, 1968/69–70*, 55. The form of words suggested by the Secretary of the Department of Finance was: 'I am perfectly satisfied as a result of the inquiries which I have made that

every penny of state funds has been spent for the purpose for which it was spent by the Dáil.'

15. *Committee of Public Accounts, 1968/69–70,* 57.
16. Interview with Garret FitzGerald.
17. Des O'Malley, interview for 'Spotlight,' BBC 1 Northern Ireland, 10 March 1998.
18. Garret FitzGerald interview.
19. See 'Spotlight,' BBC1 Northern Ireland, 26 October 1999.
20. Interview with Albert Reynolds.
21. Interview with Albert Reynolds.
22. Bertie Ahern, presidential address to Fianna Fáil ardfheis, 4 March 2000; the full text is available on the Fianna Fáil web site (www.fiannafail.ie).
23. Bertie Ahern, presidential address to Fianna Fáil ardfheis, 4 March 2000.
24. Bertie Ahern, presidential address to Fianna Fáil ardfheis, 4 March 2000.

Select Bibliography

Official documents
Government Papers, National Archives, Dublin
Cabinet Papers, Public Record Office, London
Cabinet Papers, Public Record Office of Northern Ireland, Belfast
Committee of Public Accounts, Report, 1968/69–1970
Dáil Reports
Hansard
Violence and Civil Disturbances in Northern Ireland in 1969: Report of Tribunal of Inquiry [Scarman Report] (Cmnd. 566), Belfast 1972

Interviews
Kevin Boland, Dublin, February 1998
Tim Pat Coogan, Dublin, February 1998
Paddy Devlin, Belfast, February 1998
Frank Durkan, New York, August 1999
Garret FitzGerald, Dublin, September 1999
Martin Galvin, New York, August 1999
George Harrison, New York, August 1999
Paddy Kennedy, Dublin, February 1998
James Kelly, Dublin, February, June and September 1998
John Kelly, Magherafelt, February and June 1998, October 1999
Tomás Mac Giolla, Dublin, February 1998
Seán Mac Stiofáin, Navan, August 1999
Michael Mills, Dublin, February 1998
Des O'Malley, Dublin, February 1998
Ruairí Ó Brádaigh, Roscommon, August 1999
Albert Reynolds, Dublin, October 1999

Newspapers
Economist
Hibernia
Irish Independent
Irish News
Irish Times
Magill
New Statesman
An Phoblacht/Republican News
Sunday Independent
Sunday Times
Sunday Tribune
This Week
Times
United Irishman
Voice of the North

Television programmes
'Panorama', BBC1, 6 July 1970
'Timewatch', BBC2, 27 January 1993
'Spotlight', BBC1, Northern Ireland, 10 March 1998
'Spotlight', BBC1, Northern Ireland, 26 May 1998
'Spotlight', BBC1, Northern Ireland, 26 October 1999
'Seven Ages', RTE1, 27 March 2000

Book and articles
Adams, Gerry, *Before the Dawn: An Autobiography,* London 1997.
Anonymous, *Fianna Fáil and the IRA,* Undated.
Aristotle, *The Art of Rhetoric,* London 1991.
Arnold, Bruce, *What Kind of Country: Modern Irish Politics, 1968–83,*
    London 1984.
Arthur, Paul, *The People's Democracy, 1968–1973,* Belfast 1974.
Bardon, Jonathan, *A History of Ulster,* Belfast 1992.
Bell, J. Bowyer, *The Secret Army: The IRA, 1916–1979,* Swords 1970,
    1989.
Bell, J. Bowyer, *The Irish Troubles: A Generation of Violence 1967–1992,*
    Dublin 1993.
Bell, J. Bowyer, *Back to the Future: The Protestants and a United Ireland,*
    Dublin 1996.
Bew, Paul, and Gillespie, Gordon, *Northern Ireland: A Chronology of the
    Troubles, 1968–93,* Dublin 1993.
Bew, Paul; Hazelkorn, Ellen; and Patterson, Henry, *The Dynamics of Irish
    Politics,* London 1989.

Bew, Paul, and Patterson, Henry, *Seán Lemass and the Making of Modern Ireland, 1945–66,* Dublin 1982.

Bishop, Patrick, and Mallie, Eamon, *The Provisional IRA,* London 1987, 1998.

Boland, Kevin, *Indivisible Faith,* privately printed 1997.

Boland, Kevin, *The Decline of Fianna Fáil,* Dublin 1998.

Bottomore, Tom (ed.), *A Dictionary of Marxist Thought,* Harvard 1983.

Bowman, John, *De Valera and the Ulster Question, 1917–73,* London 1983.

Brady, Séamus, *Arms and the Men,* 1971.

Brewer, John, with Higgin, Gareth, *Anti-Catholicism in Northern Ireland, 1600–1998: The Mote and the Beam,* Basingstoke 1998.

Buckland, Patrick, *The Factory of Grievances: Devolved Government in Northern Ireland, 1921–39,* Dublin 1979.

Chubb, Basil, *The Government and Politics of Ireland,* Stanford (Conn.) 1970, 1982.

Clayton, Pamela, *Enemies and Passing Friends: Settler Ideologies in Twentieth-Century Ulster,* London 1996.

Cohen, Al, *The Irish Political Elite,* Dublin 1972.

Coogan, Tim Pat, *De Valera: Long Fellow, Long Shadow,* London 1993, 1995.

Coogan, Tim Pat, *The Troubles: Ireland's Ordeal, 1966–95, and the Search for Peace,* Dublin 1997.

Cronin, Mike, *The Blueshirts and Irish Politics,* Dublin 1997.

Cruise O'Brien, Conor, *States of Ireland,* London 1972.

Cruise O'Brien, Conor, *Memoir,* Dublin 1999.

Dehl, Robert, Modern Political Analysis, Englewood Cliffs (NJ): Prentice-Hall 1991.

Devlin, Paddy, *Straight Left: An Autobiography,* Belfast 1983.

Downey, James, *Lenihan: His Life and Times,* Dublin 1998.

Dunphy, Richard, *The Making of Fianna Fáil Power in Ireland, 1923–1948,* Oxford 1994.

Dwyer, T. Ryle, *Charlie: The Political Biography of Charles J. Haughey,* Dublin 1987.

Dwyer, T. Ryle, *Short Fellow: A Biography of Charles J. Haughey,* Dublin 1999.

Engleton, Terry, *The Idea of Culture,* Oxford 2000.

English, Richard, *Radicals and the Republic: Social Republicanism in the Irish Free State,* Oxford 1995.

English, Richard, *Ernie O'Malley, IRA Intellectual,* Oxford 1998.

English, Richard, and Skelly, John Morrison (eds.), *Ideas Matter: Essays in Honour of Conor Cruise O'Brien,* Dublin 1998.

English, Richard, and Walker, Graham (eds.), *Unionism in Modern Ireland: New Perspectives on Politics and Culture,* Basingstoke 1996.

Farrell, Brian, *Chairman or Chief?,* Dublin 1971.

Farrell, Brian, *Seán Lemass,* Dublin 1991.

Farrell, Michael, *Northern Ireland: The Orange State,* London 1976, 1992.

Femia, Joseph, *Gramsci's Political Thought: Hegemony, Consciousness and the Revolutionary Process,* Oxford 1981.

FitzGerald, Garret, *All in a Life: An Autobiography,* Dublin 1991.

Follis, Brian, *A State under Siege: The Establishment of Northern Ireland, 1920–1925,* Oxford 1995.

Garvin, Tom, *1921: The Birth of Irish Democracy,* Dublin 1997.

Hall, John, *The State of the Nation: Ernest Gellner and the Theory of Nationalism,* Cambridge 1998.

Hart, Peter, *The Irish Republican Army and Its Enemies: Violence and Community in Cork, 1916–1923,* Oxford 1998.

Hennessey, Thomas, *A History of Northern Ireland,* Dublin 1997.

Holland, Jack, *The American Connection: US Guns, Money and Influence in Northern Ireland,* Dublin 1989, Colorado 1999.

Horgan, John, *Seán Lemass: The Enigmatic Patriot,* Dublin 1997.

Ignatieff, Michael, *Blood and Belonging: Journeys into the New Nationalism,* London 1994.

Kelly, James, *Orders for the Captain,* Dublin 1971.

Kelly, James, *Bonfires on the Hillside,* Belfast 1995.

Kelly, James, *The Thimble-Riggers: The Dublin Arms Trials of 1970,* Dublin 1999.

Kenna, G. B. (alias Father John Hassan), *The Belfast Pogroms, 1920–22,* Belfast, 1997.

Keogh, Dermot, *Twentieth-Century Ireland: Nation and State,* Dublin 1994.

Laffan, Michael, *The Partition of Ireland, 1911–1925,* Dundalk 1983.

Laffan, Michael, *The Resurrection of Ireland: The Sinn Féin Party, 1916–1923,* Cambridge 1999.

Lawson, Kay, and Merkl, Peter, *When Parties Fáil: Emerging Alternative Organisations,* Princeton 1988.

Lee, Joseph, *Ireland, 1912–85: Politics and Society,* Cambridge 1989.

McCann, Eamonn, *War and an Irish Town,* London 1989.

McGarry, John, and O'Leary, Brendan, *Explaining Northern Ireland: Broken Images,* Oxford 1995.

MacIntyre, Tom, *Through the Bridewell Gate: A Diary of the Dublin Arms Trial,* London 1971.

McKeown, Michael, *The Greening of a Nationalist,* Lucan 1986.

McKittrick, David; Kelters, Séamus; Feeney, Brian; and Thornton, Chris, *Lost Lives: The Stories of the Men, Women and Children who Died as a Result of the Northern Ireland Troubles,* Edinburgh 1999.

Mac Stiofáin, Seán, *Memoirs of a Revolutionary,* Edinburgh 1975.

Mair, Peter, *The Changing Irish Party System,* London 1987.

Mallie, Eamon, and McKittrick, David, *The Fight for Peace: The Secret Story Behind the Irish Peace Process,* London 1996.

Manning, Maurice, *James Dillon: A Biography*, Dublin 1999.

Maume, Patrick, *The Long Gestation: Irish Nationalist Life, 1891–1918*, Dublin 1999.

Miller, David, *Queen's Rebels*, Dublin 1978.

Morgan, Austen, and Purdie, Bob, *Ireland: Divided Nation, Divided Class*, London 1980.

Ó Dochartaigh, Niall, *From Civil Rights to Armalites: Derry and the Birth of the Irish Troubles*, Cork 1997.

O'Halloran, Clare, *Partition and the Limits of Irish Nationalism*, Dublin 1987.

O'Halpin, Eunan, *Defending Ireland: The Irish State and its Enemies since 1922*, Oxford 1999.

O'Higgins, Thomas F., *A Double Life*, Dublin 1996.

O'Leary, Brendan, and McGarry, John, *The Politics of Antagonism: Understanding Northern Ireland*, London 1996.

Panebianco, Angelo, *Political Parties: Organisation and Power*, Cambridge 1988.

Patterson, Henry, 'Seán Lemass and the Ulster Question, 1959–65', *Journal of Contemporary History*, vol. 34 (1), 145–59.

Patterson, Henry, *The Politics of Illusion: A Political History of the IRA*, London 1997.

Pearce, Edward, *Lines of Most Resistance: The Lords, Tories and Ireland, 1886–1914*, London 1999.

Porter, Norman (ed)., *The Republican Ideal: Current Perspectives*, Belfast 1998.

Purdie, Bob, *Politics in the Streets: The Origins of the Civil Rights Movement in Northern Ireland*, Belfast 1980.

Rose, Peter, *How the Troubles Came to Northern Ireland*, Basingstoke 1999.

Ruane, Joseph, and Todd, Jennifer, *The Dynamics of Conflict in Northern Ireland*, Cambridge, .

Sacks, Paul Martin, *The Donegal Mafia: An Irish Political Machine*, London 1976.

Sharrock, David, and Devenport, Mark, *Man of War, Man of Peace?: The Unauthorised Biography of Gerry Adams*, London 1997.

Smith, M., *Fighting for Ireland: The Military Strategy of the Irish Republican Movement*, London 1995.

Smith, Raymond, *Haughey and O'Malley: The Quest for Power*, Naas 1987.

Stewart, A. T. Q., *The Ulster Crisis: Resistance to Home Rule, 1912–1914*, Belfast 1967, 1997.

Sweetman, Rosita, *On Our Knees: Ireland, 1972*, London 1972.

Taylor, Peter, *Provos: The IRA and Sinn Féin*, London 1997, 1998.

Toolis, Kevin, *Rebel Hearts: Journeys within the IRA's Soul*, London 1995.

Townshend, Charles, *Political Violence in Ireland: Government and Resistance since 1848*, Oxford 1983.

Wallace, Martin, *Drums and Guns: Revolution in Ulster*, London 1970.

Walsh, Dick, *Des O'Malley: A Political Profile*, Dingle 1986.a

Walsh, Dick, *The Party: Inside Fianna Fáil,* Dublin 1986.

White, Barry, *John Hume: Statesman of the Troubles,* Belfast 1984.

White, Robert, *Provisional Irish Republicans: An Oral and Interpretative History,* 1993.

Wilson, Andrew, *Irish America and the Ulster Conflict, 1968–1995,* Belfast 1995.

Wolinetz, Steven ed.), *Political Parties,* Aldershot 1998.

Wright, Frank, *Northern Ireland: A Comparative Analysis,* Dublin 1987, 1992.

Index